# THE POWER OF OBEDIENCE

## READING SCRIPTURE THROUGH THE LENS OF OBEDIENT DISCIPLESHIP

## About the Front Cover Design

The antique Bible in the cover photo is an heirloom belonging to my husband's family. It was in the Craggs family and was passed down to us from his mother, Freda Jean Craggs Roeger (1909 - 2007). The Bible contains records of family marriages, births and deaths back to the early 1800's. Pressed between its yellowed pages is the original 1857 marriage certificate of Francis Craggs and Anna Longstaff — my husband's great grandparents who immigrated to America from Durham County, England. The antique pocket watch was also in the Craggs family and is believed to have belonged to Freda's father, Francis Arthur Craggs (1868-1954).

## Books by Deborah Roeger

*God Still Speaks* (paperback [978-1-63199-795-2] and e-book [978-1-63199-796-9])

## Watch for these soon to be released studies in the Lost in Translation Series

*The Power of Hope: Reading Scripture Through the Lens of Hope* (Expected Release: 1st quarter, 2023)

*My Dwelling Place: Reading Scripture Through the Lens of God's Desire to Dwell Among Us* (Expected Release: 3rd quarter, 2023)

# Pastor and Ministry Leader Introductions

Debbie and Derf Roeger are not new to their calling to teach, however they are newcomers in their assignment to publish studies Debbie has written. Allow them to introduce themselves to you through the words and experiences of some of the Pastors and Ministry Leaders who know them.

*Few couples have dedicated themselves to personal discipleship, to listening for Divine direction, and to preparation for Kingdom service as have Derf and Debbie Roeger. Their partnership for many years in the family of Worthington Christian Church was a great encouragement and blessing to the whole congregation. Debbie is a careful thinker, a diligent student of the Bible, and a skillful teacher with well-prepared and delivered lessons. She and her husband share a devotional life and a commitment to prayer, as the primary equipment for their service.*

**Dr. Marshall Hayden**
Retired Sr. Minister, Worthington Christian Church
Worthington, Ohio

*I have known Debbie and Derf Roeger for nearly 20 years. Over the years our friendship and ministry relationship grew into several prison ministry assignments, numerous prayer walks, and various worship assignments both in Ohio and Washington, D.C. Debbie is a devoted disciple of Christ, an effective leader, and mentor, filled with a passionate love for Christ and others. She is a bright, innovative, prolific teacher of God's Word and she reaches a multicultural audience. Her classes are informative and challenging creating a hunger for more. Her teachings are solid and sound! They set a foundation on which one cannot only stand but build greater understanding to facilitate greater participation and a greater expression of God's desire on the earth as it is in heaven. Her consistency in her commitment to the*

Lord, her husband, her family, and the expansion of God's Kingdom is unchanging. All would benefit from her insightful teachings, which I highly recommend.

**Carolyn A. Quinichett, M.A.**, Prayer Life Ministry/Ministry Leader, Rhema Christian Church, Columbus, Ohio

*Debbie is very gifted in organizing and creating a complete Bible-based study on many subjects. She and her husband both have the gift of presenting Bible studies in an interactive way that engages the participants to grow in their knowledge, understanding, and faith. They are both deep prayer warriors!*

**Pastor Tom Sharron**, Chumuckla Community Church, Pace, Florida

*I am one blessed ministry leader to have Debbie Roeger on my teaching team at Calvary and in my life personally! Her knowledge of God's Word is deep and is reflected in her writing, and her teaching. She is diligent to record her sources and takes no credit for her ministry. As iron sharpens iron, her sensitivity to Holy Spirit, encourages me, excites me, teaches me, and loves me. Debbie strives to seek God's face every day, and it shows!*

**Carol DeBlasis**, Senior Director of Women's Ministry, Calvary Chapel, Melbourne, Florida

*Debbie and Derf Roeger love the Lord and love His Word! They both have been gifted by God to teach His Word. As you study with them, expect fresh insights and a deeper understanding and desire to follow the One who first loved us!*

**David Roberson**, Retired Sr. Pastor, Worthington Christian Church, Worthington, Ohio

*Debbie and Derf are not only our dear friends, but they are also amazing leaders and mentors who are filled with a passionate love for the Lord and others. They are devoted disciples of Christ and are intent on leading others to be disciples as well. They teach from the core*

*of Christianity in a manner that is not only relatable, but is also life changing. They live their lives as beautiful examples of ones who know true intimacy with God. And their international ministry, "Hope of the Nations" is to draw others into that same close relationship with our Lord and Savior. Truly it is men and women like Derf and Debbie who personify the 'Hope of the Nations'!*

**Diane Daniels**, Women's Ministry Leadership, Worthington Christian Church, Worthington, Ohio

*As a successful lawyer, now retired, Debbie Roeger has developed and mastered key transferable skills such as organization, research, analysis, critical thinking, and the like, which she utilizes as she studies God's Word from a historical, socio-economic, cultural, and spiritual perspective. She articulates profound biblical principles in a way that is simple for readers and students to comprehend. Throughout the years I have witnessed the humility she and Derf embody, their love for people, and their passion to make disciples for God's Kingdom. As prayer warriors, they have developed a keen ability to "hear" God's voice, producing a lifestyle of obedience and worship unto the Lord. I recommend their teachings and classes without reservation as they offer a roadmap for discipleship and the development of a deeper relationship with the Lord.*

**Dorcas Hernandez**, MS, Hannah Ministries, Inc./Overseer

*I know Debbie Roeger to be a woman of integrity. Our church is blessed that she is using her teaching gifts in our Small Group Ministry. I know her to be sensitive to the voice of the Holy Spirit and having a passion for intercessory prayer. Her walk with the Lord is an encouragement to the church body as well as myself. She allows God to move through her in every gifting. It is a blessing to know her.*

**Pastor Bob Russell**, Calvary Chapel, Melbourne, Florida

# The Power of Obedience

## Reading Scripture Through the Lens of Obedient Discipleship

Lost In Translation
Bible Study Series
#1

Energion Publications
Gonzalez, Florida
2022

Copyright © 2020, edited 2022, Deborah L. Roeger. All rights reserved worldwide. No part of this book may be reproduced or used in any manner without the written permission of the copyright owner except for the use of quotations in a book review.

Unless otherwise noted, Scripture throughout this study is quoted from New American Standard Bible (NASB 1995), copyright © 1960, 1962, 1963, 1968, 1971, 1972, 1973, 1975, 1977, 1995 by The Lockman Foundation. Used by permission. All rights reserved. www.lockman.org

Scripture quotations marked NET are from THE NET BIBLE®, New English Translation (NET) http://netbible.com, copyright ©1996, 2019 used with permission from Biblical Studies Press, L.L.C. All rights reserved.

Scripture quotations marked NLT are from the Holy Bible, New Living Translation, copyright ©1996, 2004, 2015 by Tyndale House Foundation. Used by permission of Tyndale House Publishers, Carol Stream, Illinois 60188. All rights reserved.

Scripture quotations marked HCSB are from the Holman Christian Standard Bible®. Used by Permission HCSB, copyright ©1999,2000,2002,2003,2009 Holman Bible Publishers. Holman Christian Standard Bible®, Holman CSB®, and HCSB® are federally registered trademarks of Holman Bible Publishers.

Scripture quotations marked AMP are from the Amplified® Bible (AMP), copyright © 2015 by The Lockman Foundation. Used by permission. www.lockman.org

Scripture quotations marked CJB are from the *Complete Jewish Bible*, copyright © 1998 and 2016 by David H. Stern. Used by permission. All rights reserved worldwide.

Scripture quotations marked ESV are from the ESV® Bible (The Holy Bible, English Standard Version®), copyright © 2001 by Crossway, a publishing ministry of Good News Publishers. Used by permission. All rights reserved.

Scripture quotations marked NKJV are from the New King James Version®, copyright © 1982 by Thomas Nelson. Used by permission. All rights reserved.

Scripture quotations marked RSV are from Revised Standard Version of the Bible, copyright © 1946, 1952, and 1971 the Division of Christian Education of the National Council of the Churches of Christ in the United States of America. Used by permission. All rights reserved worldwide.

Scripture quotation marked NIV are from The Holy Bible, New International Version® NIV® Copyright © 1973 1978 1984 2011 by Biblica, Inc.TM Used by permission. All rights reserved worldwide.

**ISBN:** 978-1-63199-818-8
**eISBN:** 978-1-63199-819-5
**Library of Congress Control Number:** 2022941551
**Lost in Translation - P. O. Box 841 - Gonzalez, FL 32560 - pubs@energion.com**
*An Imprint of Energion Publications*

The *Lost in Translation* series of Bible Studies is dedicated to Henri Louis Goulet and Messianic Studies Institute located in Gahanna, Ohio. You taught us that an inherently Jewish perspective of the Messianic worldview and way of life is the principle that all learning is for living. Through your teaching and encouragement my husband and I became lifelong learners!

---

*The Power of Obedience* is specially dedicated in loving memory to Pam Ulmer (May 21, 1949 – July 21, 2020). Pam was a faithful intercessor. For reasons I may never know, God gave her an assignment to pray for *everything* that concerned me. For 15 years she was obedient to that calling. On July 21, 2020 before I finished writing this study, Pam went home to be with the Lord following a 3-year battle with cancer. The last years of her life were lived in incredible pain yet she never stopped praying for me and the work God was asking me to do. Pam's love of the Lord and life of obedience led her straight into her Father's waiting arms. I am confident that before she died her prayers were sown into this study and that they will leave an indelible mark for the Kingdom of God.

**Disclaimer:** In this Bible Study I will cite a wide variety of references. While I am comfortable citing the identified source for the specific point referenced, that does not mean that I have read, understand, or necessarily agree or disagree with that source on other points of theology or doctrine. Therefore, referencing various scholars, authors or Study Bibles is not intended to be a blanket endorsement of that work.

**Note:** The presentation of Hebrew and Greek words I have used is designed to make those words easier to read and pronounce. As a result, some letters are not precisely represented.

# Table of Contents

Acknowledgements ..................................................................... vii
Introduction To *Lost In Translation* Series ..................... xi
Preface ........................................................................................... xv

1  The First Biblical Test of Obedience ............................. 1
2  God Fulfills His Warning To Adam ........................... 23
3  Abraham's Willingness to Sacrifice Isaac ..................... 45
4  Lessons Learned from Genesis ..................................... 67
5  When Obedience Doesn't Produce
      the Result We Expected ............................................. 83
6  Provision on the Path of Obedience ........................... 101
7  Another Word for Obedience Is Lordship .................. 121
8  God's Discipline ......................................................... 139
9  The Attitude of the Heart, The Focus of the Eyes
      and The Direction of the Feet .................................. 159
10 The Power of Desire-Based Obedience ...................... 185
11 Cultivating a Heart of Desire-Based Obedience ......... 203
12 Ushering In The New Heaven and New Earth ........... 221

How to do basic WORD STUDIES
   when you don't read Hebrew or Greek ................... 253
Index to the Word Studies .......................................... 267
Meet the Author Deborah L. Roeger ......................... 269

# Acknowledgements

Although *The Power of Obedience* is not the first study I wrote in *The Lost in Translation* series, it is the first of those studies God has directed me to publish. As a result, my initial acknowledgment must go back to the place and time where it all started.

It began at the dinner table following the wedding of my good friend's daughter. Seating had been pre-arranged and I found myself next to a woman whose son was incarcerated. Because I was volunteering in the Ohio prisons addressing conflict resolution and family re-entry we had quite the conversation. That night was the first time I had ever heard about messianic studies. My dinner conversation partner told me about a man she knew who had attended some of the Messianic Studies Institute (MSI) classes.[1] My curiosity was piqued and my husband and I contacted that man who had been a student at MSI to learn more. We only had one meeting with him but that one meeting was life-impacting! God had ever so purposefully left us a bread crumb trail to follow and within a short time, my husband and I were enrolled in our first

---

[1] The Messianic Studies Institute (MSI) was established in 1994. As described on their website, MSI (https://mjsi.org/) "is a unique institute for lifelong learning that empowers you to be transformed by Yeshua (Jesus) Messiah and His teaching, the Jewish heritage and essence of the Scriptures, and the holistic Messianic worldview and way of life. MSI's dynamic curriculum unlocks the Biblical languages, Scripture in its continuity from Genesis to Revelation, and the inherently Messianic Jewish perspective important to understanding and knowing the only true God, and the one whom He sent, Yeshua Messiah." One of the highlights of their yearly curriculum is the annual Messianic Studies Institute Scholar Symposium.

MSI class. That was the fall of 2010 and reading the Bible has never been the same since.

That first class, *New Testament Environment*, was taught by Chris Kotting and Russ Beaudet. They introduced us to the cultural and historical background of the New Testament which deepened our understanding of the Scriptures we had been reading for years. It was like turning on extra light bulbs to illuminate a more comprehensive level of understanding. As a result, we enrolled in another MSI class, then another and then another. In 2013 God gave me the assignment to teach the book of Revelation verse-by-verse in a women's Bible Study. The first person I contacted was Henri Louis Goulet, the Executive Director of MSI. Henri teaches many of the courses offered by MSI and we had been privileged to sit under his teaching numerous times by then. Henri graciously directed me to reputable and trustworthy scholarly resources which guided the preparation of my teaching notes and handouts for that year-long Bible study.

Not long after that God began to stretch me into new areas of teaching and writing. Study by study I reached out to Henri for research guidance. I consider him to be my research mentor and over the years he has become a good friend. Henri's connection with the resources produced by highly regarded scholars assures me that the starting point for every new study is solidly grounded in the best of biblical scholarship. Thank you, Henri, for following God's leading out of your career in pharmaceutical science and trusting Him to work through you to offer the studies at MSI to all of us! Thank you for being so humble and accessible.

Our dear friend Joan Winchell deserves special mention. I knew this study would benefit from the reading skill of someone with an editorial eye. I had no idea who might be willing to do that for me but God did! Joan and I first spoke with each other in April, 2017. I recall thinking at the time that I had just made a friend for life. Even though Joan lives in the Chicago area and I live in Florida, she and I have kept in touch since that first connection.

Every so often one of us emails or texts the other to catch up. On one of those occasions, Joan extended an unexpected and immensely gracious offer to me. She knew I was writing Bible studies that would be published and offered to read what I had written. It was a grace gift I accepted immediately without hesitation. She has a keen eye for details such as missing commas as well as wonderful suggestions to simplify run-on sentences and unwind overly complicated ones. Joan began reading the manuscript at a time when her schedule was already pretty full. Several months before she finished the task, God opened the door for her to return to a part-time nursing position at Wheaton College where she had worked years before. While immensely enjoying her return to the college, it also greatly reduced the hours she had to devote to reading and commenting on the manuscript. Joan diligently pressed on and after a number of months finished the task. I am so grateful for her persistence which was truly a sacrifice bathed in love.

This is the second publishing project I have had the privilege of partnering with Energion Publications to bring to print. I am deeply indebted to Henry Neufeld for his knowledge of the Hebrew and Greek languages. He and Jody are a delight to work with and make it easy for beginning authors to learn the process associated with getting a manuscript ready for publication. Thank you for what you do for the body of Christ!

Our many prayer partners are a God-given gift whose worth to us is well beyond measure. We know that your prayers on our behalf are effective and the results are tangible. May the Lord richly bless you for how you have blessed us!

I want to especially highlight my closest sister in Christ and faithful prayer partner, Diane Daniels, for her Barnabas-type encouragement and never ceasing prayers for every study I have written and taught over the years. In 2014 God gave Diane the first glimpse that Bible Studies I had written would be published. She has held on to that revelation and diligently prayed it into being.

My husband Derf and I have been married for 48 wonderful years. Over the last 15 years God has rooted us in full time volunteer ministry together. For many of those years we labored together in love in the Ohio prisons. God surprisingly called us into teaching and discipling in the body of Christ in 2009 and expanded that call to international travel and teaching with our first trip to India in February 2018. As my ministry partner, Derf is my sounding board, my proof reader, my technical person, my computer expert, my problem solver, my closest prayer partner and so much more. He has ever so patiently endured more than one late dinner, overcooked dinner, or last-minute carry-out in place of dinner because I was engrossed in research and writing – a loving thank you that goes well beyond words. When God brought us together, He knew what He was doing!

As I finish this Acknowledgment I am reminded that Jesus designed His *ekklesia* to function as a body. That's precisely what I have experienced to bring this study to completion.

To God be the glory forever and ever.

# Introduction To
# *Lost In Translation* Series

God instilled in me a love for digging deep into His Word. He added to that a passion for "getting it right" and the ability to assimilate a wealth of diverse material into an understandable lesson. Those gifts have enabled me to write well-researched meaningful studies. Each one incorporates numerous "Word Studies" along the way to ensure that original word meanings which have been largely lost in translation are brought to life again. The end result is a series of Bible Studies that have a scholarly emphasis on rightly dividing God's Word while highlighting personal application for spiritual growth and transformation. When asked, I succinctly describe *Lost in Translation* as connecting biblical scholars with the rest of us who sit in the church pews. However, I have come to understand that these studies also move toward providing a bridge between conservative evangelicals and pentecostal/charismatics. An explanation of that last statement will be helpful.

Through my research mentor I am able to reach into the best and most current scholarship of the subject matter of the study. With diligent research I become equipped to culturally and historically contextualize Bible passages. Doing so provides relevant background to aid the reader in their understanding of original language word meanings and concepts. My goal is never about increasing intellectual knowledge. My orientation is always a right understanding of God's Word with a focus on personal application and discipleship.

At times God adds to my research with revelation and understanding that does not come directly from the pages of the

Commentaries, Bible Dictionaries or other sound scholarly materials I customarily reference. At those times, He simply speaks His heart to me on the matter. Often what He says answers a question I had been pondering but had been unable to draw to a satisfactory conclusion.[2] It wasn't until I started fine-tuning the manuscripts to begin the publication process that I caught a glimpse of what God had been doing through this combination of research and revelation. Here I'll need to insert a bit of background information.

In 2014 R. T. Kendall released, *Holy Fire: A Balanced, Biblical Look At The Holy Spirit's Work In Our Lives.* In it, Kendall wrote about an unplanned "divorce" that had silently taken place in the church between God's Spirit and God's Word.[3] Using broad brushed descriptive strokes he defined two separate and distinct categories of churches.

- Denominations majoring on the written Word of God. Their focus is on the inerrancy of the written Word, expository preaching and sound doctrine. They may be virtually silent about the Holy Spirit. Generally, these congregations are labeled: *conservative evangelical* – strong in Word, much less emphasis on Holy Spirit.
- Other congregations seeking to experience the power that was present in the book of Acts. Their desire to see the gifts of the Spirit operating in the church today leads to an active pursuit of signs, wonders and miracles. General-

---

2   In our international teaching/discipling ministry I have been asked to deliver sermons during a Sunday morning worship service. I imagine my preparation for those messages most likely happens in a way that is similar to those who are called to be Preacher/Pastors. The end result from sound prayerful preparation is a combination of searching out the Word through other resources and the divine guidance of Holy Spirit to bring greater understanding. It's a good example of the way in which God has led me to write Bible Studies.

3   I had already come to recognize an invisible but distinct separating line between groups of Christ-followers. Thankfully Kendall's book equipped me with a way to articulate what I had observed.

ly, these congregations are labeled: *charismatic/pentecostal* – major emphasis on power manifestations of the Spirit, often much less emphasis on God's written Word.

There is nothing in what Kendall says that intends to indict either evangelicals or charismatics for their respective passionate pursuits. Kendall's point is that Scripture presents a clear and compelling picture of the early church as being *simultaneously strong in both Word and Power*. He credits some congregations with having found that proper balance between Word and Spirit which existed in the early church. Kendall stresses the need for that to be the goal of *every* church.

In his first epistle to the Corinthians, Paul identifies two groups of people but the distinction he makes is *not within* the body of Christ it is between those who are *in Christ* and those who are *outside of Christ*. To all of those *in Christ* Paul urged unity in the midst of their diversity.[4] The encouraging conclusion of Kendall's book is that he envisions a day when God will sovereignly *remarry* His Word and His Spirit. As that happens, proper first-century balance will be restored to the body of Christ.

It occurs to me that the *Lost in Translation* Bible Study series works towards that coming remarriage. To that end, the reader may find the series somewhat unique in its orientation – a well-researched Bible Study inseparably joined with Holy Spirit inspired counsel and revelation.

---

[4] "For even as the body is one and yet has many members, and all the members of the body, though they are many, are one body, so also is Christ. For by one Spirit we were all baptized into one body .... God has placed the members ... just as He desired.... [N]ow there are many members, but one body. And the eye cannot say to the hand, "I have no need of you"; or again the head to the feet, "I have no need of you."... But God has so composed the body, giving more abundant honor to that member which lacked, so that there may be no division in the body, but that the members may have the same care for one another."
1 Corinthians 12:12-25

To God be the glory for what He has done, is doing and will yet do!

> [B]ut just as it is written, "Things which eye has not seen and ear has not heard, And which have not entered the heart of man, All that God has prepared for those who love Him." For to us God revealed them through the Spirit; for the Spirit searches all things, even the depths of God. 1 Corinthians 2:9-10

*In His Service by His grace,*

*Deborah L. Roeger*

# Preface

**A Word from the Author:** My goal for this study is to enable participants to have a life-transforming encounter with God. Our Western culture values *knowledge* for the sake of knowledge, but the culture of the Bible valued knowledge for the sake of guiding righteous behavior. J. I. Packer who is considered to be among the most influential evangelicals in North America has asserted that attempts to interpret God's Word without personal application do not deserve the title "Interpretation."[1] In the world of the ancient Hebrew, the goal of *every* student of *every* rabbi was to go well beyond learning what the rabbi knew and to be like the rabbi – to walk the way the rabbi walked through life. The purpose of education was not to gain head knowledge and become more intelligent but to inform perspective which would transform behavior. May the cry of your heart with every page of this study be, "O God, change me from the inside out, let me be more like you!" As your cry ascends and joins with my prayers for you, I am trusting God will hear and answer in unimaginable ways! Let the change begin!

**Use of Yahweh:** In the study I may use "Yahweh"– the most frequent Name for God in the Hebrew Bible. It is composed of four Hebrew letters: Yud (Y), Hey (H), Vav (V) and Hey (H) which combine as *Yahweh* or *YHVH*.

---

[1] "Exegesis without application should not be called interpretation at all." J.I. Packer quoted by Dr. Grant C. Richison, Website Homepage *Verse-By-Verse Commentary by Dr. Grant C. Richison*. Retrieved from https://versebyversecommentary.com/ (last accessed September 15, 2021)

Yahweh is the personal covenant Name by which the ancient Hebrews knew God. The first biblical reference is found in the exodus story.

> Moshe said to God, "Look, when I appear before the people of Isra'el and say to them, 'The God of your ancestors has sent me to you'; and they ask me, 'What is his name?' what am I to tell them?" God said to Moshe, "*Ehyeh Asher Ehyeh* [I am/will be what I am/will be]," and added, "Here is what to say to the people of Isra'el: '*Ehyeh* [I Am *or* I Will Be] has sent me to you.'" God said further to Moshe, "Say this to the people of Isra'el: '*Yud-Heh-Vav-Heh* [Adonai], the God of your fathers, the God of Avraham, the God of Yitz'chak and the God of Ya'akov, has sent me to you.' This is my name forever; this is how I am to be remembered generation after generation. Exodus 3:13-15 CJB, italics in original

With this answer, God announced His eternal Name to Moses. As noted in the *Complete Jewish Bible* translation quoted above, the Hebrew verb *'ehyeh* can be translated as "I Am" *or* "I Will Be." Notice in this more Jewish rendering of Exodus 3:13-15 how the four Hebrew letters mentioned above are used in this translation, "Say this to the people of Isra'el: '*Yud-Heh-Vav-Heh* [Adonai], the God of your fathers, the God of Avraham [Abraham], the God of Yitz'chak [Isaac] and the God of Ya'akov [Jacob], has sent me to you.'"

In context, the primary focus of God's answer to Moses is His promise *to be with* Moses and with the people Moses is sent to lead out of Egypt.[2] In the setting of the Old Testament, a name served a much greater function than simply an identification marker. A name communicated that which was essentially true of the one it

---

2  *ESV Study Bible* (Crossway Books 2008) study note Exodus 3:14, p. 149

identified.³ Yahweh equates His Name with His character as being "absolute and unchanging. This immutability provides inflexible reliability that the [promises He makes] will be realized."⁴ To the Hebrew mind, Yahweh above all else meant the God who faithfully keeps covenant with His people.⁵

Yahweh (often translated as Jehovah or LORD in most modern Bible translations) is the most intensely sacred Name to the Jewish people and many will not even pronounce it. In its place, they may say the four-letters Yud-Hey-Vav-Hey (YHVH) or will often simply use *Hashem* (literally "the Name"). Because of this sacredness, "God" is often written "G-d" in Jewish writings to avoid writing/saying the Name.⁶

**Use of "the" Holy Spirit and Use of Holy Spirit**: Throughout this study I will interchangeably refer to "the Holy Spirit" (His title) and "Holy Spirit" (His name). Because some might find that objectionable an explanation will be helpful. It is noteworthy that in the original Greek of John 20:22, for example, the phrase "*pneuma hagion*" (translated Holy Spirit) could properly be a name

---

3   Motyer, J. Alec, *The Prophecy of Isaiah: An Introduction & Commentary* (InterVarsity Press 1993) Isaiah 65:15-16d, p. 528
4   Sarna, Nahum M., *Exploring Exodus: The Origins Of Biblical Israel* (Schocken Books 1986, 1996) p. 52
5   "The verb form used here is אֶהְיֶה (*'ehyeh*) the Qal imperfect, first person common singular, of the verb הָיָה (*haya* 'to be').... [W]hen God used the verb to express his name, he used this form saying, 'I AM.' When his people refer to him as Yahweh, which is the third person masculine singular form of the same verb, they say 'he is.'... The idea of the verb would certainly indicate that God is not bound by time, and while he is present ('I AM') he will always be present, even in the future ...." *NET Bible Notes*, translator's note 47, Exodus 3:14
6   The Jewish people understand Deuteronomy 12:4 as a prohibition against "erasing, destroying or desecrating the name of G-d." Jewish Community Center, *Writing G-d*. Retrieved from https://www.jccmb.com/templates/articlecco_cdo/aid/1333937/jewish/Writing-G-d.htm (last accessed August 9, 2021). As a result, many special precautions are taken both when writing the Name and when eliminating any documented format on which the Name has been written.

or a title, depending on how one reads the Greek. Similarly, we find in Scripture references to "Jesus" as His name, while "Christ" (Messiah) is His title. We alternate between name and title often in the English language. For example, we say, "When Lincoln was the president" or "President Lincoln." If we are thinking of Holy Spirit as a name, it is already definite without the use of "the" because a name does not need to be preceded by a definite article. I suggest discomfort with a reference to "Holy Spirit" may be due to lack of familiarity with using His name. However, using His name rather than His title emphasizes the personal nature of the Holy Spirit. And that's my point.

**Use of Hebrew word *Talmid* (singular) or *Talmidim* (plural):** By the time of Jesus, discipleship was well-established within the Jewish culture. All the great sages, rabbis and teachers of Torah had *talmidim* (disciples). A *talmid* (a disciple) was on a pilgrimage that was far more than an intellectual pursuit. The *talmid's* goal was to be *like* the rabbi – he wanted to assimilate the essence of who the rabbi was into his own life. This was radical discipleship – it was a complete re-making of the one who was being discipled so as to become like his rabbi in knowledge, wisdom and ethical behavior.

In other words, a *talmid's* deepest desire was to follow his rabbi so closely that he would start to think and act just like his rabbi. Jesus summed up the goal of discipleship this way: "*every disciple fully trained will be like his teacher.*"[7] A *talmid's* behavior would be a reflection on their teacher's reputation – either positively or negatively.[8] That means perseverance was a standard requirement for every *talmid*.[9] Once a *talmid* was fully trained, he would become a teacher and he would disciple *talmidim* of his own. What Jesus had begun by making *talmidim* of His first followers, the body of

---

7   Luke 6:40
8   Keener, Craig S., *The Gospel Of John: A Commentary*, Volume Two (Hendrickson Publishers 2003) John 13:34-35, citing e.g., Aeschines Timarchus 171-173 among others, pp. 926-927
9   Keener, Craig S., *The Gospel Of John: A Commentary*, Volume Two (Hendrickson Publishers 2003) John 13:34-35, p. 926

Christ now does as they make new *talmidim* of Jesus. We see the apostle Paul following this established rabbinic pattern when he says, "*Imitate me, as I also imitate Christ. Now I praise you because you always remember me and keep the traditions just as I delivered them to you.*"[10]

When we understand disciple-making in its first-century context, most of us would have to admit that Jesus' (and likewise Paul's) idea of making disciples is vastly different than many self-designated "Christians" or what we often call a "follower," a "believer" or even a "disciple" today.

Throughout the study when I use the phrase "Christ-follower" or the word "Believer" I intend those word choices to be synonymous with the definition and culturally relevant understanding of a *talmid*.

**About Word Studies**: Hebrew scholar Tremper Longman refers to Bible translations as "commentaries with no notes."[11] I think he is spot on! Because no language easily and accurately translates word-for-word one to another, every translator makes judgment calls as to which word best fits the context as he sees it. Longman calls these "interpretive decisions" and that's why he suggests that any translation amounts to that translator's commentary on the text.[12] Even so, by the very nature of translation, the person translating typically leaves no notes behind for future readers to follow his line of reasoning.[13]

"Our sacred literature does not use obscure language, but describes most things in words clearly indicating their meaning. Therefore, it is necessary at all times to delve into the literal mean-

---

10  1 Corinthians 11:1-2
11  Longman, Tremper III, *How To Read Proverbs* (InterVarsity Press 2002) p. 18
12  Longman, Tremper III, *How To Read Proverbs* (InterVarsity Press 2002) p. 18
13  In my research experience, the *New English Translation* (NET) seems to be the exception to this rule in that according to netbible.com it contains 60,932 translator notes.

ing of words to achieve complete understanding of what is actually meant."[14] To that end, from time to time in our lessons it will be advantageous to stop and do a "Word Study" which will allow us to consider the contextual meaning of that word from its original Hebrew or Greek language.

A diligent assessment of original word meanings relies on several factors. Both the authors and the original audience of the Scriptures lived in a different world than today's modern world. Politics, culture(s), ethics, worldview, theology as well as the realities of daily life were all radically different from what we know and experience. Those factors shaped the thoughts and expectations of the biblical writers which in turn shaped their words. An important task in biblical understanding is to discern, as much as possible, what any given word meant to the *original* audience. Therefore, the more we are able to appreciate the ancient mindset of the Bible the better equipped we are to understand what God was trying to communicate in a given text.

When we work to understand the Greek language of the New Testament, it is critical to realize just how much Hebrew thought impacted the New Testament authors. Most recent scholarship suggests *all* of those authors were Hebrew men who grew up in Jewish homes and were educated in the Old Testament writings.[15] As a result, the Hebrew thought-world of the Old Testament is the beginning source for proper understanding of New Testament Greek words. Although those men wrote in Greek, the thinking behind their writings was informed by their Hebrew heritage making the Old Testament the best starter dictionary we have for the New Testament.

---

14  Rabbi Samson Raphael Hirsch (1808-1888). Retrieved from https://www.thiss.org/ (last accessed August 8, 2021)

15  According to Henri Goulet, my research mentor, recent research suggests that absent evidence otherwise even Luke must be held to be Jewish. Henri Louis Goulet, Email to Deborah Roeger March 27, 2022, citing the work of Isaac Oliver on Luke

To understand Greek words in the New Testament we may also need to consider ordinary everyday word usage in the first-century Greco-Roman world. Paul authored approximately 50% of the books in the New Testament. As an apostle to Greek-speaking Gentiles, he desired to shape those who had begun to follow Christ into new social communities. He understood that God's way is a whole new way to live, not a simple re-ordering of the *world's* way. Therefore, Paul was intent on providing direction to new Christ-followers about how they should re-orient their lives to walk out life according to their new identity *in* Christ.[16] To quote scholar Teresa Morgan, "New communities forming themselves within an existing culture do *not* typically take language in common use in the world around them and immediately assign to it radical new meanings …. This is all the more likely to be the case where the new community is a missionary one [as it was in Paul's case]. One does not communicate effectively with potential converts by using language in a way which they will not understand."[17] Paul "writes with what he assumes will be shared cultural assumptions regarding language and concepts that he uses without detailed explanation."[18] In other words, Paul, along with the other New Testament authors, would have chosen Greek words which already had common meaning to their audience. That cultural consideration may also supply important interpretive guidance which will aid in our proper understanding of New Testament word meanings. When we fail to put biblical words in their proper historical, cultural context they end up getting lost in translation.

No matter what language we are discussing, it is common for words to have more than one meaning. The semantic range of a word is observed by its usage in various contexts. The more times

---

16  Tucker, J. Brian, *Reading 1 Corinthians* (Cascade Books 2017) p. 4
17  Morgan, Teresa, *Roman Faith and Christian Faith: Pistis and Fides in the Early Roman Empire and Early Churches* (Oxford 2015) p. 4
18  Keener, Craig S., *Romans*, New Covenant Commentary (Cascade Books 2009) Introduction, p. 2

a word is used in different ways, the broader its semantic range. As a result, scholars often advise that words do not mean anything outside of a context. My friend and research mentor Henri Goulet, shares this example he uses at the Messianic Studies Institute in Gahanna, Ohio. Take the English word "trunk: It could mean a host of things from an elephant's [nose], a suitcase, an ornamental chest, the rear compartment of a car, the main stem of a tree, the main part of a human body to which the head and appendages are connected, the principal channel of a tributary, or a circuit between two telephone exchanges."[19]

In the lessons in this study, Word Studies are not intended to explore the entire semantic range of a given word. Every author determines the meaning of a word by how he uses it within a context. The focus of each word studied will be narrowed by the specific context in which the author originally used that word in the particular passage we are studying. To that end, I will always seek to place Word Studies in original literary context as well as to add relevant cultural context where possible.

Refer to the supplement at the end of this study for helpful guidance on how to complete your own research of Hebrew and Greek words using free internet resources.

**The Bible's Use of Ancient Near East Background:** Because our lessons, where applicable, will seek to point out the historical context for Scripture, I will include references to ancient Near Eastern[20] beliefs as appropriate. As Jewish scholar Nahum Sarna points out: "modern scholarship has shown that the Torah made

---

19  Henri Louis Goulet, Academic Dean, Executive Director, & Faculty Messianic Studies Institute; Ph.D. Studies (Unfinished), University of Cape Town, Biblical Studies, 2007–2010; S.T.M., Capital University, Biblical Studies, 2007; M.A., Ashland University, Biblical Studies, 2003; B.S., The Ohio State University, Pharmaceutical Sciences, 1984

20  The ancient Near East is the region which includes modern Turkey, Syria, Lebanon, Israel, Palestine, Jordan, Egypt, Iraq and Iran. Important ancient civilizations in this region were the Egyptians, Arameans, Babylonians, Assyrians and Persians. Power, Cain, *Kingship in the Hebrew Bible*.

use of very ancient traditions which it adapted to its own special purposes."²¹ For example, there are poems in Proverbs that clearly depict creation in imagery and expressions drawn from ancient pagan myths.²² When a biblical author used ideas and concepts from the ancient culture around him the purpose was to borrow from the imagery to make his communication clear. That does not mean that the author endorsed the original pagan theology.²³ As Sarna noted, "the [pagan] materials used have been transformed so as to become the vehicle for the transmission of completely new ideas" which are entirely consistent with the nature and character of Yahweh.²⁴ In fact, some scholars believe that the very purpose of "borrowing" from ancient Near Eastern concepts was to demonstrate the absolute superiority of Yahweh over every false god.²⁵ According to Jewish scholar Joshua Berman, "For weak and oppressed peoples, one form of cultural and spiritual resistance is to appropriate the symbols of the oppressor and put them to competitive ideological purposes."²⁶

---

    Retrieved from https://www.sbl-site.org/assets/pdfs/TBv3i3_PowerKingship.pdf (last accessed August 8, 2021)

21  Sarna, Nahum M., *Understanding Genesis Through Rabbinic Tradition and Modern Scholarship* (The Jewish Theological Seminary 2015) p. 39

22  See for example: Proverbs 3:20; 8:29; 30:4; Waltke, Bruce K., *The Book of Proverbs: Chapters 1-15*, The New International Commentary on the Old Testament (Eerdmans 2004) Theology, p. 68

23  Waltke, Bruce K., *The Book of Proverbs Chapters 1-15*, The New International Commentary on the Old Testament (Eerdmans 2004) Theology, p. 68

24  Sarna, Nahum M., *Understanding Genesis Through Rabbinic Tradition and Modern Scholarship* (The Jewish Theological Seminary 2015) p. 4

25  See for example: Longman, Garland, editors, *The Expositor's Bible Commentary: 5 Psalms*, Revised Edition (Zondervan 2008) *Reflections: Yahweh Is The Divine Warrior*, p. 734

26  Berman, Joshua, *Ani Maamin: Biblical Criticism, Historical Truth, and the Thirteen Principles of Faith* (Maggid Book 2020) p. 55. Berman points out during much of its early history "ancient Israel was in Egypt's shadow." Ibid., p. 55

It is worth noting that not all scholars embrace the use of ancient literature outside the Bible itself to assist in biblical interpretation. Some argue that it is a dangerous practice. I am inclined to agree with Professor Jon D. Levenson, Harvard Divinity School, who rightly warns on the one hand that historical criticism should never replace "the more traditional modes of study within religious communities." On the other hand, he advises that neither should modern research of the Bible's historical context be "disregarded or neutralized." Instead, he advocates: "the worthiest course … is one that combines the modern and the traditional modes of study in an intellectually honest and theologically sophisticated way."[27]

---

27  Levenson, Jon D., *The Shema and the Commandment to Love God In Its Ancient Contexts*, TheTorah.com, August 14, 2016, last updated June 20, 2021. Retrieved from https://www.thetorah.com/article/the-shema-and-the-commandment-to-love-god-in-its-ancient-contexts (last accessed June 29, 2021)

## LESSON 1:

## THE FIRST BIBLICAL TEST OF OBEDIENCE

 "The LORD God commanded the man, saying, 'From any tree of the garden you may eat freely; but from the tree of the knowledge of good and evil you shall not eat, for in the day that you eat from it you will surely die.'" Genesis 2:16-17

WHEN WE OPEN our Bible the first words we read are, "In the beginning, GOD ..." From cover to cover the Bible is about God. It is His consummate love letter to us. As Creator to His creation His love letter introduces us to Him. From Genesis to Revelation the Bible testifies of a Holy, yet loving, God who created the world in *His* wisdom and sustains it by *His* wisdom. God's letter to us overflows with wise counsel about how to thrive in the world *He* created. It leaves no doubt that thriving in this world will require obedience. Simply stated, "Obeying the Lord means doing the right thing in the right way at the right time for the right reason [and the right reason is always] to [glorify] God."[1]

Let's just get very practical about obedience right out of the box. "To know the skill of living, which entails making wise decisions, one must know *everything*.... But no human being sees and knows everything."[2] Because God is the One who spoke everything into being in the world around us, would it not be true that He

---
1  Wiersbe, Warren W., *The Wiersebe Bible Commentary* (David C. Cook 2007) p. 322
2  Waltke, Bruce K., *The Book of Proverbs: Chapters 1-15*, The New International Commentary on the Old Testament (Eerdmans 2004) Theology, p. 79, italics added

alone knows how to keep it in perfect working order. Wouldn't it be true that aligning with His wisdom would lead to the greatest possible blessing? In fact, according to Proverbs 29:18, true life is enabled *only* through the wisdom God reveals to us.[3] Because that's true, the only reason we ever need for obeying God is that God knows best! Ideally, that would have been the story of creation, but even the most elementary students of the Bible know that is not how the biblical story unfolds.

We are accustomed to associating Adam with the Bible's first recorded act of sin. However, before that act of rebellion against God Adam *obeyed* God. For example, we read that Adam named all of the animals as God brought them to him (Genesis 2:19-20). That seems to make clear Adam was obeying an instruction God had given him. Scripture does not record how long Adam remained obedient to God before we learn about his disobedience. Presumably, obedience was the norm for some time because the implication of Genesis 3:8 is that God routinely walked in the Garden of Eden with Adam and Eve. The picture of God walking with a person depicts His presence and normally suggests an established relationship of enjoyment involving closeness, intimacy and fellowship.[4]

God walking in the Garden is such a wonderfully descriptive image. It allows the concrete everyday activity of walking to become a window for the divine truth that God longs to have fellowship with us! The counterpart to God walking with Adam and

---

[3] Waltke, Bruce K., *The Book of Proverbs: Chapters 15-31*, The New International Commentary on the Old Testament (Eerdmans 2004) Proverbs 29:18, p. 446. "Where there is no vision [no revelation of God and His word], the people are unrestrained; But happy and blessed is he who keeps the law [of God] (Proverbs 29:18 AMP)." The KJV translates the same verse as, "Where there is no vision the people perish."

[4] Alcorn, Randy, *Is Genesis 3:8 Sufficient to Establish That God Was in the Habit of Visiting with Adam and Eve in the Garden?* Eternal Perspective Ministries, March 29, 2010. Retrieved from https://www.epm.org/resources/2010/Mar/29/gen-38-sufficient-establish-god-was-habit-visiting/ (last accessed July 8, 2021)

Eve is man "walking with God" which is observed several times in Genesis. That expression pictures the righteous acts and pleasing conduct of men like Enoch, Noah and Abraham.[5] As we will see in this study, the Bible consistently makes clear that God's divine presence among men is directly related to their obedience. Adam and Eve as the first created individuals on earth were no exception.

Our Key Scripture for this lesson sets up the very first recorded test of obedience in the Bible. We are only in the second chapter of Genesis and we read:

> Then the LORD God took the man and put him into the garden of Eden to cultivate it and keep it. The LORD God **commanded** the man, saying, "From any tree of the garden you may eat freely; but from the tree of the knowledge of good and evil you shall not eat, for in the day that you eat from it you will surely die." Genesis 2:15-17, bold added

The word "commanded," highlighted in bold text above, is the Hebrew verb *tsavah* {tsaw-vaw'} which envisions obedience. It pictures a person who has the authority to "command" something with an *expectation* that his directive will be obeyed.[6] For example, *tsavah* is found in 2 Samuel 21:14 to refer to commands given by King David which were explicitly followed.

We have already taken notice of the powerful imagery of God, Adam and Eve walking together in the Garden. The setting is the most perfect environment ever known to man. In this ideal place, God and Adam enjoyed a perfect relationship. God gave Adam one very straightforward mandate, not to withhold something good from him, but because failure to follow this command would disrupt the perfect relationship he had with God.

---

5   "Enoch walked with God (Genesis 5:21);" "Noah walked with God (Genesis 6:9);" "Abraham: The Lord before whom I have walked (Genesis 24:40)"

6   Harris, Archer, and Waltke, editors, *Theological Wordbook of the Old Testament* (Moody Press 1999) word #1887, p. 757

Scripture does not explain *why* God gives this command to refrain from eating of the tree of knowledge. There is no indication God gave any type of explanation to Adam. The narrative merely states the directive with the authority of the Creator and warns that death will be the consequence of disobedience. That brings us to an important biblical principle. In the Bible's teaching on wisdom, it is noteworthy that "*allegiance precedes understanding, not the other way around.*"[7] In other words, the biblical pattern that we see from cover to cover is that God gives a command, He expects us to obey and understanding comes *after* we obey Him – not before. I guess we could say that understanding occurs only in hindsight as we look in the rearview mirror at where we've been.

There is no definitive scholarly consensus about the meaning of this particular Garden tree or the phrase "good and evil." Understanding exactly what the "tree of the knowledge of good and evil" is doesn't seem to be the author's purpose in writing the narrative. However, if we work our way through a few Word Studies we can at least glean an accurate understanding of how the ancient Hebrews would have heard the words God used.[8] We'll begin with the word "knowledge."

Because this is our first Word Study in *The Power of Obedience* I think it is important to remind you of something I pointed out in the Preface. Word Studies are *not* intended to explore the entire semantic range of a given word. The focus of each word we study will be narrowed by the specific context in which the author originally used that word.

---

[7] Waltke, Bruce K., *The Book of Proverbs: Chapters 1-15*, The New International Commentary on the Old Testament (Eerdmans 2004) Proverbs 2:5, p. 222, citing Newsom, *Woman and Discourse*, p. 147, italics added

[8] According to David Stern, *The Complete Jewish Bible*, "The early chapters of Genesis (1-11) were possibly written in cuneiform upon clay tablets and passed on through Noach (Noah) to the early patriarchs.... [T]he book may have been written when Isra'el was about to enter the Promised Land." Stern, David H., *The Complete Jewish Study Bible* (Hendrickson Publishers Marketing 2016) Introduction to *B'resheet* (Genesis), p. 1

## WORD STUDY

*In the phrase* **the tree of the knowledge of good and evil** *the word "knowledge" is a translation of the Hebrew word da`ath {dah'-ath} which describes knowledge gained in various ways by one of the five senses. The verbal root of da`ath is often used in Genesis to refer to "intimate experiential knowledge."[9] It is one of the Hebrew words regularly associated with the biblical concept of wisdom.[10] Da`ath is found in Proverbs as a "synonymously parallel term" for wisdom gained by experience.[11]*

*The Greek translation of the Old Testament uses the Greek noun aisthesis {ah'-ee-sthay-sis} (from aisthánomai meaning "to apprehend by the senses") to translate da`ath. In his letter to the Philippians, Paul used aisthesis to refer to moral discernment.[12]*

The Bible leaves no doubt that Yahweh is the *only* source of wisdom (Proverbs 2:6). Knowledge is possessed by God and in His

---

9 Fouts, David M., "Genesis 1-11," in *The Bible Knowledge Word Study, Genesis – Deuteronomy*, edited by Eugene H. Merrill (Victor 2003) Genesis 2:9 under *The tree of the knowledge*, p. 47, citing Gen. 4:1; 19:8; 22:12

10 Baker and Carpenter, *The Complete WordStudy Dictionary of the Old Testament* (AMG Publishers 2003) word #1847, p. 245; Harris, Archer, and Waltke, editors, *Theological Wordbook of the Old Testament* (Moody Press 1999) word #848c, pp. 366-367

11 Fouts, David M., "Genesis 1-11," in *The Bible Knowledge Word Study, Genesis – Deuteronomy*, edited by Eugene H. Merrill (Victor 2003) Genesis 2:9 under *The tree of the knowledge*, p. 47, citing Prov. 2:6,10; 3:19-20

12 Philippians 1:9; Bromiley, Geoffrey W., *Theological Dictionary of the New Testament*, Abridged in One Volume (Eerdmans 1985) entry for *aisthanomai* under B. *The Word Group in the NT*, p. 29

perfect design, it remains hidden unless He reveals it to man.[13] As we have already noted, the guidance provided by God's wisdom, received through inspired revelation, is what enables true life![14] Given these truths, we are already beginning to see the problem with Adam and Eve gaining wisdom by experience that is separate and apart from God.

Let's move on to the words "good" and "evil."

> **WORD STUDY**
>
> *In our Key Scripture the word translated as **good** is the Hebrew adjective* towb *{tobe} also transliterated as* tob *or* tov *{towb}. It occurs more than 500 times in the Old Testament with a range of meanings that is broader than the English word "good."*[15] *Towb conveys such ideas as well-pleasing, fruitful, moral correctness and even kindness and benevolence.*

Scholar Bruce Waltke summarizes *towb* as referring to whatever is "desirable because it/he serves the purpose for which it was made.[16] When applied to persons, it emphasizes a special excellence

---

13   Proverbs 2:6; Job 28:21; Deuteronomy 29:29; Psalm 51:6
14   Waltke, Bruce K., *The Book of Proverbs: Chapters 15-31*, The New International Commentary on the Old Testament (Eerdmans 2004) Proverbs 29:18, p. 446. "Where there is no vision [no revelation of God and His word], the people are unrestrained; But happy and blessed is he who keeps the law [of God] (Proverbs 29:18 AMP)." The KJV translation reads, "without vision the people perish."
15   *Spirit Filled Life Bible* (Thomas Nelson 1991) *Word Wealth [Ezekiel] 34:14 good, tob*, p. 1205
16   Waltke, Bruce K., *The Book of Proverbs: Chapters 1-15*, The New International Commentary on the Old Testament (Eerdmans 2004) Theology under *b. The Wise and Righteous, (1) The Wise and Righteous and Other Correlative Terms*, p. 99, citing K.-D. Schunck, *TDOT*, 5:298, s.v. *tob*

or positive quality, depending on the context, that makes them desirable."[17] *The Theological Wordbook of the Old Testament* points out that an important biblical usage of *towb* refers to moral goodness.[18] Ecclesiastes acknowledges that those who are good (*towb*) receive wisdom and knowledge from the Lord.

> For to a person who is good [*towb*] in [God's] sight He has given wisdom [*chokmah* {khok-maw'}/shrewdness, moral skill][19] and knowledge [*da`ath*] and joy ....
> Ecclesiastes 2:26

Notice that God's wisdom (moral skill) for living was meant to be given *by God* to the person who is *good*. God did not create man to independently know good from evil by their own choice of experience. The wisdom literature of the Old Testament points to the fear of the Lord as the necessary foundation for obtaining wisdom.[20] As Pastor Robert Morris says, "God designed man to relate to Him by hearing His voice. He never intended that man would need to choose between right and wrong (good and evil). He intended man to be guided through life by His voice."[21] God's Spirit is the only One who knows God's wisdom.[22] "Through his

---

17 Waltke, Bruce K., *The Book of Proverbs: Chapters 1-15*, The New International Commentary on the Old Testament (Eerdmans 2004) Theology under *b. The Wise and Righteous, (1) The Wise and Righteous and Other Correlative Terms*, p. 99, citing Schunck, *TDOT*, 5:306
18 Harris, Archer, and Waltke, editors, *Theological Wordbook of the Old Testament* (Moody Press 1999) word #793a, p. 346
19 *Wisdom – Chokmah – Hebrew Word Study*, Precept Austin, citing *NET Bible Note*. Retrieved from preceptaustin.org/wisdom-chokmah (last accessed July 8, 2021)
20 Waltke, Bruce K., *The Book of Proverbs: Chapters 1-15*, The New International Commentary on the Old Testament (Eerdmans 2004) C. Wisdom Genre, p. 52
21 Morris, Robert, Senior Pastor, Gateway Church, Dallas/Fort Worth, TX, The Blessed Life, *Frequency Sermon Series*
22 1 Corinthians 2:9-16; Fee, Gordon D., *The First Epistle To The Corinthians*, New International Commentary on the New Testament (Eerdmans 1987) 1 Corinthians 2:10b-11, p. 111

Spirit God empowers man to know [His wisdom that is] beyond the human mind, eye, [or] ear."[23]

God is the only one who can express wisdom with the fullness of His omnipotence and omniscience. The ideal way of life, the way it would work best, would be for God as the perfect Father to provide all the wisdom His children need. To the extent that Adam and Eve needed to learn something by experience, the ultimate training environment would have been to learn through instructive experiences that God would have provided according to His set plans and times.

Our last word is "evil."

> ### WORD STUDY
>
> *Evil is a translation of the Hebrew adjective ra` {rah}. Its meaning ranges from displeasure to detrimental. Ra` can indicate both 1) being wrong concerning God's intent and 2) being detrimental as it relates to its effects on humankind.*[24]
>
> *When ra` is placed parallel to towb (as it is in: "the tree of the knowledge of good and evil") its essential meaning is highlighted to convey the opposite extremes of the moral spectrum.*[25]

Did you happen to notice that the definitions for knowledge, good and evil all share a common theme? They all relate to moral

---

[23] Barth, Markus, *Ephesians: Introduction, Translation, and Commentary on Chapters 1-3*, The Anchor Bible Vol 34 (Doubleday 1974) Ephesians 3:16 under *through his Spirit ... fortified with power*, p. 369, citing 1 Corinthians 2:9-16

[24] Harris, Archer, and Waltke, editors, *Theological Wordbook of the Old Testament* (Moody Press 1999) word #2191a, p. 854

[25] Harris, Archer, and Waltke, editors, *Theological Wordbook of the Old Testament* (Moody Press 1999) word #2191a, p. 854

behavior. As noted in the Word Study on evil, when God places evil and good side by side, He is pointing out that they are at the opposite extremes of moral choice. As polar opposites they convey the idea of complete knowledge, knowledge of all things.[26]

God's judgment is the immovable plumb line in all things and stands as a moral absolute. Scripture leaves no doubt about God's judgment of evil. In Psalm 5:5 King David characterizes God as one who, "hate[s] all who do evil."[27] As we will soon see, the word "hate," as used in Psalm 5, provides the explanation that is implied, but not expressly stated, in the narrative of Adam and Eve's sin.

The Hebrew verb translated as "hate" in Psalm 5:5 is *sane'* {saw-nay'}. It is *not* a reference to God's emotions as if they were human emotions. *Sane'* refers to God's rejection.[28] To say God "hates" indicates His lack of preference which leads to His responsive action to evil conduct. In Psalm 5:5, *sane'* depicts a conflict between opposing values that can never be reconciled or harmonized with each other.[29] That which is *in* harmony with God is *towb*,[30] that which is *out of* harmony with God is *sane'*.[31] In fact, a "grand theme of the Old Testament is God's holiness, which separates Him from all that is not in harmony with His charac-

---

26 In Hebrew this is referred to as a merism. In a merism the author states polar opposites for the purpose of highlighting everything that lies in between those opposites. Beale, G. K., *Revelation*, The New International Greek Testament Commentary (Eerdmans 1999) p. 199
27 Psalm 5:5b CJB
28 Block, Daniel I., *For the Glory of God: Recovering A Biblical Theology of Worship* (Baker Academic 2014) p. 95
29 Hill, Gary, *The Discovery Bible*, HELPS Ministries, Inc., [H]11p (SN 8130) *śānē'*
30 Recall that we have learned that which is *towb* refers to whatever is desirable because it serves the purpose for which it was made.
31 Bentorah, Chaim, *Hebrew Word Study – Evil – Ra* רע *Resh Ayin*, chaimbentorah.com. Retrieved from https://www.chaimbentorah.com/2020/09/hebrew-word-study-evil-ra/ (last accessed March 10, 2022)

ter."³² (For additional understanding of *sane'* see the Word Study in Lesson 8).

As we can see, hatred causes separation by distancing oneself. Israel knew from personal experience how God responds to sin – He distances Himself from it! In fact, God's reaction is so strong that to "hate" can refer to His treatment of someone as an adversary (enemy).³³

Returning to our Key Scripture, let's turn our attention to God's warning about death.

> "… but from the tree of the knowledge of good and evil you shall not eat, **for in the day that you eat from it you will surely die**." Genesis 2:17, bold added

In our experience, death is considered to be a natural part of living. Before sin, that consequential distancing (i.e. separation) by God was unknown, it was *not* a natural part of life. God's purpose was for Adam and Eve to have never-ending life and never-ending fellowship with Him.³⁴ However, in the test of obedience God gave Adam and Eve, He provided the very first biblical warning about death as a natural consequence of sin.

The original Hebrew text conveys God's forewarning to Adam in stronger terms than we can see in our English translation. The penalty of death was stated especially forcefully by using two Hebrew verbs that can be translated as: "dying you shall die." That is to say that death, without regard to how it is defined, is absolutely certain!³⁵ The grammatical construction of this warning is very similar to the way Mosaic law warned of capital punishment: "he

---

32  Harris, Archer, and Waltke, editors, *Theological Wordbook of the Old Testament* (Moody Press 1999) word #1169, p. 497

33  Hill, Gary, *The Discovery Bible*, HELPS Ministries, Inc., [H]11p (SN 8130) *śānē'*

34  Harris, Archer, and Waltke, editors, *Theological Wordbook of the Old Testament* (Moody Press 1999) word #1169, p. 497

35  *Holman Christian Standard Bible*, Study Bible edition (Holman Bible Publishers 2010) study note Genesis 2:17 under *[you will certainly die]*, p. 11

will surely die," or "they will surely die" (Exodus 21:12; Leviticus 20:9–16). These warnings reflect God's verbal formula for declaring the certainty of a death sentence. God was not saying Adam would die immediately. He was warning Adam that guaranteed death would follow disobedience.[36]

The Old Testament uses death to refer to "ultimate separation from God due to sin."[37] "In the Bible 'death' is never [viewed as] 'termination' [or 'extinction'] but a change of place and state with continuity of personal identity."[38] *NET Bible Notes* identifies two types of separation from God that occur as a result of sin: spiritual alienation and physical death.[39] The essential characteristic of death – whether spiritual or physical – is that of being estranged or disconnected from God. Dying physically refers to "a separation from the land of the living."[40] On the other hand, dying spiritually refers to the loss of "well-being."[41] In the Bible, neither type of separation focuses on annihilation or extinction.

When God wisely and lovingly instructed Adam not to eat of that particular tree in the Garden, He set up a test of obedience for Adam. The earth and all its creatures inherently respond to their Creator's voice to fulfill God's purpose,[42] but man was created with self-will and self-control. God gave man the unique ability to

---

36 Turpin, Simon, *Did Death of Any Kind Exist Before the Fall? What the Bible Says About the Origin of Death and Suffering*, Answers In Genesis, Answers Research Journal 6 (2013) pp. 99–116. Retrieved from https://answersingenesis.org/doc/articles/pdf-versions/death_before_Fall.pdf (last accessed July 8, 2021)
37 Harris, Archer, and Waltke, editors, *Theological Wordbook of the Old Testament* (Moody Press 1999) word #1169, p. 497
38 Motyer, J. Alec, *The Prophecy of Isaiah: An Introduction & Commentary* (InterVarsity Press 1993) Isaiah 14:9-15, p. 143
39 *NET Bible Notes*, study note 54, Genesis 2:17. The source for this information is "*Net Notes*" however it will be descriptively cited as "Net Bible Notes" throughout the study.
40 *NET Bible Notes*, study note 54, Genesis 2:17
41 *Spirit Filled Life Bible* (Thomas Nelson 1991) *Word Wealth [Luke] 9:56 destroy, apollumi*, p. 1531
42 *ESV Study Bible* (Crossway Books 2008) study note Genesis 1:31, p. 52

choose how he would respond to his Creator's voice. Mankind was given the distinctive ability to exercise self-control. In His wisdom, God determined that *choice* must be tested to be meaningful. Testing must necessarily involve the opportunity to select that which is harmfully forbidden. "In order for human beings to be truly free persons they must have the possibility of refusing God's purposes for their lives" and that means they are free to make choices that are "self-damaging and self-destructive."[43] To be confronted by what is prohibited is the very thing that allows man to recognize he was created with choice.[44] Adam will soon learn that he will be held accountable for the choices he makes. Adam and Eve had a personal invitation to fellowship with God in the Garden. However, that continuing fellowship, as we are beginning to see, was contingent upon continually choosing to obey God.

Now that we understand more about God's command to Adam, let's next consider the enemy's scheme. After that we'll look at the impact his temptation had on Adam and Eve.

> Now the serpent was more crafty (subtle, skilled in deceit) than any living creature of the field which the LORD God had made. And the serpent (Satan) said to the woman, "Can it really be that God has said, 'You shall not eat from any tree of the garden'?" And the woman said to the serpent, "We may eat fruit from the trees of the garden, except the fruit from the tree which is in the middle of the garden. God said, 'You shall not eat from it nor touch it, otherwise you will die.'" But the serpent said to the woman, "You certainly will not die! For God knows that on the day you eat from it your eyes will be opened [that is, you will have greater awareness], and you will

---

43 Goulet, Henri Louis, *At Least One Good Thing about a Global Pandemic,* Monday's Messianic Taste of Hidden Manna #34, March 30, 2020, citing Paul S. Fiddes, *The Creative Suffering of God* (OUP 1988). Delivered via email from Messianic Studies Institute

44 Nicoll, W. Robertson, *Expositor's Bible Commentary*, Genesis 3:1. Retrieved from Hill, Gary, *The Discovery Bible*, HELPS Ministries, Inc.

be like God, knowing [the difference between] good and evil." And when the woman saw that the tree was good for food, and that it was delightful to look at, and a tree to be desired in order to make one wise and insightful, she took some of its fruit and ate it; and she also gave some to her husband with her, and he ate. Genesis 3:1-6 AMP

This is the first introduction in Scripture to the creature known as the "serpent." In his well-researched book, *The Unseen Realm: Recovering the Supernatural Worldview of the Bible*, Dr. Michael Heiser has argued persuasively that the vocabulary and imagery of Genesis 3 are designed to alert the ancient reader "to the presence of a divine being, not a literal snake."[45] "Genesis telegraphed simple but profound ideas to Israelite readers" and according to Heiser an ancient Hebrew "would have known that the [Genesis 3] episode described interference in the human drama by a divine being, a malcontent from within Yahweh's [divine] council."[46] The Old Testament contains four passages that identify Satan as a celestial being.[47] In Job 1 and Zechariah 3 scholars agree that Satan is in the setting of the divine council.

Perhaps the image of the serpent is used without further explanation because the ancient Hebrews for whom Genesis was written already knew the serpent represented "the epitome of evil in the Ancient Near Eastern world" in which they lived.[48] In any event, even for the Bible student today who lacks knowledge of ancient

---

45  Heiser, Michael S., *The Unseen Realm: Recovering the Supernatural Worldview of the Bible* (Lexham Press 2015) p. 74
46  Heiser, Michael S., *The Unseen Realm: Recovering the Supernatural Worldview of the Bible* (Lexham Press 2015) p. 74
47  Korner, Ralph J., *Reading Revelation After Supersessionism: An Apocalyptic Journey of Socially Identifying John's Multi-Ethnic Ekklesiai with the Ekklesia of Israel* (Cascade Books 2020) p. 78. In footnote 115, the four passages are listed as: Num 22:22-32; Job 1-2; Zech 3:1-2; 1 Chr 21:1
48  Fouts, David M., "Genesis (1-11)," in T*he Bible Knowledge Word Study, Genesis – Deuteronomy*, edited by Eugene H. Merrill (Victor 2003) Genesis 1:4 under *The light was good*, p. 41; Genesis 3:1 under *Now the serpent*, p. 50

history, the book of Revelation reveals that this serpent is actually the evil one known as the *devil* (translation of Greek) and as *Satan* (Hebrew word).[49]

The Genesis narrative begins to introduce the truth "that behind the insoluble [perplexing] mystery of the entrance of evil into the good world of God lies the presence or activity of a force that is [hostile] to God."[50] The Old Testament and ancient Jewish literature consistently refer to the adversarial nature of *satan*.[51] The New Testament presents "Satan" as "a personal being."[52] Paul brings this *real being* to life for us when he makes clear that our daily battle is "not against flesh and blood, but against the rulers, against the powers, against the world forces of this darkness, against the spiritual forces of wickedness in the heavenly places."[53] Paul's understanding of Satan was informed by the Jewish thought of

---

49   References to "devil" in Revelation include: 2:10; 12:9,12; 20:2,10. References to "Satan" in Revelation include: 2:24; 3:9; 12:9; 20:2,7. We typically use the words "devil" and "Satan" as a proper name; however, in the original biblical languages these words actually refer to our enemy's job description. Greek word *diabolos* {dee-ab'-ol-os} is most often translated as "devil" in the New Testament. *Diabolos* refers to a slanderer or a false accuser. Hebrew word *ha-satan* (literally "the satan') means the accuser or the adversary.

50   Bromiley, Geoffrey W., *Theological Dictionary of the New Testament*, Abridged in One Volume (Eerdmans 1985) entry for *ophis* under B. *The Serpent in the OT*, p. 749

51   Korner, Ralph J., *Reading Revelation After Supersessionism: An Apocalyptic Journey of Socially Identifying John's Multi-Ethnic Ekklesiai with the Ekklesia of Israel* (Cascade Books 2020) p. 81. Dr. Korner credits scholar Thomas Farrar for his conclusion that the ancient Jewish literature contains *conceptual* consistency in the functions and attributes of Satan (See Farrar and Williams, *Talk of the Devil*, 90-82, especially Table 1, italics in original).

52   Korner, Ralph J., *Reading Revelation After Supersessionism: An Apocalyptic Journey of Socially Identifying John's Multi-Ethnic Ekklesiai with the Ekklesia of Israel* (Cascade Books 2020) p. 81. Dr. Korner quotes scholar David Aune's conclusion that the various aliases "ruler of this world," "Satan," and "Devil" are designations for a personal being (Aune, *Dualism in the Fourth Gospel*, 135).

53   Ephesians 6:12

his day. His use of the name *Belial* (also spelled *Beliar*) to refer to Satan in his second letter to the Corinthians is instructive.[54] The Hebrew word *beliya`al* {bel-e-yah'-al} "denotes one who is implacably [relentlessly] wicked and who agitates against all that is good."[55] Although that name for Satan is not found in the Old Testament, it was used frequently in Jewish writing to "stress Satan's activity as an opponent of God."[56]

Before we proceed to unpack the methods Satan used to tempt Eve, let's park here for a moment to consider the origins of our adversary, the evil one. Many believe, just as I have been taught, that Satan was created as a beautiful angel but he rebelled against God. He desired to be greater than God and because of that rebellion, God cast him out of heaven. To quote from the *Dictionary of Biblical Imagery*:[57]

> It has also been common to believe in a fall of Satan from heaven before human history began. [This belief] rests on two OT passages, which may or may not be adequate for the belief. In Isaiah's taunt against the king of Babylon, the prophet exclaims, "How are thou fallen from heaven, O Lucifer, son of the morning!" (Is 14:12 KJV).... Ezekiel's oracle against Tyre elaborates the picture further, portraying a being who once resided in Eden, placed "with an anointed guardian cherub" on "the holy mount of God" (Ezek 28:14 RSV). This being was "blameless ... from the day you were created, till iniquity was found in you" (Ezek 28:15 RSV). Thereupon he was "cast ... as a profane thing from the mountain of God,

---

54  2 Corinthians 6:15
55  Waltke, Bruce K., *The Book of Proverbs: Chapters 1-15*, The New International Commentary on the Old Testament (Eerdmans 2004) Proverbs 6:12, p. 342
56  *ESV Study Bible* (Crossway Books 2008) study note 2 Corinthians 6:15 under *Belial*, p. 2231
57  Ryken, Wilhoit, and Longman III, editors, *Dictionary of Biblical Imagery* (Intervarsity Press 1998) entry for *Satan Cast Down*, pp. 761-762

and the guardian cherub drove [him] out from the midst of the stones of fire" (Ezek 28:16 RSV). Again, he was "cast … to the ground" (Ezek 28:17).

It is in the biblical account of Jesus' earthly ministry where we find the most fully developed understanding of Satan. For example, Jesus affirms there is a ruler of demons who is known by the name *Beelzebul*.[58] In the wilderness temptations of Jesus, Satan is highlighted as the one who tempts people to disobey God. Jesus contrasts Himself as "the Truth" and Satan as a liar and the father of lies.[59] Jesus makes clear that individual people can functionally do the work of Satan.[60] Satan is credited as having an important role in the death of Jesus, but only because God permits it.[61] The cross is identified as the place where Satan was stripped of his intimidating power as it relates to "the power of death."[62] The New Testament portrays Jesus as having come to set people free from the work of Satan who had held them captive.[63]

Eve is tempted by one who it seems knew rebellion personally and therefore knew its consequences! That leads to the conclusion that Satan's plan in the Garden was intentional and his scheme was purposefully calculating. He knew the outcome! He saw Adam and Eve in the Garden. They were created in the image of God. Satan's goal in his rebellion was to become *like* God and set his throne above God's throne.[64] He learned the hard way that no

---

58  Matthew 12:24-32
59  John 8:44
60  See for example Matthew 16:2, when Peter strongly objects to the plans the Father has for His Son, Jesus rebukes Peter saying, "Get behind me, Satan!" Jesus was not saying Peter had actually become Satan but that Peter was aligning his thoughts and actions with the thoughts and actions of Satan and therefore Satan was able to use Peter to accomplish his objectives.
61  John 19:11
62  Hebrews 2:14, referring to the second death
63  See for example: Luke 4:18; Galatians 5:1; 2 Timothy 2:26
64  "But you said in your heart, 'I will ascend to heaven; I will raise my throne above the stars of God, And I will sit on the mount of assembly in

*The Power of Obedience*

one could aspire to such a place. Satan must have been miserable having failed in his attempt and having lost his favored position among the angels that worshipped God. So, he tempted Eve with the very same desire he had – to become *like* God. He apparently knew from his own experience that if he could successfully tempt Eve (and Adam through her), their rebellion would breach their perfect fellowship with God.

Satan's scheme seems to be much more than misery loves company. His temptation of Eve was a power play from start to finish – he would start his own kingdom! It would be a kingdom that would rival God's Kingdom. He cunningly knew far better than Adam and Eve that disobedience (sin) disrupts God's sovereign rule. The Bible makes clear that sin is a lack of self-control. Sin is tantamount to obeying unredeemed fleshly desires thus yielding obedience to the kingdom of darkness. We will have more to say about this in our study, our purpose here is simply to set the context for what transpired in the Garden which led to the first recorded instance of man's sin. For now, let's return to our biblical text and pick up where we left off. We will work from the NASB 1995 translation.

> ... And [the serpent] said to the woman, "Indeed, has God said, 'You shall not eat from any tree of the garden'?" The woman said to the serpent, "From the fruit of the trees of the garden we may eat; but from the fruit of the tree which is in the middle of the garden, God has said, 'You shall not eat from it or touch it, or you will die.'" The serpent said to the woman, "You surely will not die! For God knows that in the day you eat from it your eyes will be opened, and you will be like God, knowing good and evil." Genesis 3:1-5

---

the recesses of the north. I will ascend above the heights of the clouds; I will make myself like the Most High (Isaiah 14:13-14).'" These verses are commonly thought to apply to Satan's rebellion against God prior to the account of Adam's sin in the Garden of Eden.

The serpent uses exaggerated half-truths and overt contradiction to what God had said. His methods are deceptive, devious and ever so subtle. He knows what God has prohibited, but he pretends to be ignorant and craftily asks Eve to inform him. His subtle cunningness is displayed in the very first question he asked her, "Indeed, has God said, 'You shall not eat from *any* tree of the garden'?" In the original Hebrew the form of this question is an interrogative, expressing surprise. The serpent's question could be rendered, "Is it *really the fact* that God has prohibited you from eating of all the trees of the garden?"[65] The serpent acts indignant and astonished to emphasize his subtle suggestion that God is unjust. His feigned surprise hints at the cruelty of God for prohibiting Adam and Eve the pleasure of eating of *any* tree in the garden. The way the serpent asked the question is designed to introduce doubt about God's goodness.[66] It is as if the serpent has said, "What! Has God, who has given you a variety of appetites and passions, forbidden you to satisfy them? Surely, He has not, but if He has, He must be cruel. And if so, then how can you trust Him and obey what He says?"[67] Once doubt is introduced, the serpent progresses to a very bold denial of the truth of God's warning.

> The serpent said to the woman, "You surely will not die!...." Genesis 3:4

In the original Hebrew language, the serpent's statement falsely yet audaciously declares you "will *positively not* die!"[68] The serpent

---

65 We find questions of similar form in 1 Samuel 23:3; 2 Samuel 4:11. Keil and Delitzsch, *The Keil & Delitzsch Commentary on the Old Testament*, Genesis 3:1. Retrieved from Hill, Gary, *The Discovery Bible*, HELPS Ministries, Inc.

66 Perowne, John, general editor, *The Cambridge Bible for Schools and Colleges*, Genesis 3:1. Retrieved from Hill, Gary, *The Discovery Bible*, HELPS Ministries, Inc.

67 Benson, Joseph, *Joseph Benson's Commentary of the Old and New Testaments*, Genesis 3:1, my paraphrase. Retrieved from Hill, Gary, *The Discovery Bible*, HELPS Ministries, Inc.

68 Keil and Delitzsch, *The Keil & Delitzsch Commentary on the Old Testament*, Genesis 3:1, italics added. Retrieved from Hill, Gary, *The*

then attacks God's motive for placing the tree of knowledge of good and evil off limits to Adam in the first place.

> "... For God knows that in the day you eat from it your eyes will be opened ...." Genesis 3:5

The statement "your eyes will be opened" refers to Eve's sudden ability to possess discernment that will permit her to apprehend something she could not see before.[69] Having introduced a tantalizing benefit to Eve, the serpent then provides *his* version of God's *real* reason for telling Adam he was not to eat of the fruit of that particular tree.

> "... and you will be like God, knowing good and evil." Genesis 3:5b

In other words, the serpent said to Eve, "It is *not* because the fruit of that tree is harmful to you that God has forbidden you to eat it. The reason He has said you are not to eat it is that God is envious. He does not want you to become like Him."[70] The serpent asserts that God's prohibition was designed, not as a lovingly placed guard rail to keep Adam from plunging into sin, but as a barrier to keep him from something good.

Mission accomplished. The serpent's scheme hit its mark with a perfect bullseye!

> When the woman saw that the tree was good for food, and that it was a delight to the eyes, and that the tree was desirable to make *one* wise, she took from its fruit and ate; and she gave also to her husband with her, and he ate. Genesis 3:6, italics in original

---

*Discovery Bible*, HELPS Ministries, Inc.
69  Perowne, John, general editor, *The Cambridge Bible for Schools and Colleges*, Genesis 3:5; cf. Genesis 21:19; 22:13. Retrieved from Hill, Gary, *The Discovery Bible*, HELPS Ministries, Inc.
70  Keil and Delitzsch, *The Keil & Delitzsch Commentary on the Old Testament*, Genesis 3:1, my paraphrase. Retrieved from Hill, Gary, *The Discovery Bible*, HELPS Ministries, Inc.

The *Keil & Delitzsch Commentary on the Old Testament* concludes, now you have "a truly satanic double entendre [a double meaning], in which a certain agreement between truth and untruth is secured!"[71] The serpent was truthful in the fact that by eating the forbidden fruit, Adam and Eve *did* obtain the knowledge of good and evil. In that respect, they *did* become more like God.[72] But here's the problem which is indeed the lie of the enemy. The knowledge of good and evil man acquires through his disobedience is far removed from the true likeness of God! Moreover, the enemy's brazen promise that they would most certainly *not die* was a bald-faced lie! Jesus warned His disciples about the evil one. In doing so, He revealed Satan's true character.

> … the devil … was a murderer from the beginning, [who] does not stand in the truth because there is no truth in him. Whenever he speaks a lie, he speaks from his own *nature*, for he is a liar and the father of lies. **John 8:44**, italics in original

So, we are given early notice in Scripture that to walk in obedience will require us to stand against the wiles of our adversary! Thousands of years later he continues to use variations of the same lies to woo us to sin:[73]

- "*There is no harm in it.*" When you believe this lie you are half conquered before you even know you've been attacked by the adversary.
- "*You are depriving yourself of something good by not doing it.*" Have you noticed that a common theme in present-day commercials is "you ***deserve***" whatever that advertised

---

71  Keil and Delitzsch, *The Keil & Delitzsch Commentary on the Old Testament*, Genesis 3:1. Retrieved from Hill, Gary, *The Discovery Bible*, HELPS Ministries, Inc.
72  Genesis 3:22
73  Maclaren, Alexander, *Expositions of Holy Scripture,* Genesis 3:1. Retrieved from https://biblehub.com/commentaries/genesis/3-1.htm (last accessed September 2, 2021)

product is and if you don't buy it, you will be depriving yourself?

Peter warns:

> Be of sober *spirit*, be on the alert. Your adversary, the devil, prowls around like a roaring lion, seeking someone to devour. 1 Peter 5:8, italics in original

When Adam and Eve surrendered to the enemy's enticing temptation, they made a deliberate choice to please themselves even though that meant displeasing God. The consequence for Adam and Eve was a historic change. We will turn to what changed in our next lesson.

**Hear What The Spirit is Saying to the Church:** *Oh that my children would learn to trust me. I am a good God and I only desire that which is best for my creation. Disobedience never accomplishes that which it promises because the enemy is a liar.*

# Lesson 2:

# God Fulfills His Warning To Adam

"Then the LORD God said, 'Behold, the man has become like one of Us, knowing good and evil; and now, he might stretch out his hand, and take also from the tree of life, and eat, and live forever'—therefore the LORD God sent him out from the garden of Eden ... He drove the man out; and at the east of the garden of Eden He stationed the cherubim and the flaming sword which turned every direction to guard the way to the tree of life." Genesis 3:22-24

WHILE THERE MAY BE a wide chasm between temptation and sin, once the sin takes place the results are automatic![1] This lesson will pick up exactly where we left off in Lesson 1. As we return to Genesis 3:6 and re-read the description of Eve's temptation turned to sin, we will be able to consider the consequences of disobeying God's instruction.

> When the woman saw that the tree was good for food, and that it was a delight to the eyes, and that the tree was desirable to make *one* wise, she took from its fruit and ate; and she gave also to her husband with her, and he ate. Genesis 3:6, italics in original

---

[1] Maclaren, Alexander, *Expositions of Holy Scripture*, Genesis 3:1. Retrieved from https://biblehub.com/commentaries/genesis/3-1.htm (last accessed September 2, 2021)

The phrase "to make one wise" translates the Hebrew word *le-haskil*. It is worth noting that this is not the normal biblical word for wisdom. At its core, *le-haskil* refers to prudence – "the ability to *govern and discipline oneself* by the use of reason."[2] Jewish scholar Nahum Sarna defines *le-haskil* as "the capacity for making decisions that lead to success."[3] We are beginning to see that the very nature of the serpent's temptation is for Adam and Eve to acquire the ability "to make judgments as to their own welfare *independently* of God."[4] Sarna notes that the serpent has implied that God's law is overly restrictive and therefore the path to human freedom is to disregard what God says.

Notably, the root word of *le-haskil* is *sakal* {saw-kal'} which often refers to God's instruction. The irony is that God's instruction is the very thing missing in Adam and Eve's deliberate choice to do what God said not to do! In our first lesson, we recognized that God alone is the source of wisdom. In Proverbs "the son" searches for wisdom but he does not grasp it because the Lord alone has access to wisdom.[5] The Bible tells us that Yahweh gave wisdom birth from His very being (Proverbs 8:22-24).[6] In Psalm 119 the psalmist rightly concluded it is God's *commands* that make him wiser than his enemies![7] Because Moses understood this same truth he instructed Israel to follow God's wisdom in all their ways.

---

2   Merriam-Webster.com, entry for *prudence*, italics added. Retrieved from www.merriam-webster.com/dictionary/prudence (last accessed July 8, 2021)
3   Sarna, Nahum M., *The JPS Torah Commentary Genesis*, The Traditional Hebrew Text with the New JPS Translation Commentary (The Jewish Publication Society 1989) Genesis 3:6 under *as a source of wisdom*, p. 25
4   Sarna, Nahum M., *The JPS Torah Commentary Genesis*, The Traditional Hebrew Text with the New JPS Translation Commentary (The Jewish Publication Society 1989) Genesis 3:6 under *who know good and bad*, p. 25, italics added
5   Job 28:12-28
6   Waltke, Bruce K., *The Book of Proverbs: Chapters 1-15*, The New International Commentary on the Old Testament (Eerdmans 2004) Proverbs 3:6, pp. 223-224
7   Psalm 119:98

> Therefore, observe the words of this covenant and follow them, so that you will succeed [*sakal*] in everything you do. Deuteronomy 29:9 HCSB

Daniel also recognized Yahweh as the sole source of wisdom. After Daniel had been given revelation and understanding of King Nebuchadnezzar's dream, he burst into spontaneous praise.

> [Daniel] said, "Praise the name of God forever and ever for he has all wisdom and power. He controls the course of world events; he removes kings and sets up other kings. He gives wisdom to the wise and knowledge to the scholars. He reveals deep and mysterious things and knows what lies hidden in darkness, though he is surrounded by light...." Daniel 2:20-22 NLT

Let's park here for a moment to state plainly a universal truth. Wisdom belongs to the Lord.

> Because "this wisdom existed before creation and its origins are distinct from it, wisdom is neither accessible to humanity nor can it be subdued by human beings, but it must be revealed to people [by God] and [then] accepted by them."[8]

When God stamped His image into Adam, and indeed all of humanity, He designed each and every one of us to live best by *His* wisdom. God's perfect design has never changed. It is important to understand that when God is removed from society, His wisdom is removed! In that case, all that remains is the wisdom of this world which God calls "foolish."[9]

Now we see the problem. Instructional experience on wisdom was supposed to come from God, not the serpent. Adam and Eve

---

8  Waltke, Bruce K., *The Book of Proverbs: Chapters 1-15*, The New International Commentary on the Old Testament (Eerdmans 2004) Proverbs 8:22, p. 409

9  1 Corinthians 3:19

have made the wrong choice, they have not exercised self-control and therefore failed the test of obedience! But they've gone too far to turn back. What's done is done and it appears that they know so by what happens next.

> Then the eyes of both of them were opened, and they knew that they were naked; and they sewed fig leaves together and made themselves loin coverings. Genesis 3:7

In Lesson 1 we noted that the serpent's statement "your eyes will be opened" referred to the sudden acquisition of discernment permitting Eve to apprehend what had been hidden from ordinary sight. As to this promise made by the serpent, he was telling the truth. Genesis 3:7 tells us that Adam and Eve's eyes *were* opened (the same Hebrew word the serpent used).

The result of their eyes being opened is that they now *knew* (Hebrew *yada`* {yaw-dah'}) that they were naked.[10] In Genesis 2:25 it was simply stated as an objective fact that Adam and Eve were not clothed, but now their personal knowledge is involved. The reason we can be sure of this new source of their knowledge is that the word *yada`* used in Genesis 3:7 does not refer to mere intellectual knowledge, it refers to knowledge that comes from experience.[11] They have just crossed the line. The source of their wisdom is no longer limited to God's instruction, they have begun to experience life independent of His guidance. In fact, they now have a life experience that is born out of direct disobedience to His perfect wisdom and guidance!

Notice what happens next. *They sewed* fig leaves together and *made themselves* loin coverings. Rather than turning to God who had always provided everything they needed for life in the Garden,

---

10  Note in Lesson 1 we considered the word *da`ath* (knowledge) which is a noun derived from this verb *yada`*.

11  MacArthur, John, *The MacArthur Study Bible* (Thomas Nelson 2006) study note Psalm 100:3, p. 818; Sarna, Nahum M., *The JPS Torah Commentary Genesis,* The Traditional Hebrew Text with the New JPS Translation Commentary (The Jewish Publication Society 1989) Genesis 4:1 under *the man knew*, p. 31

the result of their sin is that they take another step of independence away from Him.

Consider how different Adam and Eve's experience would have been if they had exercised self-control and stood firm in their obedience to what God had commanded. "God reserves to Himself the finding and assessing of wisdom, and the revelation of it to people who apprehend it by divine gift of faith."[12] What if Adam and Eve had waited on God's perfect timing to release the understanding of good and evil they sought? I think Psalm 73 provides us with a magnificent picture of what that might have looked like. The first 15 verses of Psalm 73 express the psalmist's utter confusion about the arrogance and the success of the wicked compared to his own life experiences. The psalmist's perspective changes immediately when God brings revelation, insight and understanding of evil and unveils the mystery.

> When I tried to understand all this, it seemed hopeless until I entered God's sanctuary. Then I understood their destiny [referring to the destiny of the wicked]. Psalm 73:16-17 HCSB

Entering God's sanctuary rest and being in close fellowship with Him provided the psalmist with the wisdom he needed. That truth gave him the understanding he lacked! "To a person who is good in His sight [God] has given wisdom and knowledge and joy."[13]

Returning to Genesis 3 we see in the very next portion of our text that Adam and Eve's experiential knowledge not only changes their perspective, their experience altars everything about their relationship with God.

---

12  Job 28:1-28; See also: Proverbs 30:1-6; Waltke, Bruce K., *The Book of Proverbs: Chapters 1-15*, The New International Commentary on the Old Testament (Eerdmans 2004) Proverbs 3:14-15, p. 258
13  Ecclesiastes 2:26

They heard the sound of the LORD God walking in the garden in the cool of the day, and the man and his wife hid themselves from the presence of the LORD God among the trees of the garden. Then the LORD God called to the man, and said to him, "Where are you?" He said, "I heard the sound of You in the garden, and I was afraid because I was naked; so I hid myself." Genesis 3:8-10

First, we'll consider the nature of God's encounter with Adam and Eve and then we'll zero in on the issue of nakedness. There is some scholarly debate about the phrase "the cool of the day" in Genesis 3:8. The most common explanation is that the expression refers to the time of day – i.e. afternoon when the sun was beginning to decline.[14] However, this phrase does not necessarily refer to the *time of day* God comes to the Garden. It has been suggested that it more likely references *how* God comes into the Garden. That suggestion is based on the possibility that the original Hebrew text may be translated as, "They heard the sound of the LORD God walking in the garden *in the wind of the storm*, and the man and his wife hid themselves ...." If that interpretation is correct, then God is not pictured as taking a normal afternoon stroll through Eden, but as coming in a powerful windstorm. Consistent with that translation, Adam's reference to hearing "the sound of [God] in the garden" may actually indicate God's thunderous voice which typically accompanies His appearance in the storm.[15]

This possible translation gives way to a natural conclusion that God is coming in angry judgment. However, it occurs to me that even if the original Hebrew does refer to the storm-like manner in

---

14 *NET Bible Notes*, translator's note 22, Genesis 3:8, citing U. Cassuto, *Genesis: From Adam to Noah*, 152–54

15 *NET Bible Notes*, translator's note 22, Genesis 3:8, citing J. J. Niehaus (*God at Sinai* [SOTBT], 155–57). Niehaus suggests the Hebrew word *yom*, usually understood as "day," may well find a background in an Akkadian cognate *umu* (storm). When used in connection with the Hebrew word *rûaḥ* {roo'-akh} (commonly translated wind, breath, spirit) as in the case of Genesis 3:8, the text could be translated as "in the wind of the storm."

which God comes down, it does not automatically mean He was coming as an angry God to vengefully judge Adam and Eve. Let's consider a few other times when the manifestation of God's appearance was attended by storm-like conditions. For example, we see this image in the book of Job when the Lord answered Job from the whirlwind (Job 38:1). We find it in the exodus narrative when God approached a consecrated nation of Israel standing at the foot of Mt. Sinai (Exodus 19:16-18). We see it again when Elijah fled to Mt. Sinai, perhaps desperate to meet with God and hear His voice after he defeated the prophets of Baal and was threatened by Jezebel (1 Kings 19:11-13). In none of these cases did God draw near in angry judgment. He simply came in a way that visibly *displayed His power* as He approached one who was the object of His affection.

I think it quite likely God's *power demonstration* was calculated to be very purposeful in each of those instances. It was what He deemed the circumstances required. You might say Yahweh's impressive appearance in each case set the record straight as to who He is! It is quite plausible God decided that same type of intentional power display best served His purpose when He entered the Garden to meet with Adam and Eve after they fell for the serpent's scheme. To be sure, the Genesis narrative makes clear that Adam and Eve will suffer consequences for their sin. However, when taken in the total context of the unfolding story it would seem that a choice by God to display His power would not be about an angry God storming into the Garden demanding an audience with His rebellious children. It is more like God hitting the re-set button with Adam and Eve. Without speaking a word, He reminds them of who He is, His all-powerful nature and that He has the right to deal with their present circumstances according to His wisdom.

Moving on to our discussion of nakedness we see Adam and Eve take another step in the wrong direction! The new knowledge of their nakedness not only led them to make a covering for themselves, their independently gained wisdom led them to hide from God. For the first time, man's reaction to God's presence in the Garden is fear and the need to be concealed from Him. Covering their bodies with leaves was apparently not sufficient so they were driven to seek additional covering in an attempt to completely hide themselves from Him. Their desperate need to find covering reflects their new-found sense of alienation from Him.[16] Now we understand the true impact of their rebellion and what God's warning of "death" meant. As we have previously learned, death in the Bible does not focus on *termination*, it refers to "a change of place and of state with continuity of personal identity."[17] What the serpent knew all along, Adam and Eve have now fully discovered for themselves – a Holy God cannot be in the presence of sin! Sin will cause separation from God (i.e. the very essence of death).

The tragic reality is that while Adam and Eve desired to be *like God* what they actually gain is fear of even being in His presence![18] Disobeying God never turns out like we thought it would. In reality, Adam and Eve did *not* become more like God in the way which they expected, they became more like the crafty, shrewd serpent.

Next, we see a further movement away from God that results in two missed opportunities – first for Adam and second for Eve. They each miss the opportunity to experience the grace of confession, repentance and forgiveness.

> And [God] said, "Who told you that you were naked? Have you eaten from the tree of which I commanded you not to eat?" The man said, "The woman whom You gave *to be* with me, she gave me from the tree, and I ate." Then the Lord God said to the woman, "What is this you have

---

16 Turpin, Simon, *Did Death of Any Kind Exist Before the Fall? What the Bible says About the Origin of Death and Suffering*, Answers in Genesis, April 3, 2013. Retrieved from https://answersingenesis.org (last accessed July 8, 2021)
17 Motyer, J. Alec, *The Prophecy of Isaiah: An Introduction & Commentary* (InterVarsity Press 1993) Isaiah 14:9-15, p. 143
18 Alcorn, Randy, *Is Genesis 3:8 Sufficient to Establish That God Was in the Habit of Visiting with Adam and Eve in the Garden?* Eternal Perspective Ministries, March 29, 2010, quoting *New American Commentary*. Retrieved from https://www.epm.org/resources/2010/Mar/29/gen-38-sufficient-establish-god-was-habit-visiting/ (last accessed July 8, 2021)

done?" And the woman said, "The serpent deceived me, and I ate." Genesis 3:11-13, italics in original

If God is omniscient, and He is, why do you think He asked first Adam and then Eve for an explanation of what they had done? The Genesis narrative does not provide us with the reason. Consistent with His character, I suggest God was giving them the chance to turn back to Him, to confess their sin and repent of the rebellious choices they had made. Tragically, we know that is not how the narrative reads. Rather than taking ownership for choosing to believe the serpent's lie and do what God had specifically told them not to do, they made excuses. Wow. Isn't that telling. Have you ever been there? I have. Rather than running straight for the Father's arms, we continue to sink deeper and deeper into the deception of sin. That next step in sin's pathway is always to excuse away the personal responsibility we actually have for obeying God's instruction. Have you ever noticed that never turns out well? As each successive step takes us deeper into sin we are increasingly alienated from God.

The best thing Adam and Eve could have done under the circumstances was to avail themselves of God's free gift exchange counter. Rather than covering themselves, hiding and making excuses they should have immediately turned back to God. They should have approached Him with honesty and integrity. If they had, they would have been invited to exchange their fear for His free gift of forgiveness. Honest confession and sincere repentance result in God's forgiveness. This has always been the *best* solution when we have not obeyed Him!

As we are going to see repeatedly in our study, **the power of obedience is that obedience provides the *only* source of unhindered fellowship with God**. Disobedience, on the other hand, leads to further and further alienation and separation. At its most basic meaning, holiness is distinctiveness or separateness from all that is *not* sacred. The biblical notion of God's holiness does not describe an ethical quality He possesses. His holiness refers to the very essence of His nature as being distinct and completely removed from that which is wicked.[19] Thus, God's holiness by His very nature, demands separation from all that is not in harmony with His character.

God knew separation had occurred and He knew why it had occurred. What He did next demonstrates the amazing merciful love of a Father!

> The LORD God made garments of skin for Adam and his wife, and clothed them. Genesis 3:21

The phrase "garments of skin" refers to the hide of a skinned animal.[20] The text gives us no indication of how God did this, again that type of detail is simply not important to the author. What does seem to be important is to emphasize for the reader that God was acting deliberately and intentionally, doing what He was certain was necessary.[21] Their self-made covering was insufficient. God alone could provide the covering they now needed.

It will be instructive for us to consider what is being covered and what is not. In 2011 I was teaching a women's Bible study and we were discussing Adam and Eve's sin. God supplied me with an illustration to help those in the class understand the type of covering God provided. Using my Ken doll (from my childhood Ken and Barbie collection) as Adam, I placed a black piece of construction paper over Adam explaining it represented the fear/shame covering which resulted from their sin. I then slipped a piece of red tissue paper in between Adam and the black piece of construction paper. As I did I said, *"Notice that God did not place His covering here on the outside of the black construction paper (representing fear/*

---

19　Childs, Brevard S., *Isaiah*, Old Testament Library Commentary (Westminster John Knox Press 2001) Isaiah 6:1-3, p. 55

20　Harris, Archer, and Waltke, editors, *Theological Wordbook of the Old Testament* (Moody Press 1999) word#1589a, p. 657

21　In the original Hebrew text, the word translated as "clothed" is in the *hiphil* verb-stem which refers to action that the doer is convinced is necessary under the circumstances. Hill, Gary, *The Discovery Bible*, HELPS Ministries, Inc., explanation of *Hiphil*

*shame). He placed it **in between** Adam and the fear/shame."* When God clothed Adam and Eve with the garments of skin He was not *covering over* their fear/shame, He was covering the distinctive mar that sin made on them.[22] In covering the spiritual blemish left by their sin, God sovereignly chose to insert (as it were) the garments of animal skin in between them and the fear/shame.

The Genesis narrative presents a *before* sin and an *after* sin picture that we need to unpack before we proceed further. To do so will require us to compare and contrast Genesis 2:25 with Genesis 3:6-8.

> And the man and his wife were both **naked** and were **not ashamed**. Genesis 2:25, bold added

> ... the woman ... took from its fruit and ate; and she gave also to her husband with her, and he ate. Then the eyes of both of them were opened, and **they knew that they were naked; and they sewed fig leaves together and made themselves loin coverings**.... and **the man and his wife hid themselves from the presence of the LORD God** among the trees of the garden. Genesis 3:6-8, bold added

In Genesis 2:25 the Hebrew word translated as "not" [*not* ashamed] or in some translations "no" [*no* shame] is the word *lo'* {lo}. It is the most commonly used Hebrew word for "factual negation."[23] The Hebrew word *lo'* tells us that the absence of shame before sin was factually true. The clear implication of their post-sin condition is that shame is now involved. Because the Adam and Eve narrative is the first biblical encounter with shame it is well worth our while to take a closer look at the scriptural notion of shame. As we will learn, the purpose and meaning of shame in

---

22 Under the New Covenant, blemishes resulting from sin are removed by the cleansing work of the blood of Christ (cf. Ephesians 5:27)!

23 Harris, Archer, and Waltke, editors, *Theological Wordbook of the Old Testament* (Moody Press 1999) word #1064, p. 463

the Bible differs significantly from the primary focus of the English word "shame." In short, when shame is introduced by the author it immediately alerts the reader to God's opinion of what has taken place in the garden!

In our modern-day Western culture, the emphasis is on the shamed person's inner attitude or state of mind.[24] A common definition is the one developed by Dr. Brené Brown, a researcher at the University of Houston Texas. Based on two decades of research she defines shame as, "the intensely painful feeling or experience of believing that we are flawed and therefore unworthy of love and belonging—something we've experienced, done, or failed to do makes us unworthy of connection."[25] On the other hand, as we will see from a Word Study and biblical application, the emphasis on shame in the Hebrew culture is primarily on failed trust, God's judgment and modifying unacceptable behavior.

> ## WORD STUDY
>
> *In Genesis 2:25 the Hebrew word buwsh {boosh} is the verb that is translated as **ashamed**. Its primary meaning is to fall into disgrace (disgrace meaning without favor, not pleasing – things are not as they should be) either through your own failure or the failure of someone you have placed your trust in.[26]*
>
> *Buwsh can also refer to a sense of "rebuke" when behavior does not align with expected conduct.[27]*

---

24 Harris, Archer, and Waltke, editors, *Theological Wordbook of the Old Testament* (Moody Press 1999) word #222, p. 97
25 Brown, Brené, *Shame vs. Guilt,* brenebrown.com, January 15, 2013. Retrieved from https://brenebrown.com/articles/2013/01/15/shame-v-guilt/ (last accessed February 8, 2022)
26 Harris, Archer, and Waltke, editors, *Theological Wordbook of the Old Testament* (Moody Press 1999) word #222, p. 97
27 Fouts, David M., "Genesis (1-11)," in *The Bible Knowledge Word Study, Genesis – Deuteronomy*, edited by Eugene H. Merrill (Victor 2003) Gen-

*The Power of Obedience* 35

As an initial matter, notice that shame can be the result of misplaced trust! Whereas our modern understanding of shame relates to being flawed or unworthy as a person, in ancient culture shame applies exclusively to the wrongful action.[28] The idea of being rebuked is connected with being disgraced or dishonored reflecting disapproval of behavior that does not conform with values that are deemed essential.[29] The goal is to correct the offender's behavior and at the same time discourage others from engaging in those actions that are socially disruptive.

Before the fourth chapter of the Bible unfolds its narrative, we are already presented with a vital biblical truth about obedience. We now know what type of conduct brings honor[30] and what results in dishonor/disgrace/shame. The rule of the Bible is set. Nothing is left to the imagination. Obeying God's commands is honorable, but disobedience is dishonorable!

Thereafter honor and shame is a common thread that runs throughout both the Old and New Testaments. When we trace the shame theme, we can conclude it relates to a person's standing before God and is always at its core about failure to obey God.[31]

---

esis 1:4 under *The light was good*, p. 41; Genesis 2:25 under *They felt no shame*, p. 50

28  Kranz, Rob, *Has the Cross Lost its Shame?* posted May 22, 2021 at 3:00 a.m., citing social anthropologist Unni Wikan. Retrieved from https: https://steppingintothejordan.com/2021/05/22/has-the-cross-lost-its-shame/(last accessed March 25, 2022). Kranz received his MA in Old Testament from Abilene Christian University. His MA thesis examined how warrior dialogues in the books of Samuel reflect cultural ideas of honor and shame.

29  deSilva, David A., *Hope of Glory: Honor Discourse and New Testament Interpretation* (Wipf & Stock 1999) p. 2

30  In the biblical record, as well as in ancient society in general, honor "becomes an umbrella that extends over the set of behavior, commitments, and attitudes that preserve a given culture and society ...." deSilva, David A., *Hope of Glory: Honor Discourse and New Testament Interpretation* (Wipf & Stock 1999) p. 3

31  The Psalms repeatedly make clear the direct connection between obeying God's decrees and not being abandoned by God or put to shame. Garland, David E., "Philippians," in *The Expositor's Bible Commentary:*

"To be put to shame" functions as a biblical idiom. It refers to God's judgment for those who rebel against His commands.[32] The biblical rule can be summarized as, "shame for the wicked and no shame for the righteous."[33] Righteousness relates to expectation. It means doing what is rightly obligated or expected by God when in covenant relationship with Him.[34] On the other hand, as our Word Study pointed out, when behavior does *not* line up with what is expected, shame (rebuke) is the result. Said another way, when God's wisdom is rejected, it results in God's rebuke.[35] Since shame serves to regulate (or modify) behavior, those who are righteous (those who do what God expects in covenant relationship) are protected from shame.

The Old Testament often uses *buwsh* in parallel with *kalam* – a word referring to the disgrace that accompanies *public* humiliation.[36] In the culture of the Bible, being publicly disgraced was

---

*Ephesians – Philemon*, Vol. 12, Revised Edition, edited by Longman III and Garland (Zondervan Academic 2006) Philippians 18b-20, p. 203. For example: "If only my ways were committed to keeping Your statutes! Then I would *not be ashamed* when I think about all Your commands.... I will keep Your statutes; never abandon me (Psalm 119:5-6,8 HCSB, italics added)." See also: "May my heart be blameless regarding Your statutes so that I will *not be put to shame* (Psalm 119:80 HCSB, italics added)."

32 Ryken, Wilhoit, and Longman III, editors, *Dictionary of Biblical Imagery* (Intervarsity Press 1998) entry for *Shame*, p. 780
33 MacArthur, John, *The MacArthur Study Bible* (Thomas Nelson 2006) study note Psalm 25:2,3, p. 751
34 Meier, Sam, *Misunderstood Terms in the Bible 2020*, Lesson 1, Messianic Studies Institute, Term 4 2020. Dr. Meier is a Professor in the Department of Near Eastern Languages and Cultures, The Ohio State University. He holds a Ph.D. from Harvard University (1987) in Hebrew and Semitic Languages and Literatures.
35 Garland, David E., "Philippians," in *The Expositor's Bible Commentary: Ephesians ~ Philemon*, Vol. 12, Revised Edition, edited by Longman III and Garland (Zondervan Academic 2006) Philippians 18b-20, p. 203
36 The *Theological Wordbook of the Old Testament* notes that there are 30 cases where *kalam* is used in parallel with *buwsh* minimizing any distinction between the meanings of the two roots. Harris, Archer, and Waltke, edi-

synonymous with your enemy gloating over you after he defeated you![37] One common shaming technique used in ancient warfare was for a conquering nation to subject their captives to public nakedness. In a prideful display of power, ancient carvings depict naked captives with their hands bound behind their backs and yokes around their necks.[38] The absence of clothing highlighted their captivity, subjugation and defeat. Putting shame in its ancient cultural context permits us to paint a vivid word picture of exactly what the serpent had done to Adam and Eve!

However, there is a deeper understanding of the author's reference to Adam and Eve's nakedness that we need to explore. The best way for us to proceed is to allow the Bible to interpret itself. Isaiah, Ezekiel and Hosea all use the idea of nakedness with moral overtones in the context of Israel's faithfulness to God's commands.[39] Biblically nakedness (absence of clothing) is used in two different

---

tors, *Theological Wordbook of the Old Testament* (Moody Press 1999) word #987, p. 443

37  Psalm 25:1-3 HCSB: "Lord, I turn to You. My God, I trust in You. Do not let me be disgraced; do not let my enemies gloat over me. No one who waits for You will be disgraced; those who act treacherously without cause will be disgraced."

38  Ferris, Paul W., Jr., "Lamentations," in *Zondervan Illustrated Bible Backgrounds Commentary*, Vol. 4, edited by John H. Walton (Zondervan 2009) Lamentations 4:21-22 under *Daughter of Edom … stripped naked*, p. 392; See for example: 2 Samuel 10:2-5

39  With reference to Ezekiel's use see: Patterson, Dorothy Kelley, general editor, *The Study Bible for Women* (Holman Bible Publishers 2015) study note Ezekiel 16:7, p. 1304; Block, Daniel I., *The Book of Ezekiel: Chapters 1-24*, The New International Commentary on the Old Testament (Eerdmans 1997) Ezekiel 16:7, p. 482. Additionally, Isaiah 47:3 refers to God "uncovering" the nakedness of Israel to expose her shame because she has prostituted herself with foreign gods; Hosea 2:9 uses the metaphor of removing the covering God had provided to Israel in order to expose her nakedness + shame. "The Israelites were literally uncovering their nakedness in temple prostitution in the Baal fertility cult rituals. Yahweh will, in effect, give them what they wanted (nakedness) but not in the way they wanted it: Yahweh will withhold the agricultural fertility they sought from Baal which would lead to nakedness caused by impoverishment." *NET Bible Notes*, study note 36, Hosea 2:9

ways. Nakedness is a reference to innocence and conversely nakedness is used to express guilt.[40] In a figurative way, nakedness without shame and no need of covering pictures being vulnerable or morally innocent, but uncovered nakedness + shame refers to moral guilt that needs a covering.

As an example, Ezekiel 16:1-8 uses the absence of clothing (with no mention of shame) to refer to Israel (more specifically Jerusalem) in her helpless innocence.[41] When she was young, Yahweh "adopted her" and provided for her. Even so, she began to worship other gods.[42] Her guilt is referred to as her nakedness and in this sense, it is a shameful thing (something deserving God's righteous judgment). This figurative use of nakedness + shame is based on the ancient custom of exposing a woman's promiscuous behavior with

---

40  The Bible uses nakedness as a description 104 times. Its meaning is context dependent. Being naked can indicate "innocence, purity, defenselessness, vulnerability, or helplessness." But it can also refer to "humiliation, shame, guilt, and judgment." Ritenbaugh, John W., *What the Bible says about Nakedness as Innocence and Vulnerability*, from *Forerunner Commentary*, Leadership and Covenants (Part Six), bibletools.org. Retrieved from https://www.bibletools.org/index.cfm/fuseaction/Topical.show/RTD/cgg/ID/5874/Nakedness-as-Innocence-Vulnerability.htm (last accessed March 14, 2022); See also: Harris, Archer, and Waltke, editors, *Theological Wordbook of the Old Testament* (Moody Press 1999) word #1588c, p. 656; Ryken, Wilhoit, and Longman III, editors, *Dictionary of Biblical Imagery* (Intervarsity Press 1998) entry for *Naked, Nakedness*, p. 581

41  "The Hebrew language generally perceives geographic entities as female." Block, Daniel I., *The Book of Ezekiel: Chapters 1-24*, The New International Commentary on the Old Testament (Eerdmans 1997) *Excursus: The Offense of Ezekiel's Gospel*, p. 468

42  The idea of adoption is expressed in the statement "[Yahweh] said to you while you were in your blood, 'Live!' Yes, [Yahweh} said to you while you were in your blood, 'Live!' (Ezekiel 16:6)." Block, Daniel I., *The Book of Ezekiel: Chapters 1-24*, The New International Commentary on the Old Testament (Eerdmans 1997) Ezekiel 16:6, p. 481, concluding "The expression seems difficult to understand, but interpreted in the light of ancient Near Eastern custom, it signifies a formal declaration of adoption."

*The Power of Obedience* 39

shameful public nakedness.[43] Nakedness + shame is a frequently used biblical metaphor for conduct that is detestable to Yahweh as well as the judgment He imposes for that disobedience.[44]

On the other hand, based on practice in the ancient Near East, "the gesture of covering a woman with one's garment [was] a symbolic act ...."[45] This type of metaphoric language is used in Ezekiel when God said He spread His garment over Israel's nakedness with the implication that He is alleviating her shame.[46] In the culture of the Bible, for a man to provide a covering for a woman was akin to a marriage proposal.[47] The suitor of a promiscuous woman could demonstrate forgiveness, restoration of honor and his intention to provide for her in the future as her husband by covering her.[48] In short, covering with a garment signified "'the establishment of a new relationship and the symbolic declaration

---

43   Ferris, Paul W., Jr., "Lamentations," in *Zondervan Illustrated Bible Backgrounds Commentary*, Vol. 4, edited by John H. Walton (Zondervan 2009) Lamentations 1:8 under *Nakedness*, p. 383. See for example: Jeremiah 13:22,26; Lamentations 1:8; Hosea 2:10; Nahum 3:5

44   Ezekiel 23:10 – The Assyrian conquer of Samaria described as uncovered or exposed nakedness (i.e., Yahweh's judgment for Samaria's idolatry); Ezekiel 23:18 - Israel's idolatry described as flaunting her nakedness (as if her idolatry removed her covering); Ezekiel 23:29 - metaphor of Israel being left "stark naked" and stripped of the provisions Yahweh had given her; the shame of her idolatry will be exposed for all to see. See also: Isaiah 47:3 - metaphor of uncovered nakedness + shame applied to Babylon; Isaiah 20:4 – Egyptian captives referred to in terms of nakedness + shame

45   Block, Daniel I., *The Book of Ezekiel: Chapters 1-24*, The New International Commentary on the Old Testament (Eerdmans 1997) Ezekiel 16:8, p. 482

46   See: Ezekiel 16:8; Block, Daniel I., *The Book of Ezekiel: Chapters 1-24*, The New International Commentary on the Old Testament (Eerdmans 1997) Ezekiel 16:8, p. 482

47   See Ruth 3:9 where Ruth asked Boaz to spread his cloak over her. In this sense Ruth was asking Boaz to provide for her as a husband provides for his wife.

48   *How does the Bible use symbolism?* under *Woman's nakedness and covering of nakedness*, Compelling Truth. Retrieved from https://www.compellingtruth.org/biblical-symbolism.html (last accessed March 13, 2022)

of the husband to provide for the sustenance of his future wife.'"[49] Accordingly, nakedness + shame + covering is used figuratively to describe God's willingness to forgive Israel's promiscuous chasing after other gods. Covering her indicates His desire to continue His relationship with her.

Applying these metaphors to Adam and Eve's before and after nakedness can help us understand what the original author's intent may have been. Using figurative language of the ancient Near East, the Genesis sin narrative involving nakedness and no shame pictures Adam and Eve's innocence and vulnerability. At that point in the story, they are innocent of all disobedience, but vulnerable to the serpent's craftiness. On the other hand, the nakedness + shame of Adam and Eve refers to their disobedience to God using the imagery of relational unfaithfulness. They had rebelled against God by trusting the serpent more than they trusted Him. When God provides garments to cover their nakedness, He is symbolically establishing a new relationship, restoring their honor and declaring His desire to continue in fellowship with them.

As we continue on in our study of Adam and Eve's disobedience to God it is noteworthy that the serpent had deceptively suggested to Eve that God's warning of death was nothing more than an idle threat.

> The serpent said to the woman, "You surely will not die!…" Genesis 3:4

Satan's distinctive thumbprint is that he makes assurances of positive outcomes that he cannot deliver! His promise is always a lie cloaked in deceit as he conceals the true consequence that naturally follows disobedience to God's command. By contrast, when God warns of consequences to sin, He means it! He *will* make good

---

[49] Block, Daniel I., *The Book of Ezekiel: Chapters 1-24*, The New International Commentary on the Old Testament (Eerdmans 1997) Ezekiel 16:8, pp. 482-483, quoting P.A. Kruger, *The Hem of the Garment in Marriage: The Meaning of the Symbolic Gesture in Ruth 3:9 and Ezek 16:8*, JNSL 12 (1984) p. 86

*The Power of Obedience*

on His word! You could say it is His unique trademark to *always* do what He says He will do.⁵⁰

Even though Adam and Eve are now properly covered, permitting continued fellowship with God, there are still consequences they must suffer because of their disobedience. Among those consequences is that their fellowship must now take place *outside* the Garden. That leads us to our Key Scripture for this lesson which I will restate here.

> Then the LORD God said, "Behold, the man has become like one of Us, knowing good and evil; and now, he might stretch out his hand, and take also from the tree of life, and eat, and live forever"—therefore the LORD God sent him out from the garden of Eden, to cultivate the ground from which he was taken. So He drove the man out; and at the east of the garden of Eden He stationed the cherubim and the flaming sword which turned every direction to guard the way to the tree of life.⁵¹ Genesis 3:22-24

What the author describes aligns precisely with how the Bible characteristically describes death. As a reminder, we have said that in the biblical account death is not synonymous with termination. Death is a change of place and a change of state with continued personal identity. Adam and Eve continue in their existence (i.e. continuity of personal identity) but they are required to change their address (i.e. change of place) and now wear a covering of skin (i.e. change of state). Moreover, as we discover in Genesis Chapter

---

50  In our culture we use the word "trademark" as an idiom to refer to consistently reliable characteristics about a person. For example, we might refer to a person's "trademark smile."

51  "The concept of a *tree of life* ... to represent eternal life is part of the ancient Near Eastern culture in which Israel participated. ... [It] figuratively represents immortality ... it also signifies healing." Waltke, Bruce K., *The Book of Proverbs: Chapters 1-15*, The New International Commentary on the Old Testament (Eerdmans 2004) Proverbs 3:18, p. 259, citations omitted

4, proper fellowship with Yahweh must now be mediated through appropriate sacrifice.[52]

I think it is fair to say that Adam and Eve didn't see that one coming! Hindsight is 20-20. However, at the time the choice is made to disobey God it is impossible to see the full extent of sin's aftermath. Notably, even though their sin was prompted by the serpent's deception and they could not fully anticipate all the consequences, God still held them accountable for their disobedience![53]

> Therefore, just as through one man sin entered into the world, and death through sin, and so death spread to all men, because all sinned. Romans 5:12

In his letter to the Romans, Paul taught that sin and death entered the human world when Adam disobeyed God. Jewish scholar Nahum Sarna views the story of the Garden of Eden as God's revelation that "evil is a human product."[54] Sarna explains that when God created the world it was good. However, man was permitted to exercise the free will God had given him. When he chose to rebel against God, he corrupted the good of creation and empowered evil in its place.

While the first biblical sin narrative seeks to explain the origin of evil as it relates to man, it is far from an exhaustive dissertation on the subject. It leaves us with many unanswered questions. Even so, it does introduce us to the devil who is real, is the heartless originator of evil, is a predator looking for human weakness and is the one who tempts people with evil.[55] We are also able to affirm that God is *not* the author of sin and we are accountable for the

---

52  Genesis 4:3-5
53  *Holman Christian Standard Bible*, Study Bible edition (Holman Bible Publishers 2010) study note Genesis 3:16, p. 13
54  Sarna, Nahum M., *Understanding Genesis Through Rabbinic Tradition and Modern Scholarship* (The Jewish Theological Seminary 2015) p. 24
55  Cymbala, Jim, *Spiritual Warfare Is Real: How the Power of Jesus Defeats the Attacks of Our Enemy* (Harper Christian Resources 2021) DVD Session 1: Know Your Enemy

*The Power of Obedience*

choices we make.[56] The same freedom of choice that permitted man to rebel against God, arms him with the freedom of choice to stand against every evil temptation. It boils down to a matter of individual preference!

The story of Adam and Eve's sin sets the backdrop for a perfect storm. On the one hand, we are created as God's image-bearers and to maintain honor and right relationship with Him requires obedience. On the other hand, Satan rules and reigns (having the dominion on earth that Adam had forfeited to him) and he will continually fight against that obedience with everything in him!

Before we conclude this lesson, we have some personal work to do. We have established that as God's covenant people we are tailor-made by Him to live by His wisdom not our own! If we would lay down our right to live life on our terms – if we would turn to Him in submission, letting Him rule and reign as the perfect Creator and Lord of life in *every* aspect of our life – we would then joyfully know by experience what it means to *know* Him. If there is any area of your life that you have been holding back from Him, would you be willing right now to drop to your knees, bow your heart and your head before Him in complete surrender? Life will never be the same! And praise God for that!

**Hear What The Spirit is Saying to the Church**: *I realize what was lost in the Garden, but My power to restore is greater than the enemy's power to destroy. Trust Me to do My part as you obey all that I command and you will see the enemy defeated.*

---

56 Sarna, Nahum M., *Understanding Genesis Through Rabbinic Tradition and Modern Scholarship* (The Jewish Theological Seminary 2015) p. 30

## Lesson 3:

## Abraham's Willingness to Sacrifice Isaac

"Now it came about after these things, that God tested Abraham, and said to him, 'Abraham!' And he said, 'Here I am.' He said, 'Take now your son, your only son, whom you love, Isaac, and go to the land of Moriah, and offer him there as a burnt offering on one of the mountains of which I will tell you.'" Genesis 22:1-2

OUR FIRST TWO lessons emphasized that unhindered fellowship with God is only possible through obedience. In this lesson, we will push deeper into the biblical truth we mentioned in Lesson 1 that obedience precedes understanding, not the other way around. We have noted the biblical pattern is for God to give a command, an instruction, an exhortation that He expects us to obey and we are only able to understand His reasoning *after* we obey Him – not before. The rearview mirror may provide us with 20-20 hindsight, but as we are walking it out, the windshield in front of us and the side view mirrors only serve to keep our feet from veering off the path.

Our Key Scripture for this lesson is no doubt a familiar one. What may come as surprisingly new is an understanding of the unprecedented revelation of God's character that He can give to Abraham because of his obedience. By digging deeper, I think we are going to see that there is a lot more going on in this narrative than that which we see at first blush. We'll begin by understanding what it means when the text says, *"God tested Abraham."*

## Word Study

*In our Key Scripture the word translated as* **tested** *is the Hebrew verb nāsâ {naw-saw'} which means to put to the test; to try; to prove the quality of, or try as fact. Divine testing brings "someone into a critical situation in order to observe reaction and behavior."[1] Accordingly, the trying or proving of the one tested often takes place through adversity or hardship.[2]*

*Nāsâ carries the sense of being brought before a judge as in a trial.[3] Nāsâ can also refer to a student being tested after a period of instruction.[4]*

*At its core meaning, nāsâ is concerned with the results of the "test" and in particular, whether the reaction or behavior of the one being tested meets with God's approval or disapproval.[5]*

---

1 Nelson, Richard D., *Deuteronomy*, The Old Testament Library (Westminster John Knox Press 2002) Deuteronomy 8:2-6, p. 111
2 Harris, Archer, and Waltke, editors, *Theological Wordbook of the Old Testament* (Moody Press 1999) word #1373, p. 581
3 Bradford, Tom, *Torah Class: Rediscovering the Old Testament: Exodus*. Retrieved from https://torahclass.com/old-testament-studies-tc/35-old-testament-studies-exodus/134-lesson-15-exodus-17-18 (last accessed July 8, 2021)
4 *God Used Manna In The Wilderness To Teach Israel Discipline & Test Their Obedience*, Power of Prayer, Praise and the Word of God Ministries, February 6, 2011. Retrieved from http://pppministries.wordpress.com/2011/02/06/god-used-manna-in-the-wilderness-to-teach-israel-discipline-test-their-obedience/ (last accessed July 8, 2021)
5 Hill, Gary, *The Discovery Bible*, HELPS Ministries, Inc., [H]58b (SN 5254) *nāsâ*

Our Key Scripture presents no ordinary request. It is *not* the only time the reader is told in Scripture that God tests someone but notably, this is the *first* time the author of Genesis alerts the reader to a "test" from God. In Lesson 1 we noted that the forbidden fruit set up a test of obedience for Adam which we can see in hindsight. However, here we are told at the outset of the narrative that God is setting up a *test* for Abraham. Even though the reader is informed, there is no indication in Scripture that Abraham knew God had done so. According to Jewish scholar Nahum Sarna, the author of Genesis employed an unusual word order in the original Hebrew that works to emphasize "the purely probative nature of the divine request."[6] Sarna concludes the effect of the unusual word order is to signal God's intention to the reader that He does *not* intend Abraham to actually sacrifice Isaac. By addressing that issue up front, the reader's mind is put to ease and his attention is able to focus on Abraham.[7] This type of focused emphasis in the Hebrew text tells the reader to really think about all that this *testing* involved.[8]

The purpose of a God-directed test is to prompt "a decision that proves character and faith."[9] In this way, it can be said that, "Divine testing leads to knowledge."[10] Isaac was the heir God had miraculously given Abraham. The question that needs to be answered in this testing is whether Abraham's faith in God can

---

6 Sarna, Nahum M., *The JPS Torah Commentary Genesis*, The Traditional Hebrew Text with the New JPS Translation Commentary (The Jewish Publication Society 1989) Genesis 22:1 under *God put Abraham to the test*, p. 151

7 When the law is given it will make clear that human sacrifice is strongly condemned. See for example: Leviticus 18:21; 20:2,5; Deuteronomy 12:31; 18:10. It is likewise denounced in the books of the prophets. See for example: Micah 6:7.

8 Author's emphasis on the word "tested" in the original Hebrew text of Genesis 22:1 noted in Hill, Gary, *The Discovery Bible*, HELPS Ministries, Inc.

9 Nelson, Richard D., *Deuteronomy*, The Old Testament Library (Westminster John Knox Press 2002) Deuteronomy 8:2-6, p. 111

10 Nelson, Richard D., *Deuteronomy*, The Old Testament Library (Westminster John Knox Press 2002) Deuteronomy 8:2-6, pp. 110-111, citation omitted

overcome his natural love for his only heir. We know from the biblical account that Abraham passed the test and he becomes a perpetual example!

Another biblical context in which we learn that God tests His covenant people is that of the wilderness period between Egypt and the Promised Land. In Deuteronomy, Moses makes clear that Yahweh had led the people into the wilderness to humble them and test [*nāsâ*] them. In its most basic meaning, humility is another way of expressing reliance on God, it denotes obedience to God. The purpose of the testing was to know what was in their heart and whether they would keep God's commands.[11]

In the Western mindset I am said to *know* something when I comprehend it intellectually. In Hebraic thought, you *know* something when you put it into practice. You don't *know* something until you actually walk it out in life. In the ancient Near Eastern culture of Abraham's day, a test allowed a person to demonstrate what they knew. This is still true today. When God tests someone He is saying, "I want to see you put into action what is hidden in your heart." God's expected outcome is that our faith will result in obedience.

Testing teaches obedience. In fact, testing is often the instrument of choice God uses in His divine classroom. It raises questions like, "Did the test show me where I am at this moment and then change my perspective?" "Did it increase my obedience so I am where God wants me to be?" God already knows what is in my heart. He needs *me* to see what is there. Once I see my true heart condition, He then invites me to change it in whatever way is necessary so that my heart aligns more perfectly with His. In this way, each test we face is uniquely and specifically designed to become a very personal learning experience.[12]

---

11 Deuteronomy 8:2-6; 15-16
12 Vander Laan, Ray, *That The World May Know with Ray Vander Laan*, DVD Teaching Series, Fire On The Mountain, Volume 9 (Zondervan 2009) Session 1: The Lord Who Heals You

## The Power of Obedience

When God tests a person, it is to refine that person's character that he might walk more closely in God's ways.[13] In that way, testing is designed to shape and mold us into the person God wants us to be.[14] There is only one proper response to a God ordained test, "Even though it is painful and I don't like it, I'm going to show you what is in my heart through my obedience."

The carrot the serpent dangled in front of Eve was the promise of becoming like God. What Eve had yet to learn was that true godliness is expressed in our character as we try to imitate God's ethical nature in our day-to-day human relationships.[15] It is our *obedience* that paves the path to develop each of those attributes. In fact, they are only attained by life experiences ordained by God.

Now that we understand testing, let's look at Abraham's response. When God first called Abraham's name he replied, "Here I am." The Hebrew word is *hinneh* {hin-nay'} which lacks a good English equivalent.[16] This interpretative challenge makes it easy for Abraham's actual response to get lost in translation. *Hinneh* is a Hebrew idiom of availability.[17] When God called his name, Abraham immediately indicated his "readiness, alertness, attentiveness, receptivity and responsiveness" to anything God wanted to say to him.[18] Notice that this is the only word Abraham utters to God

---

13 Harris, Archer, and Waltke, editors, *Theological Wordbook of the Old Testament* (Moody Press 1999) word #1373, p. 581, referring to Exodus 16:4; Deuteronomy 8:2; Judges 2:22; 2 Chronicles 32:31; Psalm 26:1-3
14 Vander Laan, Ray, *That The World May Know with Ray Vander Laan*, DVD Teaching Series, Fire On The Mountain, Volume 9 (Zondervan 2009) Session 2: Not By Bread Alone
15 Sarna, Nahum M., *Understanding Genesis Through Rabbinic Tradition and Modern Scholarship* (The Jewish Theological Seminary 2015) p. 27
16 Berlin and Brettler, editors, *The Jewish Study Bible: Featuring The Jewish Publication Society Tanakh Translation* (Oxford University Press 2004) study note Genesis 22:1, p. 45
17 Utley, Bob, *The Study Bible Commentary Series, Old Testament*, Genesis 22. Retrieved from bible.org/seriespage/genesis-22 (last accessed July 8, 2021)
18 Berlin and Brettler, editors, T*he Jewish Study Bible: Featuring The Jewish Publication Society Tanakh Translation* (Oxford University Press 2004)

in the entire narrative, but it is his immediate response both times God calls his name (Genesis 22:1,11).

After Abraham demonstrated his attentiveness and receptivity to God, God began His instruction to Abraham with the words, "Take now (Genesis 22:2)." The Hebrew word translated as "now" is *na'* {naw}. It often goes untranslated,[19] even though it has an important use in the Hebrew language. It is *not* an adverb related to time as it might seem to be by its English translation. It is an entreaty. That is to say it is a plea or an appeal, usually coupled with one or more requests. Because *na'* often indicates the speaker's intent to soften his petition, the request becomes more like an exhortation (encouragement) than a command.[20]

*Na'* can also be used to intensify an entreaty or exhortation so as to highlight the urgency of the request.[21] This connotation of *na'* may well explain why Abraham got up early the very next morning to obey God's instruction (Genesis 22:3).

Rightly comprehending what "now" means allows us to accurately picture the scene. The author is not describing a threatening and forceful God demanding Abraham take his son to Moriah and sacrifice him there. The picture painted by the original Hebrew words is much more like a relational God who is appealing to His servant Abraham to offer Isaac to Him as a free-will offering.[22]

God's exhortation is for Abraham to, "Take now your son, your only son, whom you love, Isaac, and go … and offer him …

---

study note Genesis 22:1, p. 45

19  See NIV for example: "Then God said, 'Take your son, your only son ….'"
20  Ellicott, Charles John, *Ellicott's Commentary for English Readers*, Genesis 22:1. Retrieved from Hill, Gary, *The Discovery Bible*, HELPS Ministries, Inc.
21  Hill, Gary, *The Discovery Bible*, HELPS Ministries, Inc., H72o (SN 4994) *nā̓*, citing A. E. Cowley, *Gesenius' Hebrew Grammar*, 324
22  A freewill offering is an optional offering that could be offered to God at any time. See: Spence and Exell, general editors, *The Pulpit Commentary*, Genesis 22:2, citing Lange for the idea that the use of the word *na'* may indicate a freewill offering. Retrieved from Hill, Gary, *The Discovery Bible*, HELPS Ministries, Inc.

*The Power of Obedience* 51

as a burnt offering ...."[23] Isaac is the only son of Sarah, the only offspring of God's promise to Abraham, the only heir of all the future promises God has made, the only son who remained after Ishmael's departure, the only child who could take care of Abraham and Sarah in their old age, the only child through whom Abraham could have descendants. In the original text, the word order of the Hebrew communicates the reality of what God is saying to Abraham. That word order in the original text indicates increasing tension, "your son ... your favored one ... the one whom you love ... Isaac." Not only is Isaac the son upon whom Abraham's life and future wellbeing are centered, but this is also the child Abraham deeply loves.[24]

God's test will provide Abraham with the opportunity to obey without any understanding of *why* God was giving him this instruction and that's the obedience we see in the narrative. There is no record of Abraham questioning God, negotiating with Him, or in any way attempting to convince God to change His mind. We are simply informed rather matter-of-factly that, "Abraham rose early in the morning and saddled his donkey, and took two of his young men with him and Isaac his son; and he split wood for the burnt offering, and arose and went to the place of which God had told him."[25] It is worth noting here that Abraham responded immediately to God, but this test is not going to end that quickly. Scripture makes clear that his willingness to remain committed to

---

23 Genesis 22:2; A burnt offering is the most frequently mentioned type of sacrifice in the Old Testament. The distinct feature of this type of offering is that the whole sacrifice had to be burned, leaving no part left over for either offeror or priest. Fouts, David M., "Genesis (1-11)," in *The Bible Knowledge Word Study, Genesis – Deuteronomy*, edited by Eugene H. Merrill (Victor 2003) Genesis 1:4 under *The light was good*, p. 41; Holmyard, Harold R., "Genesis (12-24)," in *The Bible Knowledge Word Study, Genesis – Deuteronomy*, edited by Eugene H. Merrill (Victor 2003) Genesis 22:2 under *As a burnt offering*, p. 91

24 Berlin and Brettler, editors, *The Jewish Study Bible: Featuring The Jewish Publication Society Tanakh Translation* (Oxford University Press 2004) study note Genesis 22:2, p. 45

25 Genesis 22:3

Yahweh without knowing the precise outcome will be tested for three days.[26]

What was probably most alarming to Abraham about God's exhortation is not what we might think. To understand Scripture correctly, the best practice is to view it through the lens of the author's culture and of the people the author was writing to. When we do that, in this case, we will quickly see that our perspective must be dramatically re-oriented.

In our Western worldview, our value for life ranks high. Therefore, it is natural to assume that the most distressing thing to Abraham would have been that God asked him to make a human sacrifice. However, it seems more likely given the culture in which Abraham lived that the greater concern would have been that God was asking him to be willing to give up the heir God had promised him.[27]

By placing God's request in the cultural context of that day I think you'll see why I believe it is reasonable to reach that conclusion. Moreover, as we will see, God is going to use the prevailing culture of Abraham's day to reveal that He is remarkably different from the pagan gods of the culture that surrounds Abraham. He could have given Abraham a long lecture describing His nature, but that is not the teaching method we see God using in the Bible. The recurring biblical pattern is that God uses life lessons walked out in obedience to teach His covenant people who He is and

---

26  "On the third day Abraham raised his eyes and saw the place from a distance." Genesis 22:4

27  The author of Hebrews provides some additional insight that is not found in the Genesis narrative: "By faith Abraham, when he was tested, offered up Isaac, and he who had received the promises was offering up his only begotten *son*; ***it was he* to whom it was said, 'IN ISAAC YOUR DESCENDANTS SHALL BE CALLED.'** (Hebrews 11:17-18, italics in original, bold added)." He considered that God is able to raise people even from the dead (Hebrews 11:17-19). In this we gain a glimpse into what seemed upper most on Abraham's mind when God commanded that he be willing to sacrifice Isaac – it was forfeiting the only heir through which Abraham would have had the descendants God had promised.

how He differs from the pagan gods that are being worshipped all around them.

Putting first things first, scholars recognize that Genesis Chapters 1-38 "reflect a great deal of what we know from other sources [outside the Bible] about ancient Mesopotamian life and culture."[28] Recall Abraham was called out of Ur of the Chaldeans[29] (Genesis 12:1-3) which according to Stephen was in Mesopotamia (Acts 7:2) and according to Joshua was a place where they served other gods (Joshua 24:2). Notably, of the Abrahamic family names reported in the biblical account, all reflect traces of a connection with moon worship: Terah (Abraham's father), Sarah (Abraham's wife), Milcah (daughter of Abraham's oldest brother Haran) and Laban (the grandson of Abraham's older brother Nahor). Scholars believe what may be referenced in each of these names is the official moon cult known to exist in both Ur and Haran.[30]

Human sacrifice to a god was part of the normal worship practices among an ethnic group of people who lived in Mesopotamia in the first millennium B.C. known as the Chaldaeans.[31]

---

28  *NIV Study Bible* (Zondervan Publishing 1995) Genesis Introduction, p. 1

29  The Chaldeans derived their name from an ancient name *Chaldai*, which referred to a group of Aramean tribes who moved into lower Mesopotamia around 1000 to 900 B.C. After moving from their tribal settlements to urban settings they acquired the name Babylonians or Neo-Babylonians; therefore, Chaldeans and Babylonians are interchangeable terms. *Holman Christian Standard Bible*, Study Bible edition (Holman Bible Publishers 2010) study note Jeremiah 38:2, p. 1299

30  Sarna, Nahum M., *Understanding Genesis Through Rabbinic Tradition and Modern Scholarship* (The Jewish Theological Seminary 2015) p. 98

31  The sacrifice of a living person was a religious custom widely prevalent among the ancient Semites. The excavations, carried out in recent years at Gezer, Megiddo and Taanach, have shown that the practice was followed by the primitive Semitic inhabitants of Palestine. Moreover, at least at Megiddo, the practice continued in the Israelite period. Perowne, John, general editor, *The Cambridge Bible for Schools and Colleges*, Genesis 22:1 under 2. *The Command to sacrifice Isaac,* quoting Driver's Schweich Lectures, pp. 68, 69. There is evidence to show that human sacrifice prevailed from the earliest times in Egypt, though the victims may generally have been taken from the ranks of the enemy. Perowne, John, general

The Bible makes clear that child sacrifice was also a known practice of the Canaanites, who were in the Promised Land at the time of Abraham's arrival there.[32] Surrounded by these practices, God's request to sacrifice Isaac would likely not have seemed strange to Abraham's ears in and of itself. At the time God made His request to Abraham no formal prohibition existed against those sacrificial practices.[33] The Mosaic Law would come later in Israel's history. The fact that those type of sacrifices existed does not mean God condoned them. It simply reflects the current pagan practice. That practice provides us with the background to understand that in Abraham's eyes (absent any revelation from God to the contrary) it would not have been inherently wrong, nor even hard-hearted, for a father to sacrifice his own son.[34]

Based on the evidence that the sacrifice of a living person was a religious custom widely prevalent among the ancient cultures of Abraham's day, *The Cambridge Bible for Schools and Colleges* reaches this well-reasoned conclusion:[35]

> We may assume, then, that in Abraham's time the religious custom of human sacrifice prevailed among the peoples of the land. We have to think of the patriarch as he was, as a man of his own time and race. God spoke to him in language that he could understand. God proved

---

    editor, *The Cambridge Bible for Schools and Colleges*, Genesis 22:1, citation cf. Handcock, p. 75, quoting Budge's *Osiris*, pp. 197 ff. Retrieved from https://biblehub.com/commentaries/cambridge/genesis/22.htm (last accessed February 4, 2022)

32  See for example: Psalm 106:34-39
33  Spence and Exell, general editors, *The Pulpit Commentary*, Genesis 22:2. Retrieved from https://biblehub.com/commentaries/genesis/22-2.htm (last accessed September 3, 2021)
34  Maclaren, Alexander, *Expositions of Holy Scripture*, Genesis 22:1. Retrieved from Hill, Gary, *The Discovery Bible*, HELPS Ministries, Inc.
35  Perowne, John, general editor, *The Cambridge Bible for Schools and Colleges*, Genesis 22:1 under *2. The Command to sacrifice Isaac*. Retrieved from https://biblehub.com/commentaries/cambridge/genesis/22.htm (last accessed February 4, 2022)

his faith by a test, which, horrible as it sounds to our ears, was consonant with the feelings and traditions he had inherited from his forefathers. The [exhortation] to sacrifice Isaac [in those days] would not have suggested anything outrageous or abominable, as it does to our minds. We must remember that, startling as it may appear, it would have seemed to the ancient inhabitants of Palestine far more wonderful that Abraham's God should have interposed to prevent the sacrifice, than that He should have given the [request] for its being offered.

Now let's put that point of view into its larger Genesis context. In His first narrated encounter with Abram (renamed Abraham), God had instructed him in detail all he must leave behind: his country, his relatives and his father's house. God obviously was not interested in merely reworking an existing nation. His goal was to establish an entirely new nation (Genesis 12:1). In other words, the culture, religion and philosophy of the people of Ur were *not* to be a part of what God planned to do with His covenant people, Israel. Therefore, it is not surprising that throughout the Old Testament we see God first teaching Abraham, then Isaac, then Jacob and later teaching all of Israel the truth of who He is. Because He is not like the pagan gods of the cultures that surround them, He must rewrite their cultural script. Writing that new script will require revelation that, by His sovereign choice, will be accomplished through demonstration of His mighty acts and deeds. God's ability to demonstrate His truth will be conditioned on their obedience – if they don't obey, He will be robbed of a teachable moment. Disobedience will mean He will not be able to complete the object lesson they were supposed to have gained by experience. We have recognized that true godliness is an expression of character. It is an attempt to imitate in human relationships those ethical attributes associated with God in the Bible. That means God must be given the opportunity to reveal His true character so that we can imitate Him.

When Abraham obeyed and prepared to sacrifice Isaac, he was willingly putting his future at risk! At God's directive, He had already removed one son, Ishmael, from his life leaving Isaac as his *only* son. It wasn't until Abraham released the promise he held in his hand that he saw God's provision. This became one of those remarkable teachable moments planned perfectly by God.

> Abraham said, "God will provide for Himself the lamb for the burnt offering, my son." So the two of them walked on together. Then they came to the place of which God had told him; and Abraham built the altar; there and arranged the wood, and bound his son Isaac and laid him on the altar, on top of the wood. Abraham stretched out his hand and took the knife to slay his son. But the angel of the Lord called to him from heaven and said, "Abraham, Abraham!" And he said, "Here I am." He said, "Do not stretch out your hand against the lad, and do nothing to him; for now I know that you fear God, since you have not withheld your son, your only son, from Me." Then Abraham raised his eyes and looked, and behold, behind *him* a ram caught in the thicket by his horns; and Abraham went and took the ram and offered him up for a burnt offering in the place of his son. Genesis 22:8-13, italics in original

As we have previously noted, there is more going on in this story than first meets the eye. We already know God's appeal to sacrifice Isaac is a test of obedience and indeed as we have seen, it is just that. But it is more than that. The request to sacrifice Isaac is a perfect example of God using the things that Abraham was culturally familiar with and reorienting those cultural norms so that God could remarkably rewrite the script Abraham had known!

In the midst of an ancient world in which firstborn children were offered to appease the gods,[36] God revealed volumes about

---

36 The Bible notes that King Mesha of Moab sacrificed his firstborn son to prevent a military disaster (2 Kings 3:27); King Ahaz of Judah also sacri-

*His* nature by substituting a ram to be sacrificed in the place of Abraham's son! Yahweh, the one true God, is *not* like those other gods. He is *not* appeased by child sacrifice, nor has it ever crossed His mind that it should be so. Centuries later Israel had forgotten that Yahweh's ways and thoughts were not those of the pagan gods. In the days of Jeremiah God reminded His covenant people of the revelation He had given Abraham on Mt. Moriah!

> [The people of Israel and the people of Judah] built the high places of Baal that are in the valley of Ben-hinnom to cause their sons and their daughters to pass through *the fire* to Molech [as a sacrifice to appease that pagan god], which **I had not commanded them nor had it entered My mind that they should do this abomination, to cause Judah to sin**. Jeremiah 32:35, italics in original, bold added

The next thing of note that happens in the Genesis narrative concerning Abraham is that he gave the place where God tested him a new name.

> Abraham called the name of that place The LORD Will Provide, as it is said to this day, "In the mount of the LORD it will be provided." Genesis 22:14

This type of renaming became the established practice of other Israelite patriarchs and leaders after him. The physical location where a revelation of God's nature had occurred became a sacred site and was given a new name that was in some way reminiscent of that revelation.[37] In the culture of the Bible, an act of "naming"

---

ficed his son in similar pagan ritual (2 Kings 16:3).

37 Sarna, Nahum M., *The JPS Torah Commentary: Genesis*, The Traditional Hebrew Text with the New JPS Translation Commentary (The Jewish Publication Society 1989) The Naming Of The Alter ([Genesis 22] v. 14), p. 154. See for example, Genesis 32:30 – Jacob named the place where he wrestled with the angel of the Lord, Peniel (the face of God); Genesis 35:15 - Jacob renamed Luz to Bethel (House of God); Exodus

like this preserved the memory of the amazing revelatory event that took place there.[38] Such renaming also culturally provided that location with "a new identity, essence, function."[39]

By considering the name Abraham gave the site where the substitutionary sacrifice took place we will discover what Abraham thought was the most important thing to be remembered about his test. From that new name, we discover that *God will provide* was Abraham's understanding of what was most significant. Abraham learned by personal experience God is the one who goes before His covenant people with strategically placed provision. However, their eyes will only be open to provision as they need it. That means their feet *must* be on the path of obedience because that is where the provision will be. In fact, *that* path of obedience is the *only* place they will find God's provision! From Abraham's experience, we also learn that God's all-sufficient provision will be revealed just in time. His provision will not be late, but neither will it necessarily be as early as might be preferred! Every Christ-follower is in covenant relationship with Abraham's God. These truths are as relevant to us today as they were to Abraham when God first revealed Himself as the "*The* LORD *[Who] Will Provide.*"

As we continue to study the text, we realize that God was not yet finished with the revelation He had planned for Abraham on Mt. Moriah. God is going to dramatically reorder Abraham's thinking about the connection between obedient behavior and His grace. As soon as God saw Abraham's faith in action:

> [Yahweh] said, "Do not stretch out your hand against the lad, and do nothing to him for now I know that you **fear God**, since you have not withheld your son, your only son, from Me." Genesis 22:12, bold added

---

17:7 – Moses renamed Rephidim to Massah (Testing God) and Meribah (Complaint)

38  *NET Bible Notes*, translator's note 33, Genesis 22:14
39  Barth, Markus, *Ephesians Translation and Commentary on Chapters 1-3*, The Anchor Bible Vol 34 (Doubleday 1974) Ephesians 3:14-21 under *Comment III C The Naming*, p. 383

*The Power of Obedience*

As we have learned, this test was a deliberate trial to see if Abraham would be obedient. In Genesis 22:12 we read that God now knows that Abraham *fears* Him. God's knowledge is based on what Abraham did. Abraham's actions revealed what was in his heart and put that heart attitude on display for all to see. This was precisely what the test was designed to do and it led to God's declaration that He now knew by experience that Abraham willingly obeyed Him!

To more fully grasp what the text is teaching us, we will explore two aspects of God's declaration a little deeper: 1) what it means to "fear God" and 2) the capricious nature of the pagan gods in Abraham's day.[40] We will consider these two aspects in that order.

## WHAT IT MEANS TO FEAR GOD

Abraham's actions had demonstrated that he feared God. In the sense used here, "fear of the Lord" is synonymous with "love of the Lord."[41] A Word Study will be helpful.

---

40  The Bible does not expressly deny the existence of other gods. Nelson, Richard D., *Deuteronomy*, The Old Testament Library (Westminster John Knox Press 2002) Deuteronomy 6:4-5, p. 91. While verses like Exodus 9:14; Deuteronomy 4:35, 32:39; Psalm 18:31 and Isaiah 43:10, 45:5 seem, at face value, to deny the existence of any other "god" except Yahweh, these are in reality "statements of incomparability." Heiser, Michael S., *The Unseen Realm: Recovering the Supernatural Worldview of the Bible* (Lexham Press 2015) pp. 34-35. In other words, what we may think of as "denial statements" are in fact declarations that compared to Yahweh other gods are nothing. Heiser, Michael S., *The Unseen Realm: Recovering the Supernatural Worldview of the Bible* (Lexham Press 2015) pp. 34-35; McConville, J. G., *Deuteronomy*, Apollos Old Testament Commentary 5 (IVP Academic 2002) Deuteronomy 4:35, pp. 112-113. "To claim that a deity is one, or alone, in other ancient Near Eastern texts … generally relates to the supremacy of their rule." Walton, Matthews, and Chavalas, *The IVP Bible Background Commentary: Old Testament* (InterVarsity Press 2000) Deuteronomy 6:4 under *Yahweh is one*, p. 177, citations omitted

41  See also: Deuteronomy 10:12; Waltke, Bruce K., *The Book of Proverbs: Chapters 1-15*, The New International Commentary on the Old Testament (Eerdmans 2004) Theology under *b. The Wise and Righteous, (2) The Fear of the Lord*, p 101

## Word Study

*In Genesis 22:12 the word translated as **fear** in the phrase "fear God" is the Hebrew yare' {yaw-ray'}. No single English word conveys every aspect of yare' as it is used in this phrase.[42] As it relates to doing what God expects in covenant relationship, the essence of fearing God denotes an attitude of openness and complete submission to His divine instruction.[43]*

*The "fear of God ... decisively affects human conduct," acting as an ultimate restraint against unfaithfulness and motivating an active obedience to God's divine will.[44]*

*This "fear" supplies the power necessary to overcome every other kind of fear.[45] In Old Testament thought, a person who was said to "fear the Lord" did not fear anything else.[46]*

In Genesis 22:12, Abraham's *fear* of God includes his worshipful submission to, reverential awe of and obedient respect for

---

42 Harris, Archer, and Waltke, editors, *Theological Wordbook of the Old Testament* (Moody Press 1999) word #907, p. 399
43 Longman III and Garland, general editors, *The Expositor's Bible Commentary: Psalms*, Vol. 5, Revised Edition (Zondervan 2008) *Reflections: The Ways of Wisdom and Folly*, p. 85; Waltke, Bruce K., *The Book of Proverbs: Chapters 1-15*, The New International Commentary on the Old Testament (Eerdmans 2004) Introduction, p. 65
44 Sarna, Nahum M., *Exploring Exodus: The Origins of Biblical Israel* (Schocken Books 1996) p. 120
45 Christensen, Duane L., *Word Biblical Commentary: Deuteronomy 1-21:9*, Volume 6A, Second Edition (Zondervan 2014) Deuteronomy 10:12-11:9 under *Explanation*, p. 205
46 Brown, Michael L., *Compassionate Father or Consuming Fire: Engaging The God of The Old Testament* (AWKNG Press 2021) p. 14

Yahweh.[47] It refers to his active obedience which is the outward display of the faith hidden in his heart.[48] Abraham has now demonstrated that this faithfulness to Yahweh is what is most important to him. His actions have shown that obedience is even more important than his fatherly love for Isaac and his legitimate need for an heir.[49]

**THE CAPRICIOUS NATURE OF THE PAGAN GODS IN ABRAHAM'S DAY**

In Mesopotamian society, the nature of the pagan gods did not allow for certainty or security in the universe. As far as man could tell, the gods he worshipped were not in any noticeable way regulated by anything other than sudden and unexpected changes in their desires and actions. Those gods had no discernible norms, nor was there any expectation that man's fate was in any way decisively determined by his own behavior.[50]

> The ancients sought the favour of the god or goddess, usually for an immediate need such as good health or harvest, and not for eternal salvation. The devotee made the request, offered a sacrifice, and vowed to honor the deity should it answer the prayer. It was a bit of hit or miss approach, and supplicants kept trying until they got results.[51]

---

47  *Holman Christian Standard Bible*, Study Bible edition (Holman Bible Publishers 2010) HCSB Bullet Notes, entry for *fear(s) God or the Lord/ fear of the Lord*, p. 2232
48  *NET Bible Notes*, study note 28, Genesis 22:12
49  *NET Bible Notes*, study note 28, Genesis 22:12; Berlin and Brettler, editors, *The Jewish Study Bible: Featuring The Jewish Publication Society Tanakh Translation* (Oxford University Press 2004) study note Genesis 22:12, p. 46
50  Sarna, Nahum M., *Understanding Genesis Through Rabbinic Tradition and Modern Scholarship* (The Jewish Theological Seminary 2015) p. 147
51  Cohick, Linn H., *The Letter To The Ephesians*, The New International Commentary of the New Testament (Eerdmans 2020) p. 36

The capricious nature of those pagan gods is a direct contradiction to the biblical reality of Yahweh, the one true God.[52] As will be explored more fully in Lesson 7, it is likely Abraham knew about Yahweh from his godly ancestry through the line of Shem. However, in his formative years in Mesopotamia, he would have been surrounded by the common pagan understanding of human interaction with deity. God needed to design lesson plans for Abraham's benefit – lessons that would teach Abraham about a different reality than that pagan worldview. We can know *about* God, but we only come to *know Him* through the practical life lessons He gives us. Our obedience to those carefully designed lessons provides us with progressive revelation and teach us about God's true nature.

Unlike those pagan gods, the God of Abraham is a divine being who has an absolute will. Yahweh's faithfulness to keep His promises assures mankind that obedience to His will is *not* without meaning or purpose.[53] That reality of God's true nature is the next revelation Abraham receives. Let's see how God specifically connects the confirmation of His covenant benefits with Abraham's obedience.

> Then the angel of the LORD called to Abraham a second time from heaven, and said, "By Myself I have sworn, declares the LORD, **because you have done this thing and have not withheld your son, your only son**, indeed I will greatly bless you, and I will greatly multiply your seed as the stars of the heavens and as the sand which is on the seashore; and your seed shall possess the gate of their enemies. In your seed all the nations of the earth shall be blessed, **because you have obeyed My voice**." Genesis 22:15-18, bold added

---

[52] Sarna, Nahum M., *Understanding Genesis Through Rabbinic Tradition and Modern Scholarship* (The Jewish Theological Seminary 2015) p. 17

[53] Sarna, Nahum M., *Understanding Genesis Through Rabbinic Tradition and Modern Scholarship* (The Jewish Theological Seminary 2015) p. 18

God's covenant with Abraham has been unfolding progressively since it was first introduced in very general terms in Genesis 12:1-3. God promised Abram (Abraham) that He would give him many descendants and that He would also give him the land of Canaan. Abraham would be the focal point for the blessing or cursing of all mankind. Those who bless Abraham would be blessed and those who curse him (or esteem him lightly) would be cursed. In Genesis 15 the covenant was formally ratified with the offered sacrifice and in Genesis 17 Abraham was given circumcision as the God-ordained sign of the covenant.

After God declared that Abraham is one who fears Him, it is in keeping with God's nature that He reaffirms all the previous promises He had given Abraham. All those blessings which were pure acts of divine grace are now "reinterpreted as a consequence of [Abraham's obedience]."[54] For the first time, these blessings are authenticated by God's solemn oath. Next, God adds two new elements to Abraham's blessings: 1) sand is metaphorically used for his multitude of offspring and 2) his descendants are promised victory over their enemies.[55]

In God's Kingdom, His faithfulness is visibly demonstrated in the way in which He is steadfastly loyal to the covenant promises He makes and the non-capricious manner in which He deals with the world. Similarly, man visibly demonstrates his loyalty to God through his actions – actions that must be steadfast enough to stand the test of trial and suffering.[56] As we have said, when God tests, it is to prompt "a decision that proves [the person's] character and

---

54 Berlin and Brettler, editors, *The Jewish Study Bible: Featuring The Jewish Publication Society Tanakh Translation* (Oxford University Press 2004) study note Genesis 22:15-18, p. 47
55 Sarna, Nahum M., *The JPS Torah Commentary: Genesis*, The Traditional Hebrew Text with the New JPS Translation Commentary (The Jewish Publication Society 1989) Genesis 22:15-18 under *Reaffirmation of the Blessings*, p. 154
56 Sarna, Nahum M., *Understanding Genesis Through Rabbinic Tradition and Modern Scholarship* (The Jewish Theological Seminary 2015) p. 163

faith."[57] In a test, the quality of a man's character that exists only as a *potential* before the test must be put into practice for him to pass the test.[58] God had credited Abraham with righteousness at the moment Abraham believed God's promise for a son. But his ongoing covenant relationship with God will require Abraham to maintain that status of righteousness by his actions.[59]

The revelation of God's character which was made known through Abraham's test of obedience was not for Abraham's benefit alone. Hereafter Abraham is the "uncontested paradigm of the truly 'God-fearing' man."[60] He reflects the wholehearted openness and submission to God's will that is characteristic of one who fears God. In God's eyes it is neither relevant nor important that Abraham never completed the requested action, he never physically sacrificed Isaac. In Yahweh's lesson plan "the value of the act [He commands] may lie as much in the inward intention of the doer as in the final execution."[61]

In our next lesson, we'll take time to review what God has taught us about obedience from Genesis.

---

57  Nelson, Richard D., *Deuteronomy*, The Old Testament Library (Westminster John Knox Press 2002) Deuteronomy 8:2-6, p. 111
58  Sarna, Nahum M., *The JPS Torah Commentary: Genesis*, The Traditional Hebrew Text with the New JPS Translation Commentary (The Jewish Publication Society 1989) Genesis 22:12 under *for now I know*, p. 153
59  Sarna, Nahum M., *The JPS Torah Commentary: Genesis*, The Traditional Hebrew Text with the New JPS Translation Commentary (The Jewish Publication Society 1989) Genesis 22:12 under *for now I know*, p. 153
60  Sarna, Nahum M., *The JPS Torah Commentary: Genesis*, The Traditional Hebrew Text with the New JPS Translation Commentary (The Jewish Publication Society 1989) Genesis 22:12 under *for now I know*, p. 153
61  Sarna, Nahum M., *The JPS Torah Commentary: Genesis*, The Traditional Hebrew Text with the New JPS Translation Commentary (The Jewish Publication Society 1989) Genesis 22:12 under *for now I know*, p. 153

***Hear What The Spirit is Saying to the Church***: *I am indeed the God who provides, but I will only provide what is needed to fulfill My will. I will never reward disobedience. For those who obey, My provision will always be sufficient.*

# LESSON 4:

## LESSONS LEARNED FROM GENESIS

"... I will establish My covenant between Me and you and your descendants after you throughout their generations for an everlasting covenant, to be God to you and to your descendants after you.... and I will be their God.... Now as for you, you shall keep My covenant, you and your descendants after you throughout their generations...." Genesis 17:7-9

IN THE HEBREW tradition, the title of the book of Genesis is the same as the first word in the text: *"bere'shith"* which is commonly translated as "In Beginning." The word "Genesis" actually translates the Greek word *Geneseos* meaning "Of Birth."[1] In other words, Genesis refers to "the origin or coming into being of something."[2]

The book of Genesis tells about the beginning of all things and beginnings are a big deal in Scripture. For example, in Genesis, we learn that God was "in the beginning" (Genesis 1:1). He existed before all things for He is the Creator of all things. Some other beginnings recorded in Genesis are the coming into being of: 1) the heavens and the earth; 2) all plant, animal and human life; 3) all races, nations and languages and 4) marriage and the family. Genesis also records the beginning of sin and sacrifice and foretells

---

1  *Holman Christian Standard Bible*, Study Bible edition (Holman Bible Publishers 2010) Genesis Introduction, p. 1

2  *Merriam-Webster*, entry for *Genesis*. Retrieved from https://www.merriam-webster.com/dictionary/genesis (last accessed July 2, 2022)

the coming of a Savior as well as the nation through whom the Savior would come. Genesis is the foundation of the five Books of the Law, the foundation of the entire Old Testament and it is in fact the foundation of the entire Bible.

True to its purpose, Genesis provides us with core foundational principles related to obeying God. To that end, our first three lessons have been packed with important truths about the power of obedience and it will be beneficial to use this lesson to review those truths.

We will jump-start this lesson with a Word Study. As we have seen from the very beginning of Scripture it is abundantly clear that God expects those in relationship with Him to obey Him. As a result, it may surprise you to learn that the Hebrew language does not have a distinct word for "obey." Biblical Hebrew uses a remarkably small number of words – only about 8,000.[3] By way of contrast, *Webster's Third New International Dictionary*[4] and *Oxford English Dictionary*, Second Edition both include some 470,000 entries.[5]

"Because Hebrew has so few words, each is like an over-stuffed suitcase, bulging with extra meanings that it must carry in order for the language to fully describe reality."[6] That's certainly the case with the Hebrew word commonly translated as "obey."

---

[3] Silva, Moisés, *Biblical Words and Their Meaning: An Introduction to Lexical Semantics* (Zondervan 1983, 1994) p. 42

[4] *Webster's Third New International Dictionary Unabridged*, together with its 1993 Addenda Section

[5] *How many words are there in English?* Merriam-Webster. Retrieved from https://www.merriam-webster.com/help/faq-how-many-english-words# (last accessed October 13, 2021)

[6] Tverberg, Lois, *Shema: To Hear is to Obey*, Our Rabbi Jesus, February 6, 2013. Retrieved from https://ourrabbijesus.com/articles/ /shema-to-hear-is-to-obey/ (last accessed July 8, 2021)

## Word Study

*The Hebrew verb shama` {shaw-mah'} is most often translated as **hear** because that is its most basic meaning.[7] However, in almost every case when we see the word **obey** in the Old Testament it is a translation of the word shama`.[8]*

*In biblical use shama` has five primary shades of meaning: 1) to listen by focusing your attention, 2) to hear sound with your ear, 3) to understand, 4) to take to heart (meaning to take something into account) and 5) to act in response to what was heard.[9]*

As we can see from our Word Study, *shama`* is primarily about hearing. In Hebrew thought obedience becomes synonymous with hearing when hearing leads to action. In the Bible, hearing obediently is intimately connected with keeping God's covenant. "To respond with other than obedience demonstrates a failure to have 'heard' and is tantamount to unbelief."[10] Thus, in biblical thought faith and obedience are the manifestations of true hearing.[11]

---

7  Harris, Archer, and Waltke, editors, *Theological Wordbook of the Old Testament* (Moody Press 1999) word #2412, p. 938

8  Tverberg, Lois, *Shema: To Hear is to Obey*, Our Rabbi Jesus, February 6, 2013. Retrieved from https://ourrabbijesus.com/articles/ /shema-to-hear-is-to-obey/ (last accessed July 8, 2021)

9  Rabbi Sacks, *Va'etchanan (5770) – The Meanings of Shema*, July 24, 2010. Retrieved from http://rabbisacks.org/covenant-conversation-5770-vaetchanan-the-meanings-of-shema/ (last accessed July 8, 2021)

10 Nanos, Mark D., *The Mystery of Romans: The Jewish Context of Paul's Letter* (Fortress Press 1996) p. 222. Retrieved from books.google.com (webpage no longer available)

11 Bromiley, Geoffrey W., *Theological Dictionary of the New Testament*, Abridged in One Volume (Eerdmans 1985) entry for *akouo* under *2 a*.

Now that we've had the opportunity to unpack the biblical understanding of *obey* (which by the way does not change in the New Testament)[12] let's get to the task of reviewing the foundational teachings of obedience presented in our first three lessons.

**TRUTH #1: OBEDIENCE GIVES US ACCESS TO GOD'S WISDOM AND HIS WISDOM ENABLES US TO BE WISER THAN OUR ENEMIES!**

In Lesson 1 we learned that God holds all wisdom and when He created mankind He designed us to live according to *His* wisdom. We also learned that it is impossible to possess godly wisdom apart from God's instruction. Any time we lack wisdom, it should drive us to enter God's sanctuary presence and fellowship with Him. Yahweh is the one who gives wisdom and His commands make a person wiser than his enemies (Psalm 119:98). On the other hand, when we sin, the most we can end up with is the enemy's version of wisdom which is foolishness!

While Adam and Eve model for us the wrong way to acquire wisdom, Solomon provides for us the consummate example that pleases God. When God invited Solomon to ask for whatever he wanted God to give him, Solomon asked to be endowed with God's wisdom.

> "… So give Your servant an understanding heart to judge Your people to discern between good and evil. For who is able to judge this great people of Yours?" 1 Kings 3:9

And God's response leaves no doubt about the extent of His pleasure:

---

*The Hearing of Revelation in the NT*, p. 35

12  See Romans 2:13; James 1:22. Scholar Leander Keck notes that Paul's use of the word *hypakouein* (obey) in Romans 10:16 is clearly related to the word *akouein* (hear). Keck, Leander E., *Romans*, Abingdon New Testament Commentaries (Abingdon Press 2005) Error as Disobedience ([Romans] 10:14-21), p. 259

It was pleasing in the sight of the Lord that Solomon had asked this thing. God said to him, "Because you have asked this thing ... I have done according to your words. Behold, I have given you a wise and discerning heart, so that there has been no one like you before you, nor shall one like you arise after you. I have also given you what you have not asked, both riches and honor, so that there will not be any among the kings like you all your days. If you walk in My ways, keeping My statutes and commandments, as your father David walked, then I will prolong your days." 1 Kings 3:10-14

Solomon sets the biblical pattern. Following suit, James counsels us that we only need to ask God for wisdom and He will give it.

But if any of you lacks wisdom, let him ask of God, who gives to all generously and without reproach, and it will be given to him. James 1:5

Armed with God's wisdom we won't be taken captive by the wiles of the enemy, we will triumph over him!

**TRUTH #2: OBEDIENCE IS THE ONLY PATH TO CONTINUED FULL FELLOWSHIP WITH GOD. OBEDIENCE IS ALWAYS REQUIRED TO DRAW NEAR GOD. SIN SEPARATES US FROM GOD, BUT OBEDIENCE PERMITS US TO DRAW NEAR.**

As was illustrated so clearly in the narrative of Adam and Eve's disobedience, sin progressively leads us further and further away from God. Their first act was to eat that which was forbidden, their next act was to independently try to do for themselves what only God could do. Those two self-directed acts were followed by an attempt to hide from God – the very opposite of the fellowship they had known from the beginning.

It is in Genesis that we first find God's vow of fellowship expressed in covenant relationship. In our Key Scripture for this lesson, we learn that fellowship with Him includes His expectation that Abraham and all of his descendants reciprocate by pro-actively guarding the covenant obligations He stipulates.[13]

> "... I will establish My covenant between Me and you and your descendants after you throughout their generations for an everlasting covenant, to be God to you and to your descendants after you.... [A]nd I will be their God.... Now as for you, you shall keep [*shamar*, "guard pro-actively"][14] My covenant, you and your descendants after you throughout their generations...." Genesis 17:7-9

What began in Genesis continues to Revelation as a recurring theme of Scripture. It is God's heart to be in relationship with us such that He is our *only* God and we fellowship with Him as His obedient covenant people.

> God spoke further to Moses and said to him, "I am the LORD; and I appeared to Abraham, Isaac, and Jacob ... I also established My covenant with them ... Say, therefore, to the sons of Israel, 'I am the LORD, and I will bring you out from under the burdens of the Egyptians, and ... I will take you for My people, and I will be your God; and you shall know that I am the LORD your God ....'" Exodus 6:2-7

> If you walk in My statutes and keep My commandments so as to carry them out .... I will also walk among you and be your God, and you shall be My people. Leviticus 26:3,12

---

13 In our Key Scripture the covenant stipulation relates to circumcision, however as God's relationship with Abraham and his descendants unfolds God sets forth the other commands that enable them to maintain unhindered fellowship with Him.

14 Hill, Gary, *The Discovery Bible*, HELPS Ministries, Inc., [H]8104 *shāmar*. The verb tense used in the original Hebrew expresses ongoing action. Hill, Gary, *The Discovery Bible*, HELPS Ministries, Inc., explanation of *Imperfect*

I will make a covenant of peace with them; it will be an everlasting covenant with them. And I will ... set My sanctuary in their midst forever. My dwelling place also will be with them; and I will be their God, and they will be My people. Ezekiel 37:26-27

But this is what I commanded them, saying, 'Obey My voice, and I will be your God, and you will be My people; and you will walk in all the way which I command you, that it may be well with you.' Jeremiah 7:23

"Thus says the LORD of hosts, 'I am exceedingly jealous for Zion, yes, with great wrath I am jealous for her.... I will return to Zion and will dwell in the midst of Jerusalem. Then Jerusalem will be called the City of Truth, and the mountain of the LORD of hosts *will be called* the Holy Mountain.'... [A]nd I will bring them *back* and they will live in the midst of Jerusalem; and they shall be My people, and I will be their God in truth and righteousness.'...." Zechariah 8:2-3,8, italics in original

And I heard a loud voice from the throne, saying, "Behold, the tabernacle of God is among men, and He will dwell among them, and they shall be His people, and God Himself will be among them .... He who overcomes will inherit these things, and I will be his God and he will be My son...." Revelation 21:3,7

The Bible pictures God's relationship with His covenant people as a marriage. One of the reasons I think that is so is because marriage is the clearest example we have in natural life of an intimate one-on-one exclusive relationship. As noted in the *Holman Christian Standard Bible*, Study Bible edition, "A wife's obligation to remain true to her husband offered a fitting parallel to Israel's obligations to God."[15] Referring to His covenant people as "wife" highlights God's intention that there be absolute marital (covenantal) fidelity in their relationship with Him.[16]

Adam and Eve's sin brought a curse, death and separation, but Christ's death opened the way for our restored relationship with God. James exhorts Christ-followers that to draw near to God requires resisting the devil (James 4:8). Jesus promised us divine fellowship when we do.

> Jesus answered and said to [His disciple], "If anyone loves Me, he will keep My word; and My Father will love him, and We will come to him and make Our abode with him...." John 14:23

On the other hand, as Adam and Eve taught us, failure to resist the devil will lead to further and further alienation and separation.

**TRUTH #3: OBEDIENCE PRECEDES UNDERSTANDING, NOT THE OTHER WAY AROUND. WE OBEY FIRST AND THEN WE CAN GLEAN UNDERSTANDING BY LOOKING IN THE REARVIEW MIRROR.**

God often does things or asks things of us we don't understand. It is humanly natural to want to know the *why* of something *before* we do it. However, our relationship with God is not governed by what comes naturally. God is God – He does not *owe* us an explanation! The good news is that as Christ-followers we don't live by explanation, we walk by faith (2 Corinthians 5:7)!

If we are not alert to the enemy's schemes, we will all too often find ourselves parked in the obedience-waiting-room. As we wait there we demand God provide us with an adequate explanation *before* we do what He has asked us to do. We need to recognize

---

15 *Holman Christian Standard Bible*, Study Bible edition (Holman Bible Publishers 2010) study note Ezekiel 16:8
16 Personal Journal September 03, 2021. Because adultery involves breaking a pledge, adultery is used as a biblical metaphor for breaking the pledge of exclusive loyalty to God. Motyer, J. Alec, *The Prophecy of Isaiah: An Introduction & Commentary* (InterVarsity Press 1993) Isaiah 57:3, p. 471

that tactic for what it is. Plain and simple, it is a tool the enemy artfully uses to delay or prevent our obedience!

Abraham provides the ideal model for us to follow. Even when we don't understand how it will all work out, we proceed straight to obedience without delay. *After* we have obeyed we can look back and see what God has done. Then, and only then, might we have some understanding of the *why* in the matter. This demands faith, which is absolutely perfect because God is in the faith-giving business!

**TRUTH #4: WHEN GOD GIVES US A COMMAND, OBEDIENCE IS NOT OPTIONAL – THERE ARE CONSEQUENCES FOR DISOBEDIENCE. GOD'S TRADEMARK IS THAT HE SAYS WHAT HE MEANS AND THEN HE DOES WHAT HE SAYS.**

We noted in Lesson 3 that the pagan gods had a reputation for capriciousness. To the pagan worshipper, the god's actions seemed arbitrary and random. That meant man's relationship with those gods was unpredictable and erratic. In Genesis, the Book of Beginnings, God is already at work revealing to us that He is remarkably different from those false gods. The primary way in which He demonstrates His faithfulness to His word and His character is in His response to obedience/disobedience. The character sketch we see taking shape as early as Adam and Eve is that God sets a clear boundary and right up front He makes known the consequence for crossing that boundary. We then see that pattern play out in the narrative of Adam and Eve's rebellion. From that, we learn that God is faithful to do what He says He will do. That's actually the grace of God at work. It allows us to know what to expect from Him. He says what He means and He does what He says!

**TRUTH #5: OUR OBEDIENCE WILL BE TESTED – IT IS NOT A MATTER OF *IF* IT WILL BE TESTED, IT IS A MATTER OF *WHEN* IT WILL BE TESTED AND *HOW* IT WILL BE PUT TO THE TEST.**

The specific vocabulary of "testing" is found more than 200 times in English translations of the Bible.[17] Clearly, it is an important topic in Scripture.

We mistakenly think God's instruction to sacrifice Isaac was Abraham's *only* test because the word "tested" is used in Genesis only in that particular narrative. Jewish scholars, on the other hand, typically characterize the instruction to sacrifice Isaac as Abraham's *most difficult* test. They find in Scripture nine tests that precede the Isaac test.

*Maimonides' Commentary to the Mishnah* lists the ten tests of Abraham as follows:[18]

1. G-d tells him to leave his homeland to be a stranger in the land of Canaan. Genesis 12:1[19]
2. Immediately after his arrival in the Promised Land, he encounters a famine. Genesis 12:10
3. The Egyptians seize his beloved wife, Sarah, and bring her to Pharaoh. Genesis 12:15

---

17  Ryken and Longman III, editors, *Dictionary of Biblical Imagery* (Intervarsity Press 1998) entry for *Test Motif*, p. 855
18  Posner, Menachem, Rabbi, staff editor, *What Were Abraham's 10 Tests?* Jewish History, Chabad.org. Retrieved from https://www.chabad.org/library/article_cdo/aid/1324268/jewish/What-Were-Abrahams-10-Tests.htm (last accessed July 8, 2021). The *Mishnah* is an important Jewish text. It is the collection of rabbinic traditions redacted by Rabbi Judah ha-Nasi in the third century A.D. It supplements and clarifies the commandments found in the Torah. *Maimonides' Mishnah Commentary* was written by Moses Maimonides (Rabbi Moshe ben Maimon, often referenced as "RaMBa"M). The commentary was written in Arabic between the years 1145 and 1168.
19  Note: as pointed out in the Preface to this study the Jewish people revere Yahweh's name and often transliterate it into English as "G-d" to avoid fully spelling out His name.

## The Power of Obedience

4. Abraham faces incredible odds in the battle of the four and five kings [Abraham's intervention to rescue Lot from captivity]. Genesis 14:14
5. He marries Hagar after not being able to have children with Sarah. Genesis 16:3
6. G-d tells him to circumcise himself at an advanced age. Genesis 17:24
7. The king of Gerar captures Sarah, intending to take her for himself. Genesis 20:2
8. G-d tells him to send Hagar away after having a child with her. Genesis 21:12
9. His son, Ishmael, becomes estranged. Genesis 21:12
10. G-d tells him to sacrifice his dear son Isaac upon an altar. Genesis 22:2

We might be inclined to ask the question, how many times will God put us to the test. It is interesting to note that in Jewish thought Abraham was tested *ten* times. By identifying ten tests, there may well be an intention to supply the answer to our question. Ten is considered to be a biblical number of completeness. Ten implies that nothing is wanting and that the whole cycle has been completed.[20] Since character is determined by responses to the tests God gives us,[21] He will test us until we demonstrate that our character has reached completion according to the perfect plan God has for us.

Notice that according to Jewish thought God did not start with the most difficult test He had for Abraham. That tells us something about their understanding of God. When we are but an infant in Christ our *tests* are small – although at the time what He has asked us to do might seem like an unconquerable mountain.

---

20 Bullinger, E. W., *Number in Scripture: Its Supernatural Design and Spiritual Significance*, 4th Ed. (Eyre & Spottiswoode (Bible Warehouse) Ltd. 1921) entry for *Ten*. Retrieved from https://www.levendwater.org/books/numbers/number_in_scripture_bullinger.pdf (last accessed July 8, 2021)
21 Ryken, Wilhoit, and Longman III, editors, *Dictionary of Biblical Imagery* (Intervarsity Press 1998) entry for *Test Motif*, p. 856

The size/difficulty of our tests grows as our faith grows. The point is that in God's tailor-made character development plan for us He is always and ever at the helm steering us into greater and greater faith and as such, greater and greater revelation of who He is.

**TRUTH #6: OUR OBEDIENCE SETS THE STAGE FOR OUR ABILITY TO KNOW GOD BY EXPERIENCE. WHEN WE REFUSE TO WALK THE PATH OF OBEDIENCE, WE ROB GOD OF THE OPPORTUNITY TO REVEAL HIMSELF TO US.**

As we saw in Lesson 3, there were characteristics of God's nature that could only be seen through the lens of experience. Every time we refuse to obey God we rob Him of the opportunity of self-revelation and the demonstration of His faithfulness. And that's a problem because our willingness to obey Him actually grows in direct proportion to our knowledge of who He is and our personal experience of His faithfulness.

Let's look at how God designed this cycle of spiritual growth to work. Imagine a tiny sphere drawn on a piece of paper. When we are early in our walk with God, we have enough belief to do anything He asks us that is within that tiny sphere. Great! But here's what God does next. He gives us an assignment that falls just outside the boundaries of that little sphere and encourages us to step out in faith to do it. Our courage and boldness grow and we take what we call a "leap of faith" and complete that assignment. By doing so we have provided God with the opportunity to reveal Himself and His faithfulness to us. And all is well – the boundaries of our sphere have become a little larger. Great! But here's what God does next. He gives us an assignment that falls just outside the boundaries of that new slightly larger sphere and encourages us to step out in faith to do it. Our courage and boldness grow and we take another leap of faith and complete *that* assignment. By doing so we have given God another opportunity to reveal Himself and His faithfulness to us. And all is well – the boundaries of our sphere have become a little larger. Great! But do you know what God does next? He gives us an assignment that falls just outside

*The Power of Obedience*

the boundaries of that new sphere and encourages us to step out in faith to do it. This cycle never ends. God's self-revelation and disclosure of His faithfulness are without limit.

By the way, this faith-building cycle means that there will *always* be the next new "hardest-thing-He-has-ever-asked-me-to-do" assignment on the path in front of us.[22] To keep growing in Him and in the likeness of His Son, our Savior, we need to put our hand in His and willingly accept *every* assignment He gives us. The fact is, we are commanded to do this with joy![23]

**TRUTH #7: THE ONLY WAY TO OVERCOME THE POWER OF SATAN IS TO OBEY GOD.**

Every follower of Christ is in a spiritual war. That war is as old as the Garden of Eden. We learned in our first two lessons that obedience is the *only* way to overcome the enemy's power. If Adam and Eve had done exactly what God said to do, refraining from doing what He said *not* to do, they would have easily overcome the temptation of the serpent. Obedience to God's commands will bring victory every time. There is no alternative path or shortcut that will ever overcome Satan.

**TRUTH #8: EVERY ACT OF DISOBEDIENCE BEGINS WITH THE THOUGHT THAT GOD CANNOT BE TRUSTED.**

God had spoken truth, the whole truth and nothing but the truth to Adam when He set up the rules of the Garden. The serpent tempted Eve by undermining her trust in God. Once he was able to convince her that God was not completely trustworthy she did what God had said not to do. Satan's strategy has never changed. Every temptation to disobey God ultimately involves a choice as to whether God can be trusted on that particular matter. Bottom-line, disobedience is outward evidence that we have concluded for whatever reason we can't completely trust Him.

---

22   Personal Journal March 5, 2022
23   James 1:2-3

**TRUTH #9: OBEDIENCE WILL REQUIRE EVERY CHRIST-FOLLOWER'S WILLINGNESS TO SACRIFICE THE ISAAC IN THEIR LIFE.**

That may sound like a shocking statement. Let me be very clear that I am *not* talking about your firstborn child. Recall that we learned in Lesson 3 that Abraham's primary concern as he obeyed God was most likely the loss of his sole heir. God asked Abraham to sacrifice the son through whom he would be provided for in old age and the son through whom all the blessings of God were to be fulfilled. That means this son was valued highly. Isaac's wellbeing was vitally important to Abraham and ***that*** is the reason Abraham needed to demonstrate his willingness to offer him up as a freewill offering to God! This test was designed to determine if Abraham's confidence was in his son Isaac or in God who gave him his son. It is a test of Abraham's first love.

The first command on the list of "Ten Commandments" given by God is straightforward, "You shall have no other gods before Me."[24] Every false god "patiently endure[s] the existence of other false gods."[25] As a matter of fact those gods seem to think, "The more the merrier." On the other hand, a covenant relationship with Yahweh is intentionally and purposefully designed by Him to be an *exclusive* relationship with *exclusive* wholehearted devotion.

God's covenant command is clear, "[F]or you shall not worship any other god, for the LORD, whose name is Jealous, is a jealous God."[26] The Hebrew word translated as "jealous" does not merely reference an emotion, it refers to God anxiously watching over the welfare of His beloved bride. To say that Yahweh's *name* is "Jealous" stresses that jealousy is inherent in His character and nature.[27]

---

24  Exodus 20:3
25  Spurgeon, Charles H., *A Jealous God*, Sermon No. 502 delivered on March 29, 1863, Metropolitan Tabernacle, Newington. Retrieved from www.spurgeon.org/sermons/chs502.pdf (last accessed July 8, 2021)
26  Exodus 34:14
27  *NET Bible Notes*, study note 30, Exodus 34:14. "Yahweh's jealousy is a part of his holiness (Exod 34:14) and is demanded by what he is."

A Word Study will help us rightly understand God's self-revelation as a jealous God.

> **WORD STUDY**
>
> *When Yahweh identifies Himself as **jealous**, the Hebrew adjective used is qanna' {kan-naw'}. According to the* Theological Wordbook of the Old Testament *qanna' is used exclusively of God and only in the context of idolatry.*[28]
>
> *The root verb is qana which can refer to envy or zealousness. "The point of [qana] is to express a strong emotion in which the subject is desirous of some aspect or possession of the object."*[29]
>
> *Qanna' is aroused when a marital relationship is threatened by another lover.*

Jealousy involves vigilance to maintain or guard something of value.[30] The basis for God's jealousy is His rightful expectation of undivided loyalty in our covenant relationship with Him.[31] Accordingly, His *qanna'* is expressed exclusively where there is broken covenant. His jealousy is aroused when His people had solemnly promised they would worship no other God but Him, then they reneged on that promise.

*Any* compromise in our promise to worship God alone "leads inevitably to a divided or even a redirected loyalty that Yahweh

---

Durham, John I., *Word Biblical Commentary: Exodus*, Volume 3 (Word Books 1987) Exodus 20:5 under *Comment*, p. 287

[28] Harris, Archer, and Waltke, editors, *Theological Wordbook of the Old Testament* (Moody Press 1999) word # 2038b, p. 803

[29] Baker and Carpenter, *The Complete WordStudy Dictionary of the Old Testament* (AMG Publishers 2003) word #7065, p. 1000

[30] *Dictionary.com* entry for *jealousy*. Retrieved from https://www.dictionary.com/browse/jealousy (last accessed February 24, 2022)

[31] Durham, John I., *Word Biblical Commentary: Exodus*, Volume 3 (Word Books 1987) Exodus 20:5 under *Comment*, p. 287

has every right, even every obligation, to punish."[32] His jealousy is completely understandable. He is immeasurably possessive of the worship that was exclusively promised to Him. He is wholeheartedly devoted to that which is for our best.

Because of God's jealousy, whatever "Isaac" stands between you and your total devotion to God must eventually be put on the altar and sacrificed as a freewill offering. For me that moment came in May 2005 when after wrestling with God for a long season I finally laid down my obsession to be in control. I had been holding on to what I was convinced was my need to control a situation. I can clearly remember where I was sitting when I decided to surrender that situation to God. What flowed from my heart and out of my mouth in that moment was this confession, "God I will wait patiently on you no matter how long it takes." Those were not hollow words, I knew I meant it. It was then that I surprisingly heard God lovingly say to me, "*You have now sacrificed your Isaac.*"[33]

To be honest, I didn't know I had an "Isaac" that needed to be sacrificed! Since then I've come to understand that every Christ-follower has their own "Isaac." It may not be the issue of personal control. Your Isaac will be whatever is more important to you than your wholehearted submission to God's will. Because of His righteous jealousy, He *will* bring you to the moment of testing.

**Hear What The Spirit is Saying to the Church**: *If my people would obey my voice and learn the lessons I have to teach them I would pour out such blessing and joy my people would not be able to contain it.*

---

32 Durham, John I., *Word Biblical Commentary: Exodus*, Volume 3 (Word Books 1987) Exodus 20:5 under *Comment,* p. 287; McConville, J. G., *Deuteronomy*, Apollos Old Testament Commentary 5 (IVP Academic 2002) Deuteronomy 32:16-18, p. 456
33 Personal Journal May 18, 2005 #2

LESSON 5:

# WHEN OBEDIENCE DOESN'T PRODUCE THE RESULT WE EXPECTED

"So Moses turned on Yawheh and said, 'LORD, why have You done harm to this people? Why have you sent me here for this? From the minute I came to Pharaoh to deliver Your message, he has hurt this people, and You have not even begun to rescue Your people!'" Exodus 5:22-23[1]

THE WORDS of Moses in our Key Scripture reflect not only the aggravation and exasperation of Israel's leaders, they also convey the confusion, doubt and betrayal Moses felt. Israel's leaders accused Moses of bringing even more suffering on an already anguished people. Like the message on a relay team, Moses then accused Yahweh of doing harm instead of the good He had promised. Let's begin by setting our Key Scripture for this lesson in its historical context.

## SUMMARIZING EXODUS 2:23-5:23 ~ THE EVENTS LEADING UP TO OUR KEY SCRIPTURE

*Timeline: before Moses returned to Egypt*[2]

- Israel cried out because of their slavery and God heard the cries of the people (Exodus 2:23; 3:7,9)

---

1 Translation by John I. Durham, *Word Biblical Commentary: Exodus*, Volume 3 (Word Books 1987) p. 67
2 In the biblical narrative God met Moses when he was living in Midian tending sheep for his father-in-law. It was in that land God instructed him to return to Egypt to lead the exodus. See: Exodus 3 – 4:23

- God said He had come down to rescue Israel (Exodus 3:8)
- God told Moses to "go" as he was being sent to lead Israel out of Egypt (Exodus 3:10)
- God instructed Moses to tell Israel's leaders He had promised to bring them out of Egypt (Exodus 3:17)
- God revealed His foreknowledge that Pharaoh would need to be **forced by a strong hand** to let Israel go (Exodus 3:19)
- God disclosed His plan to **harden Pharaoh's heart**[3] so he would *not* let the people go (Exodus 4:21)
- God made plain that Pharaoh's firstborn son would be killed because he would stubbornly refuse to let God's firstborn son, Israel, leave Egypt (Exodus 4:23)

*Timeline: In Egypt*[4]

- Just as God had said, Pharaoh's response to the first request to let Israel leave was an adamant, defiant "No Way!" (Exodus 5:2)
- That same day Pharaoh penalized Israel by making their work much more difficult (straw no longer provided; daily brick quota remained the same) (Exodus 5:6)
- Then the Israelite foremen were beaten by Egyptian taskmasters for failure to produce the daily brick quota (Exodus 5:14)
- The Israelite foremen went to Pharaoh pleading that he lighten their load, but Pharaoh refused to provide straw or reduce the daily quota of bricks (Exodus 5:15-18)

---

3 "In biblical usage a person whose heart is 'hardened' is one who persists in resisting God's will and so becomes disobedient. Acts 7:56 uses 'stiffnecked' to make the same point." Keck, Leander E., *Romans*, Abingdon New Testament Commentaries (Abingdon Press 2005) God's Justness ([Romans] 9:14-18), p. 234

4 Moses obeyed Yahweh's instruction and returned to Egypt to do what he was instructed to do. See: Exodus 4:24 – 5:23

The Power of Obedience

- The angry Israelite foremen confronted Moses and Aaron because the conditions of their slavery had become even more bitter to them (Exodus 5:20)
- Moses, disheartened and frustrated, complained to God (Our Key Scripture - Exodus 5:22-23)

In the summary above, bold text highlights two different phrases that merit further study before we proceed. Both phrases ("**forced by a strong hand**" and "**harden Pharaoh's heart**") are found in Yahweh's instruction to Moses while he was still in Midian. As we will see, the concept of God's strong hand and Pharaoh's hardened heart are more closely related than appears in our English language translation. This is a place where a Word Study can help us recapture what has been lost in translation.

### WORD STUDY

*In Exodus 3:19 the Hebrew adjective חָזָק hazaq {khaw-zawk'} translated as **strong** derives from the Hebrew verb חָזַק hazaq {khaw-zak'} translated as **hardened** in Exodus 4:21. The Hebrew rendering of these words has been added to make it easy to see that the two words come from the same three-letter stem hzq.[5]*

*The verb hazaq, at its core, means "to be firm, strong."[6] It most often refers to strength in battle and is used con-*

---

5  If you look closely at the Hebrew form of these two words you will notice that the only variance between the two is the vowels (those marks which are below two of the letters for each word written in Hebrew).

6  Johnston, Gordon H., "Exodus," in *The Bible Knowledge Word Study, Genesis – Deuteronomy*, edited by Eugene H. Merrill (Victor 2003) Exodus 4:21 under *I will harden his heart*, p. 171

sistently in Exodus in reference to Pharaoh's "hardened" heart.⁷

The adjective hazaq basically means "to be resolute." This idea of being strong in power includes resistive power as in "volitional obstinance."⁸ In the Bible, a reference to a "strong hand" (as in Exodus 3:19) usually refers to the type of power God demonstrates in the exodus story.⁹

From our Word Study, it is easy to see that battle, resistance and power struggle were to be an *expected* part of what God asked Moses to do. In the very words God used to give Moses his assignment He had given fair warning that Pharaoh would not let Israel go without being forced to do so. In fact, God had even informed Moses that Pharaoh's hardhearted resistance would necessitate the death of Pharaoh's firstborn son before Israel would be released from Egypt. As noted in the timeline above, all of this instruction was given to Moses even before he left Midian and returned to Egypt.

With such clear revelation from God at the outset of the assignment, it seems that Moses had a case of what we would call "selective audition." In our Western culture, that phrase refers to filtering out what we don't want to hear while at the same time tuning in more attentively to retain that part of the message we choose to hear.

The biblical truth that God is a good God is often interpreted to mean something like this, "Therefore whatever He asks me to

---

7   Harris, Archer, and Waltke, editors, *Theological Wordbook of the Old Testament* (Moody Press 1999) word #636, p. 276
8   Johnston, Gordon H., "Exodus," in *The Bible Knowledge Word Study, Genesis – Deuteronomy*, edited by Eugene H. Merrill (Victor 2003) Exodus 4:21 under *I will harden his heart,* p. 171; Harris, Archer, and Waltke, editors, *Theological Wordbook of the Old Testament* (Moody Press 1999) word #636, p. 276
9   Harris, Archer, and Waltke, editors, *Theological Wordbook of the Old Testament* (Moody Press 1999) word #636a, p. 277

do is something I will think is good!" It seems that Moses was probably a lot like you and me. When he said "yes" to God's plan he certainly did not anticipate things would get worse before they got better. If we are honest about the matter, many of us are remarkably like Moses. God may attempt to convey something about the difficulty of the assignment He is giving us – but we skip right over that part and *selectively* hear what we want to hear. By doing so we set ourselves up for disappointment that can quickly lead to discouragement then despair. In despair, it is easy to accuse God of wrongdoing. That's the very thing we see happening in our Key Scripture for this lesson.

So, we arrive at the point in the narrative where it appears God has not done what He said He would do. He has completely failed to rescue His firstborn son, Israel, from the bondage of Egypt. It is not simply that God has failed. In the eyes of Israel and Moses He has failed miserably and harmfully! Pharaoh's power seems greater and even more cruel than before causing everyone, including Moses, to lose confidence in God's power to keep His promise.

But they don't yet see what God sees. God sees the beginning from the end. He sees the finish line! Simply stated, Israel just wants the whole ordeal to be over – to quickly become a thing of the past. What they don't yet understand is that there is a difference between something being *over* and it being *finished*. When we are in the midst of obeying God and the circumstances around us don't look like what we thought they would, we just want what we are experiencing to end and the sooner the better. However, what God starts always has a finish line that He alone establishes. Our goal in obedience is to stay the course with our eyes fixed on Him until we cross *His* predetermined finish line! To do so will demand the grace of finishing faith!

Here is the good news: God is in the grace business. He is not only *able*, but He is also faithfully *willing* to provide every ounce of grace needed to complete what His will desires to accomplish. That means we will always have sufficient equipping and enabling resources to finish well. The choice will be ours as to what we do with that truth. If we choose to remain wide open and fully yielded to the Holy Spirit from start to finish, we will lack no good thing! We are guaranteed to cross God's finish line.

What God does next is what He knew Moses needed most. It is what we always need when we misunderstand God's plan. We must adjust what we are focusing on. We need a view of the finish line from God's perspective!

> Then the LORD said to Moses, "Now you shall see what I will do to Pharaoh; for under compulsion he will let them go, and under compulsion he will drive them out of his land.... I am the LORD; and I appeared to Abraham, Isaac, and Jacob, as God Almighty, but *by* My name, LORD, I did not make Myself known to them. I also established My covenant with them, to give them the land of Canaan, the land in which they sojourned. Furthermore I have heard the groaning of the sons of Israel, because the Egyptians are holding them in bondage, and I have remembered My covenant. Say, therefore, to the sons of Israel, 'I am the LORD, and I will bring you out from under the burdens of the Egyptians, and I will deliver you from their bondage. I will also redeem you with an outstretched arm and with great judgments. Then I will take you for My people, and I will be your God; and you shall know that I am the LORD your God, who brought you out from under the burdens of the Egyptians. I will bring you to the land which I swore to give to Abraham, Isaac, and Jacob, and I will give it to you *for* a possession; I am the LORD.'" Exodus 6:1-8, italics in original

God assures Moses that all that has happened so far, even though Moses has not yet realized it, *is in fact* God's hand working on their behalf. All is going exactly as planned. Pharaoh's hardened-heart-defiance is but one ingredient in Yahweh's plan and one that will ultimately serve His purpose.

## The Power of Obedience

In the exodus story,[10]

> ... Yahweh is orchestrating, in a combination of opposing and unlikely forces, *a deliverance that will above all be a proof of his active Presence.* A reluctant Moses, an unbelieving Pharaoh, a crushed and dispirited Israel, a proud and ruling Egyptian people, a non-nation against the greatest of nations, are brought together, and the opposing sides are set still more firmly in their respective ways, *so that the proof of Yahweh's Presence,* which is to turn everything upside down, *may be established irrevocably.* Even as Moses and Aaron speak Yahweh's words of command to Pharaoh, Yahweh will increase Pharaoh's resistance, thus creating an impasse. His preparation made, Yahweh will then "pile up" in the land of the impasse "signs and wondrous deeds," which are to *function as convincing proofs and palpable reminders* ... the telling climax of which will be the exodus itself, brought about ''[sic] ["]with great deeds of vindication."

In other words, there is so much more to the story than either Moses or Israel can see with natural eyes. Obedience will always require us to do what God said and then leave all the methods, the timing and the results entirely up to Him. That's difficult for our flesh which continually asserts its right to be in control. When combined with the microwave expectation of how we live life in the 21st century Western world, the idea of leaving the methods, timing and results up to God can seem impossible. Praise be to God that what is impossible for man is possible for God (Matthew 19:26). However, for God's possibility to trump our natural impossibility will require us to remain wide open to the power of Holy Spirit

---

10  Durham, John I., *Word Biblical Commentary: Exodus,* Volume 3 (Word Books 1987) Exodus 7:1-5 under *Comment,* p. 87, italics added

and we will have much more to say about that before we conclude our study.[11]

Remember we learned in Lesson 3 that God sets up opportunities to make Himself known and our obedience ensures that He can accomplish the self-revelation He desires. The exodus narrative makes for an excellent case study on this very point. What might God want to reveal about Himself in the midst of the exodus He has planned for Israel? We can turn to the Exodus narrative itself to find some answers. As we do, we'll see that the author of Exodus highlights several of God's goals:

1. Yahweh has set up a challenge – a power showdown – between Himself and the Egyptian gods by which He will demonstrate to everyone watching His absolute supremacy over every one of those gods.
2. Yahweh wants Israel, Pharaoh and the Egyptians to come to know Him by experience.
3. Yahweh desires to physically reposition Abraham's descendants from Egypt to the land He had promised to Abraham, Isaac and Jacob. To do so will demonstrate that He is a God who keeps His promises!
4. Yahweh plans to judge Pharaoh for his harsh treatment of the Israelites, Abraham's descendants.

It's worth our time to consider each of these goals. We'll take them one by one in the order listed above.

### Yahweh has set up a power showdown to demonstrate His absolute supremacy over every one of the Egyptian gods

God told Moses that He would execute judgment against *all* the gods of Egypt (Exodus 12:12). In the book of Numbers, after all is said and done, the author speaks in the past tense that Yahweh

---
11 As noted in the Preface, at times in this study I will refer to "the Holy Spirit" (His title) simply as "Holy Spirit" (His name) emphasizing His personal nature. Refer to Preface for additional explanation.

*The Power of Obedience*

*had* executed judgment on the Egyptian gods (Numbers 33:4). Even though some sources suggest otherwise, scholar John Currid reasons that it is without question that those who authored the exodus narrative understood the plagues in that way.[12] As shown by the Chart below, each of the plagues was divinely and specifically directed at one or more of the false gods worshipped by Egypt.[13]

## Yahweh's Judgment on the gods of Egypt

| # | Scripture Reference | Type of Plague | Possible Egyptian god(s) Rebuked by Plague |
|---|---|---|---|
| 1 | Exodus 7:14–25 | water turned to blood killing all fish and other water life | *Khnum*, the guardian of the Nile; *Hopi*, the spirit of the Nile |
| 2 | Exodus 8:1–15 | frogs infest the land of Egypt | Frogs were associated with the goddess *Heqt* who helped women in childbirth |
| 3 | Exodus 8:16–19 | lice or gnats infest the land of Egypt | *Geb*, the god of the earth; *Set*, god of the desert |
| 4 | Exodus 8:20–30 | swarm of flies infest the land of Egypt | *Khepfi*, the god of insects; the goddess *Uatchit* represented by the fly |
| 5 | Exodus 9:1–7 | deadly disease attack livestock | *Apis* was the symbol of fertility and took the form of a bull god; *Hathor* was the mother-goddess who was often portrayed in the form of a cow |

---

12 Currid, John D., *Ancient Egypt and the Old Testament* (Baker Books 1997) p. 108

13 Chart originally prepared in 2012 when I was teaching the book of Exodus verse by verse. A wide variety of sources were used at that time to identify Egyptian gods who might have been the target for each of the plagues. Some sources on the subject identify one particular god for each plague. However, because the Bible does not provide that direct association for us it seems advisable to suggest a range of "possible" Egyptian gods for each plague.

|   | | | |
|---|---|---|---|
| 6 | Exodus 9:8–12 | boils that could not be healed | *Imhotep*, the god of medicine; *Sekhmet*, goddess with power over disease; *Sunu*, the pestilence god; *Isis*, god of healing |
| 7 | Exodus 9:13–35 | hail mixed with fire to destroy the grain fields of Egypt but the land of Goshen where the Israelites lived spared | *Nut*, the sky goddess; *Osiris*, god of crops and fertility; *Set*, god of storms |
| 8 | Exodus 10:1–20 | infestation of locusts to destroy the crops and all vegetation in Egypt | *Seth*, the protector of the crops; *Anubis*, the god of the fields; *Isis* protector against locusts; *Nut*, the sky goddess; *Osiris*, god of crops and fertility |
| 9 | Exodus 10:21–29 | extreme darkness to cover the land of Egypt for three days | The Egyptians had many sun gods - four of the common ones were: *Re* (or *Ra*), *Aten*, *Atum* and *Horus*. Additionally, *Nut* & *Hathor* were goddesses of the sky |
| 10 | Exodus 11,12 | death of the firstborn of every family whose home was not protected by the blood of the Passover lamb | *Osiris*, the Egyptian god considered the giver of life; *Isis*, goddess who protected children. Pharaoh and his firstborn son were both considered gods. Pharaoh was considered an incarnation of *Ra*, the sun god |

The plagues were not random acts of power. They were proof positive to Pharaoh, the Egyptians, the Israelites and the entire world down through the ages that there is a God in heaven, His Name is Yahweh and He alone is God!

## Yahweh desires to become known by experience

Perhaps nowhere else in the Bible does God reveal His *knowledge-by-experience* pattern as clearly as He does through the plagues He unleashed on Egyptian soil. Consider, for example, this sampling of verses in which Yahweh declared His purpose and intent.

> "... **The Egyptians shall know** that I am the LORD, when I stretch out My hand on Egypt and bring out the sons of Israel from their midst." Exodus 7:5, bold added

> Thus says the LORD, "By this **you [Pharaoh] shall know** that I am the LORD: behold, I will strike the water that is in the Nile with the staff that is in my hand, and it will be turned to blood...." Exodus 7:17, bold added

> "I have heard the grumblings of the sons of Israel; speak to them, saying, 'At twilight you shall eat meat, and in the morning you shall be filled with bread; and **you [Israel] shall know** that I am the LORD your God.'" Exodus 16:12, bold added

In each of the verses just cited the word translated as "know" is the Hebrew word *yada`*. We were briefly introduced to *yada`* in Lesson 2. However, it is worth our time to take a little closer look at this important biblical word.

### Word Study

*The Hebrew verb yada` {yaw-dah'} translated as **know** is used more than 900 times in the Bible with a wide range of meanings.*[14] *It does not refer to mere intellectual knowledge or awareness; it denotes knowing which*

---

14 Harris, Archer, and Waltke, editors, *Theological Wordbook of the Old Testament* (Moody Press 1999) word #848, p. 366

> *is acquired by one or more senses.*[15] *"One of the primary [biblical] uses means to know relationally and experientially ... it especially signifies knowing what to do or think in general, especially with respect to God."*[16]
>
> *Yada` is the kind of knowing that provides confident assurance of truth allowing the one who knows to acknowledge or confess the reality of what he has learned.*[17]

Are you getting the picture here? God repeatedly announced that His mighty acts on behalf of Israel would not only release them from captivity but His deeds would serve as a *knowing experience* of who He is.[18] Pharaoh will know by first-hand experience. The Egyptians will know by first-hand experience. Israel will know by first-hand experience. God understands that He created us to learn best by experience. His pattern is that we listen, we do, *then* we know.

God was at work shaping a people who would belong to Him through redemption and whose relationship with Him was based on the truth of who He is not on the assumptions of who they might think He is. The experiential knowledge God wanted Pharaoh and the Egyptians to develop should have led them to turn to Him. The experiential knowledge God wanted Israel to develop would be sufficient for them to become a light to the nations of

---

15  Harris, Archer, and Waltke, editors, *Theological Wordbook of the Old Testament* (Moody Press 1999) word #848, p. 366

16  Baker and Carpenter, *The Complete WordStudy Dictionary of the Old Testament* (AMG Publishers 2003) word #3045, p. 420

17  Longman III and Garland, general editors, *The Expositor's Bible Commentary: Psalms,* Vol. 5, Revised Edition (Zondervan 2008) Psalm 100:3, p. 742

18  Of note is that *yada`* is used in its passive form in Exodus 6:3 when Yahweh informed Moses that He had not made Himself known to the patriarchs. In other words, they did not have the same kind of experiential knowledge that Moses would be given. Yahweh had not made Himself known to Abraham, Isaac and Jacob through His mighty deeds, signs and wonders as He would do to and through Moses.

the world as God intended them to be. Based on God's mighty acts they would be able to give first-hand testimony to the nations surrounding them of His character.

## YAHWEH WANTS TO DEMONSTRATE HE KEEPS HIS PROMISES

> ... "I am the LORD; and I appeared to Abraham, Isaac, and Jacob, as God Almighty .... I also established My covenant with them, to give them the land of Canaan .... I have remembered My covenant. Say, therefore, to the sons of Israel, 'I am the LORD, and I will bring you out from under the burdens of the Egyptians, and I will deliver you from their bondage .... I will bring you to the land which I swore to give to Abraham, Isaac, and Jacob, and I will give it to you *for* a possession; I am the LORD.'" Exodus 6:2-8, italics in original

God's desire is to physically reposition Abraham's descendants from Egypt to the land He had promised to Abraham, Isaac and Jacob. The right of Israel to the Promised Land rests entirely in her covenantal relationship with God. As Yahweh shows up to do what He promised to do, He is going to teach Israel by experience that He is always faithful to His covenant obligations.

In the pattern of nations around the world, even to this day, conquest or settlement is the chief means for acquiring land. Israel is noticeably distinguishable from all other nations in this regard. Israel has never claimed her right to her physical territory is based on either conquest or settlement. Instead, she rests her claim to her national territory entirely on Yahweh's promise to Abraham, Isaac and Jacob.[19] Her covenantal relationship with Yahweh and these covenantal promises is made certain through the exodus story.

---

19  Sarna, Nahum M., *Understanding Genesis Through Rabbinic Tradition and Modern Scholarship* (The Jewish Theological Seminary 2015) pp. 86-87

## Yahweh plans to judge Pharaoh for his harsh treatment of Abraham's descendants

As our starting point here, let's consider several verses in the exodus narrative:

> The LORD said, "I have surely seen the affliction of My people who are in Egypt, and have given heed to their cry because of their taskmasters, for I am aware of their sufferings.... Now, behold, the cry of the sons of Israel has come to Me; furthermore, I have seen the oppression with which the Egyptians are oppressing them...." Exodus 3:7,9

> Say, therefore, to the sons of Israel, 'I am the LORD, and I will bring you out from under the burdens of the Egyptians, and I will deliver you from their bondage. I will also redeem you with an outstretched arm and with great **judgments**....' Exodus 6:6, bold added

> When Pharaoh does not listen to you, then I will lay My hand on Egypt and bring out My hosts, My people the sons of Israel, from the land of Egypt by great **judgments**.... Exodus 7:4, bold added

The word "judgments" highlighted in bold in both Exodus 6:6 and 7:4 is the Hebrew noun *shephet* {sheh'-fet}. The *Theological Wordbook of the Old Testament* indicates it is always used in the plural sense and is punitive in nature. The word expresses "a definite theology of punishment as retribution."[20] The plagues in the exodus story are divine punishments administered by Yahweh in response to Egypt's abuse of Abraham's descendants. Because of the covenant God made with Abraham, his descendants belong to God, not Pharaoh. Implicit in the verses quoted above is the beginning of the

---

20  Harris, Archer, and Waltke, editors, *Theological Wordbook of the Old Testament* (Moody Press 1999) word #2443a, p. 948

*The Power of Obedience*

biblical pattern whereby God holds nations accountable for how they treat His covenant people. Because of the plagues Egypt will lie in utter ruin and Pharaoh will have lost his own firstborn son!

We see this type of nation-to-nation accountability expressed more explicitly in the context of the Babylonian exile. God informed Habakkuk that He would indeed use the Babylonians to punish Israel for her sins, but then He would bring judgment against Babylon for the overly harsh way in which they will execute His judgment (Habakkuk 2:15-17).[21] What Babylon has done to others God will do to them.[22] Indeed God is true to His word. He brought the Medes and Persians to crush Babylon. He then worked through them to release His covenant people so they could return to their land (Ezra 1:1-4).

Little did Moses know that God's assignment was designed to accomplish so much more than merely releasing Israel from Egyptian bondage. The reality of what Moses did not know made his careful obedience to all God commanded that much more imperative. What was true for Moses is likewise true for every Christ-follower. We only see as through a glass darkly[23] making our careful obedience to every command of God not only important but absolutely imperative!

We have one more quick point to make before concluding this lesson. When God commissioned Moses for this great task, Moses was understandably hesitant. God graciously promised to give Moses a "sign" that He had certainly heard God correctly and

---

21  Although God may permit a nation to oppress His rebellious people as a means of discipline, that nation will later be punished because it is accountable for its own sins. Patterson, Dorothy Kelley, general editor, *The Study Bible for Women* (Holman Bible Publishers 2015) *Hard Question, How Can God raise up a nation as a "destroyer," then judge and punish that nation for its actions?* p. 1242

22  The image of God stripping Babylon from head to foot (Habakkuk 3:13 HCSB) parallels what Jeremiah prophesied in Jeremiah 50-51.

23  1 Corinthians 13:12

was to obediently do all God had instructed him to do.[24] Moses was undoubtedly relieved when he heard the Lord begin to say, "This shall be the sign to you that it is I who have sent you ...."[25] However, the rest of the sentence most likely dashed any hope for the immediate assurance Moses had sought! Listen carefully to what God spoke to him about that promised sign:

> And [God] said, "Certainly I will be with you [*singular, meaning Moses*], and this shall be the sign to you that it is I who have sent you [*singular, meaning Moses*]: **when you** [*singular, meaning Moses*] **have brought the people out of Egypt**, you [*plural, meaning Moses and all the people*][26] shall worship God at this mountain." Exodus 3:12, bold added

God's promised sign is in the form of an oath. Great it contains certainty! God's presence is promised to go with Moses. Great that will definitely help! But notice *when* the sign will be given to Moses. God's promised sign is purposefully positioned *on the other side of the finish line!* Yikes! If your flesh nature is like mine, we want the sign **before** we go and do, not *afterward*. But according to God's plan, the successful completion of Moses' mission is what will show beyond all doubt that God was truly with him and had sent him.

Exodus 3:1-12 looks forward to the experience of Israel at Horeb/Sinai, an experience parallel to the one Moses had at the burning bush. Leading Israel out of Egypt would not be completed until Moses and all the people came to the very same mountain where Moses had received God's commission to go. What Moses had experienced there, Israel will experience there – a face-to-face

---

24 "In view of Moses' hesitancy, a sign is necessary to support the promise. A sign is often an unusual or miraculous event that introduces, authenticates, or illustrates the message." *NET Bible Notes*, study note 41, Exodus 3:12

25 Exodus 3:12

26 *NET Bible Notes*, translator's note 42, Exodus 3:12

*The Power of Obedience*

encounter with Yahweh.[27] God does not spell out for Moses all the details of what will happen on the return trip to Sinai. What God does supply up front is the ultimate goal along with the revelation that He will win the battle against Pharaoh. Everything else about what God asked Moses to do will require Moses and the people to trust Him. They will need to trust not only that He had an adequate plan but that He had all the power necessary to carry it out.[28]

In this, we learn something about the trust that God requires in *every* act of obedience. In short, obeying God looks something like this: "Go! Do what I commanded you. *After* you have done what I have asked, *then* you will know from experience who I am and that I am the one who sent you!" That's why obedience is a walk of faith, not a walk by sight (2 Corinthians 5:7).

**Hear What The Spirit is Saying to the Church**: *Those who choose to "play it safe" will never come to know me by experience. For just as surely as I sent Moses and asked him to trust me, so do I send you and ask you to trust me. Obedience builds your faith step by step. Such is my good plan for every Believer.*

---

27 Durham, John I., *Word Biblical Commentary: Exodus*, Volume 3 (Word Books 1987) Exodus 3:11-12 under *Comment*, p. 33
28 *NET Bible Notes*, study note 42, Exodus 3:12

# LESSON 6:

## PROVISION ON THE PATH OF OBEDIENCE

"Then [God] brought them out with silver and gold, And among His tribes there was not one who stumbled.... He spread a cloud for a covering, And fire to illumine by night. They asked, and He brought quail, And satisfied them with the bread of heaven. He opened the rock and water flowed out; it ran in the dry places *like* a river." Psalm 105:37,39-41, italics in original

THE CENTRAL PILLAR upon which Israel has established her faith in Yahweh has been and will always be the exodus story. The pre-release exodus experience in Egypt combined with the post-release wilderness experience were the primary ways in which God had sovereignly chosen to reveal His nature and His character to Abraham's descendants. Those extraordinary acts have firmly established the identity of who God is in relationship to Israel.[1] In fact, "the Old Testament never distinguishes the nature of Yahweh from His acts."[2]

Understandably then the story of the exodus is arguably *the* event of all human history according to the Jewish people.[3] Jewish

---

1 Sarna, Nahum M., *Understanding Genesis Through Rabbinic Tradition and Modern Scholarship* (The Jewish Theological Seminary 2015) p. 8
2 Longman III and Garland, general editors, *The Expositor's Bible Commentary: Psalms*, Vol. 5, Revised Edition (Zondervan 2008) *Reflections: The Praise of Yahweh*, p. 506
3 Greenberg, Irving, Rabbi, *Why The Exodus Was So Significant*. Retrieved from https://www.myjewishlearning.com /article/the-exodus-effect/ (last accessed July 8, 2021)

scholar Nahum Sarna identifies seven important biblical themes that are revealed in this historic event.

Israel's exodus from Egypt:[4]

1. affirms God's absolute sovereignty over all nature
2. proves man is ultimately not able to thwart God's plan
3. teaches that history is the unfolding story of God's grand design, thereby giving history itself its meaning and purpose
4. demonstrates God's purposes are redemptive and He is the One who frees His people from injustice and oppression
5. establishes the biblical model of future redemption offering comfort and hope in the present
6. sets the calendar for the annual celebration of Israel's feasts, which are not only cause for celebration but for remembering and rehearsing God's mighty deeds
7. provides the authoritative and motivating source for ethical behavior because God demands a personal response that imitates His actions

Each of those seven themes is rooted in what God chooses to disclose about His nature and character. Scholars have astutely observed that the Old Testament contains no description whatsoever of God's divine physical appearance.[5] In Yahweh's perfect wisdom He knew Israel did not need a physical description of Him. What would benefit them most was His self-revelation through unforgettable deeds that would make His invisibility manifestly visible to them.[6] The entire narrative aims to highlight the active, dynamic

---

4  Sarna, Nahum M., *Exploring Exodus: The Origins of Biblical Israel* (Schocken Books 1996) pp. 2-4
5  "Eminently significant and characteristic of the whole genius of the Old Testament is the absence of any description of the divine appearance." Maclaren, Alexander, *Expositions of Holy Scripture*, Isaiah 6:3. Retrieved from https://biblehub.com/commentaries/isaiah/6-3.htm (last accessed September 6, 2021)
6  Keener, Craig S., *The Gospel Of John: A Commentary*, Volume One (Hendrickson Publishers 2003) 2B. The Father's Witness ([John] 5:36-44), p. 658

presence of God in the life and history of His people. That presence provides sufficient reason to trust in Him as the God who is eternally faithful to His covenant.[7]

Those powerful acts and His revealed nature were so foundational in Israel's history that David declared centuries later:

> [Yahweh] made known His ways to Moses, His acts to the sons of Israel. Psalm 103:7

When the Bible refers to the "ways" of God, as in Psalm 103:7, the Hebrew word is *derek* {deh'-rek}. In a physical sense *derek* refers to a material road/pathway itself or to movement on a road/pathway that leads to a particular destination. That concrete use of the word provides a wonderful picture of how *derek* is used in its figurative sense. Metaphorically, it is the path God walks on. It refers to how He interacts with His creation. His ways are carefully calculated to lead His covenant people to the destination He has in mind for them – a restored Garden of Eden with everlasting fellowship, a forever Kingdom over which He sovereignly rules!

In the Bible *derek* not only refers to God's way, it often refers to the actions and behavior of people who are in covenant relationship with God.

### WORD STUDY

*Biblically when the Hebrew word derek {deh'-rek} is applied to people it refers to:[8] 1) a course of life, meaning the character and context of our life; 2) how we conduct life, referring to our specific choices and behaviors; and*

---

7   Sarna, Nahum M., *Exploring Exodus: The Origins of Biblical Israel* (Schocken Books 1996) p. 110
8   Waltke, Bruce K., *The Book of Proverbs: Chapters 1-15,* The New International Commentary on the Old Testament (Eerdmans 2004) Proverbs 1:15-16, p. 194

*3) the consequences of those choices and behaviors that inevitably define the destiny of our chosen lifestyle.*

From our Word Study, a non-negotiable principle of God's Kingdom stands out. God's design for man centers on a "deed-destiny nexus."[9] Let me explain. *Derek* notably refers to "a path worn by constant walking."[10] That means walking on the path with God is an ongoing day-in-day-out lifestyle choice! An occasional visit to that path is more than a misstep. That lifestyle will cause God's covenant people to miss their destiny. If we as Christ-followers are going to reach our God-appointed destination, we must be willing to constantly and continually walk on the same path God walks on. He will lead and we are to follow.

As we have learned, our fellowship with God is only available as we obey what He commands. When God created the universe and prescribed the function of every part of it, He determined that the only way to truly *know* Him is by experience born out of fellowship. To that end the wilderness between Egypt and the Promised Land provided the perfect classroom. God, Himself, would be their ever-present perfect teacher skillfully using the unique elements found in the wilderness as instructional tools.

Yahweh had manifested His power in Egypt as a deliverer and conqueror to establish His Kingdom. Israel would be His people and He would be their King-Husband. However, it wasn't honeymoon-bliss and a carefree life lived happily ever after that He desired for them. He had a unique role in mind for the nation of Israel. The experience of Israel's election, her chosen-ness, is "prior and privileged but [was never intended to be] exclusivist."[11] God

---

9   Waltke, Bruce K., *The Book of Proverbs: Chapters 1-15,* The New International Commentary on the Old Testament (Eerdmans 2004) Proverbs 1:15-16, p. 194
10  Harris, Archer, and Waltke, editors, *Theological Wordbook of the Old Testament* (Moody Press 1999) word #453a, p. 196
11  Motyer, J. Alec, *The Prophecy of Isaiah: An Introduction & Commentary* (InterVarsity Press 1993) Isaiah 60:2, p. 494

## The Power of Obedience

freely chose to reveal Himself to Israel and sovereignly chose them to RE•present[12] Him to the rest of the world. His desire was for them to not only be His *messenger* but to be His walked-out *message*.

God had freed Israel with His "strong hand and powerful arm."[13] His purpose was to expand His Kingdom as they revealed His true nature by their obedience to His commands. By living according to His Kingdom principles, they would effectively RE•present Him to the nations around them. His plan is to overcome the chaos in the world and restore the shalom that was once found in the Garden. Obeying God's instruction would bring these newly liberated people "into genuine liberty, by a full commitment to the good of the other and of all; and in doing so to offer the world an example of the nature of the divine will for ordering the whole creation."[14]

However, preparing Israel to *be the message* would take more time and more work than it took to get them out of the land of Egypt![15] Before they could *be* the right message God had to get Egypt – those Egyptian gods and that Egyptian story – out of those Egyptian-born Hebrews.[16] Only then could His redeemed people

---

12  I am intentionally repurposing the word "represent" at times in this study by making a clear separation between the prefix "re" and the remainder of the word "present." The prefix "re" indicates repetition and has an ordinary meaning of "again" or "back." My goal in showing the word in this unique form is to highlight the truth that one who is God's representative does not act on his own accord, that representative is actually commissioned by God to repeat what God has done, to show again who God is. I have placed the prefix "re" in all caps to indicate the emphasis on that syllable when pronouncing the word.

13  "So the LORD brought us out of Egypt with a strong hand and powerful arm, with overwhelming terror, and with miraculous signs and wonders." Deuteronomy 26:8 NLT

14  McConville, J. G., *Deuteronomy*, Apollos Old Testament Commentary 5 (IVP Academic 2002) Deuteronomy 5:1-33 under *Explanation*, p. 136

15  Vander Laan, Ray, *That The World May Know with Ray Vander Laan*, DVD Teaching Series, Fire On The Mountain, Volume 9 (Zondervan 2009) Session 1: The Lord Who Heals You

16  Vander Laan, Ray, *That The World May Know with Ray Vander Laan*, DVD Teaching Series, Fire On The Mountain, Volume 9 (Zondervan

be His Kingdom representatives to all the nations of the world. To accomplish His purpose would require the cooperative obedience of Israel. In essence they were to become walking billboards delivering a message to the world through the obedient life they lived.

They had come to know of God's power and His redemptive heart as they watched Him defeat Pharaoh and all the Egyptian gods. As we will see in this lesson, in terms of *knowing* God's ways, Israel had just graduated from Kindergarten and God was ready to plunge them right into Graduate School. By overthrowing the most powerful ruler in the known world at that time, God had just impressively asserted His rightful Kingship over His creation. He was ready to teach His chosen people the benefits of obedient life under His sovereign rule.

If we had our way, God would simply sit us down, ask us to pick up a pen and paper and He would proceed to dictate in a logical, orderly way all that we needed to know about Him. If He would just do *that* we think we would then know Him and His ways. But let me ask you something, which provides more rocket fuel for your own belief: hearing someone say God is compassionate or experiencing God's compassion for yourself as He walks you through a particularly difficult time in your life? Does someone else describing their personal track record of God's faithfulness empower your belief more than being able to recite your own? Did Peter believe Jesus when He was warned that his faith would fail as increasing pressure was applied in a time of crisis? Or did Peter have to deny Him and hear the rooster crow before he understood just how weak he was in the flesh?

In Lesson 3 we learned that testing was God's preferred instructional method in the wilderness. We have already taken notice in our study that tests of obedience provide prime opportunities for God to self-disclose the reality of His nature. As we will see, that pattern of revelation is a theme that runs all the way through the exodus story. We said when God tests a person, it is to refine that person's character so he might walk more closely in God's ways.

---

2009) Session 1: The Lord Who Heals You

*The Power of Obedience*

Testing is designed to shape and mold us into the person God wants us to be. In this lesson, we will consider three types of obedience tests God divinely planned for Israel during her journey through the wilderness. He had led them out of Egypt; but, as we've said, the next thing He needed to do was to get Egypt out of them!

In our second lesson, we looked at the Hebrew word *yada`* highlighting that *yada`* is not mere head knowledge. So far in our study of this word we have focused on how knowledge is acquired by experience. These wilderness tests will add another element to the biblical understanding of what it means to "know" something. That is, in biblical thought, you don't know something until you actually put it into practice. You *know* it when you walk it out in your life. As we will see, God is going to demand that Israel demonstrate by her actions what she has learned from the instructive experiences He provides.

With that background, we'll consider three areas of testing God had waiting for Israel in the wilderness: 1) lack of water, 2) lack of food and 3) war. So, let's zoom in on their life-size classroom. As we do, let's first take notice that it was Yahweh who created (or allowed) each crisis they faced. Then it was Yahweh who provided the solution. As classroom observers, we'll be able to see the miracles God performed, what He intended His covenant people to learn as a result and how well they demonstrated their knowledge of Him and His ways. We'll see that in some cases they passed the test by putting their knowledge to practice, but other times they failed hands down.

## God's Instructional Water Tests

Israel's need for water and their persistent complaint at its lack presented several tests in their wilderness travels. Three days after the miracle at the Red Sea, Israel faced her first water crisis at *Marah* (Exodus 15:22-25). God had led them straight to *bitter* water.

The root of the word *marah* is much stronger than bitter. It can mean deliberate, defiant disobedience.[17] Israel was not merely complaining about the bitter water, they were defiantly questioning God's ability and motive. The intense language used in the original Hebrew text highlights their "profound lack of faith in God and base ingratitude."[18] Their conduct was something akin to a vote of no confidence in parliamentary procedure.[19] Remember they were following the cloud by day and the pillar of fire by night meaning this destination with its bitter water was no mistake. They were camped at *Marah* because it was an integral part of God's purposeful instruction. This sequence of events was exactly what God's lesson plans called for that day. Every stage of Israel's development is being determined step-by-step according to divine blueprint and purpose.

At their grumbling, Moses called out to the Lord for help. God answered Moses by giving him instructions on how to make the water sweet. The miracle at *Marah* is that the waters were made drinkable by simply tossing in the specific tree God had pointed out to Moses. God authored that crisis moment, He alone had the solution. All they needed to do was to ask. How much more pleasing to God would it have been if they had arrived at the well and as soon as they discovered the water was bitter, they simply turned their faces toward God with confident expectation awaiting His wisdom on the matter. In fact, at that place where He healed the bitter water, God revealed Himself as *Yahweh-Rapha*, "The

---

17 Vander Laan, Ray, *That The World May Know with Ray Vander Laan*, DVD Teaching Series, Fire On The Mountain, Volume 9 (Zondervan 2009) Session 1: The Lord Who Heals You
18 Sarna, Nahum M., *Exploring Exodus: The Origins of Biblical Israel* (Schocken Books 1996) p. 118. As an explicit example of Israel's attitude see Psalm 78:17-25.
19 A vote of no confidence is a way that a majority of a legislative body (or other deliberative body) indicates they no longer support a leader or governing body. *NET Bible Notes*, translator's note 66, Exodus 15:24

LORD who Heals," promising them health and well-being if they obeyed His commands.[20]

The God who had just parted the Red Sea could certainly provide sweet water for them to drink. However, they did not apply what they had previously learned about Yahweh. By their murmuring and complaining, they failed this test.

It is instructive that the very next stop they made after *Marah* is the oasis of *Elim* – a place described as having twelve springs of water and seventy date palms. The exodus narrative simply says "and they camped there by the waters."[21] No crisis here, just the grace of the God who loved them and was teaching them along the way. God no doubt desired a celebration of praise to arise from the lips of His covenant people evidencing their gratitude for this amazing provision, but sadly none is recorded in Scripture.

Their next water test came at *Rephidim*. Here again, they complained and quarreled with Moses to the point that they were ready to stone him. They failed the test again. As a matter of fact, they turned *their* test into a test of God.[22] The language of the original Hebrew text makes clear that they were "demanding proof that God was [actually] present among them and controlling the events."[23] In a manner of speaking, they were asking Yahweh to "jump through their hoops" in order to prove Himself to them.[24]

---

20   Exodus 15:26
21   Exodus 15:27
22   Moses' response was to ask them why they were "testing the LORD (Exodus 17:2)?" The Hebrew language used to describe the nature of Israel's complaint can refer to bringing a lawsuit. This type of legal action was known in the ancient Near East. In such cases, the aggrieved party made a demand on the potential defendant and then waited for a response. An unfavorable response could then lead to a lawsuit. Wells, Bruce, "Exodus," in *Zondervan Illustrated Bible Backgrounds Commentary*, Vol. 1, edited by John H. Walton (Zondervan 2009) Exodus 17:2, p. 220
23   Berlin and Brettler, editors, *The Jewish Study Bible: Featuring The Jewish Publication Society Tanakh Translation* (Oxford University Press 2004) study note Exodus 17:2, p. 142
24   Johnston, Gordon H., "Exodus," in *The Bible Knowledge Word Study, Genesis – Deuteronomy*, edited by Eugene H. Merrill (Victor 2003) Ex-

Even though they mistrusted God's provision and His motives,[25] God graciously taught them once again that He was their sustainer and provider. Water rushed from a rock simply because Moses obediently struck it with his staff (Exodus 17:1-6). God did not merely supply a few drops of water. His all-sufficient grace provided enough to quench the thirst of the estimated two million Israelites![26]

### God's Instructional Food Tests

Not long after Israel had escaped Egypt and crossed the Red Sea, they ran out of food. What I find so amazing is at the end of each day's journey God could have said to Moses, "I know the people are weary from today's travel, so instruct them to sit down at the banquet table I have prepared for them and enjoy the rich food I've provided." But He didn't do it that way because He knew it wasn't the most effective instructional strategy to reach His goal. Instead, He allowed Israel to experience the absence of food before He met their need. Doing so presented Israel the perfect opportunity to apply what they had learned at *Marah* and *Elim.* To pass this test, they would have chosen to fix their eyes expectantly on God and wait confidently for His provision as soon as they realized their need. Their waiting would have demonstrated patience based on their past experience that God would meet that need in the fullness of His time and in His perfect way.

Sadly, that's not what happened. Hungry flesh not brought under control demands to be served! And that's exactly how they responded. One month into the journey[27] they began to grumble

---

odus17:7 under *He named the place Masa ... because there they tested the* Lord, p. 196

25 *How does the Bible use symbolism?* under *Put God to the test*, Compelling Truth. Retrieved from https://www.compellingtruth.org/biblical-symbolism.html (last accessed February 3, 2022)

26 The tribal census numbers given in Numbers 1 report a total of 603,550 adult males who left Egypt. This suggests a total population figure with women and children of close to 2 million.

27 Exodus 16:1

and even nostalgically reminisce about the food they ate in Egypt as slaves. They absurdly accused Moses of wanting to starve them to death. (Note: we are rarely rational in our thinking when we demand something we think is being improperly withheld from us). Again, despite their murmuring and complaining, God provided for them. Quail came and covered the camp that evening (Exodus 16:13) and manna appeared in the morning (16:14) supplying two more rich God-related knowing experiences (*yada`*).[28]

Even though God's gracious response was "watch Me, I'll rain down heavenly bread for everyone,"[29] God's teaching instructions came attached to that food. There were commands Israel needed to carefully obey to have the enjoyment of what God provided for them. "Gather only what you need, eat what you gather and rest from gathering on the seventh day."[30] I find it interesting that God could have measured out the exact supply He desired for each person in the same way He prevented the manna from appearing on the seventh day. However, He desired to teach obedience and trust. The question that needed to be answered is, "When He provides instruction for Israel that is for her best, will she hear and obey?" We know from the exodus story, in most cases Israel passed the test by following God's instruction for collecting and storing the food. On the other hand, some continued to demonstrate the dissatisfaction hidden in their heart by stubbornly refusing to do exactly what God told them to do. They suffered the consequences God had warned would result from disobedience (remember, we have already learned that God reliably carries through on His warnings)! He was patiently and lovingly inviting them to integrate and apply previous lessons learned to each new situation.

---

28  Exodus 16:11
29  My paraphrase of Exodus 16:4. This miracle of manna took place not just once or twice but 6 days a week for 40 years! Just as miraculously as it began, God stopped delivering the manna when Joshua and the people crossed the Jordan and began to eat the food of the Promised Land (Joshua 5:12).
30  My paraphrase of Exodus 16:4-5

By supernaturally supplying food and water God was revealing His faithfulness to them. He wanted Israel to know that they could trust Him to meet their needs. One of the main functions of any king is to provide for the people in his kingdom. Yahweh was no exception. If He truly is King of these people, then they will benefit from His gracious provision which will meet their basic needs. He supplies provision, extends protection and then sovereignly demands obedience. Yahweh wanted them to learn that when it came to matters of basic survival, He was willing and able to sustain them. But He would teach them that their provision was to be found only on the path of obedience. As they obeyed Him they would be in the right place at the right time to receive His provision for them.

### GOD'S INSTRUCTIONAL WAR TEST

During the exodus from Egypt God had fought their battles for them. According to the Bible, Amalek was the first enemy that Israel encountered after they supernaturally crossed the Red Sea in safety. The Amalekites ambushed Israel while they were camped at *Rephidim*. That unprovoked attack became the perfect opportunity for a miraculous deliverance that would result in a new revelation about Yahweh.

During that battle, Aaron and Hur supported Moses' uplifted hands as he stood on top of a hill overlooking the battlefield. Israel prevailed in battle when the hands of Moses were held up, but Amalek prevailed when the hands of Moses were lowered.[31] While the biblical account does not specify exactly why Moses did what he did, God was revealing His strategy for victory in every war they would ever fight.[32] They were to fight with all their might, but they

---

31   Exodus 17:11
32   One suggestion that merits consideration is that Moses was holding up an ensign, a banner which signified the presence and support of Yahweh serving to rally the Israelites and bolster their morale. Support for this suggestion comes from the facts that: 1) this type of banner containing religious symbols was widely used in the world of the Old Testament

*The Power of Obedience*

were to never take their eyes off God. They were *His* soldiers, fighting under *His* command.[33] God's battle strategy was pretty simple, yet very effective. It was captured by the Psalmist when he wrote: "I lift up my eyes to the hills. From where does my help come? My help comes from the LORD, who made heaven and earth."[34]

Because they ultimately got it right, Israel under Joshua's leadership, secured a great victory that day. Recall that we have already learned of the ancient practice of naming or renaming a physical location based on a life-changing encounter with Yahweh. We also learned that the given name related to the self-revelation God provided at that site. At the place of Israel's first victory in battle, Moses built an altar to the Lord and called it *Yahweh-Nissi* – "The LORD Our Banner."[35] The tribes of Israel were marked by identifying banners as they camped (Numbers 2:2). But in this case, Moses understood the revelation that God Himself was Israel's banner, their only source of victory. Whether He was fighting while Israel stood still to watch[36] or whether He chose to put Israel's sandals on the battlefield, He was the one who won their battles.

---

and 2) the Hebrew word for this type of banner is *nes*. There may be a connection between that word for banner and the altar Moses built to commemorate God's victory over Amalek. The name of the altar, *Yahweh-nissi*, means "The Lord is my ensign/banner." Sarna, Nahum M., *Exploring Exodus: The Origins of Biblical Israel* (Schocken Books 1996) pp. 122-123

33  Brain, Bill, Sermon: *God is my Banner (Jehovah Nissi)*. Retrieved from http://www.sermoncentral.com/sermons/god-is-my-banner-jehovah-nissi-brian-bill-sermon-on-god-s-omniscience-77773 (last accessed July 8, 2021)

34  Psalm 121:1-2 ESV

35  "Banners were used in military campaigns to identify members of an army. These banners often included symbols or representations of the national gods who were fighting for the respective armies. Yahweh took on this role with Israel (Exodus 15:3; Joshua 23:10) and was identified as Israel's banner (Exodus 17:15)." *Holman Christian Standard Bible*, Study Bible edition (Holman Bible Publishers 2010) study note Psalm 20:5, p. 899

36  As at the shores of the Red Sea. "But Moses said to the people, Do not fear! Stand by and see the salvation of the LORD which He will accom-

It was centuries before this that Abraham had experienced the provision of the ram in the thicket on the path of his obedience. We noted in Lesson 3 that he gave that place a new name to commemorate God's provision. In addition to renaming the place, Abraham also gave God a new name: *Yahweh-Jireh*.[37] This new name could be translated as: "The LORD Who Sees," or "The LORD Who Will See To It."[38] That new name is based on Abraham's miraculous experience in that place and conveys the unchangeable truth that God will make provision when He sees the need. Just as Yahweh had done with Abraham, He was patiently, methodically and miraculously instructing Israel in His covenantal faithfulness and their covenantal obligation in return.

As we have watched God reveal Himself to Israel, let's take note of the obvious lest we miss it. God was ever-ready to provide whatever Israel needed – food, water, victory in battle – but their feet *had* to be on the path of obedience to receive the provision He wanted to release to them! The foundational lesson which God repeated many times over is that the enjoyment of covenant blessing is contingent upon obedient responsiveness to doing His will![39] He simply will not bless disobedience.

In Egypt, Israel had learned that water, food and safety came from Pharaoh and the Egyptian gods. However, in the desert, God was beginning to teach them the truth that *He* is their provider. At every turn in the exodus story, God was presenting the perfect learning environment to invite Israel to come to know Him and to

---

plish for you today; for the Egyptians whom you have seen today, you will never see them again forever." Exodus 14:13

37  Genesis 22:12-14
38  Nester, Emery, *The Compound Names of Jehovah: Jireh, Rapha, Nissi*, Bible.Org, published October 20, 2006. Retrieved from https://bible.org/seriespage/60-compound-names-jehovah-jireh-rapha-nissi (last accessed July 8, 2021)
39  Longman III and Garland, general editors, *The Expositor's Bible Commentary: Psalms*, Vol. 5, Revised Edition (Zondervan 2008) Psalm 103:15-18, p. 759

learn His love language – obedience. He wanted them to become a reflection of who He is to all other nations.

All of God's wilderness-infused lessons were goal-driven. Through these tests He was prompting Israel to check her heart and consider her answers to questions such as, "Are you learning that I alone meet your needs? Where are your eyes focused? Are they fixed on me, your provider, your sufficiency? Are you learning to expect me to provide for your every need according to my perfect plan and purpose? Are you learning to act in a way that is consistent with my character and my Name? Are you learning to be both my fully developed messenger and my perfected message to a lost and dying world?"

Centuries later the words of James succinctly summed up God's goal in testing this way:

> Consider it nothing but joy, my brothers and sisters, whenever you fall into various trials. Be assured that the testing of your faith [through experience] produces endurance [leading to spiritual maturity, and inner peace]. And let endurance have its perfect result *and* do a thorough work, so that you may be perfect and completely developed [in your faith], lacking in nothing. James 1:2-4 AMP, italics in original

The cardinal principle of imitating God is front and center in the exodus narrative. In God's Kingdom, every person is obligated to mimic, as closely as possible, His divine attributes. If we allow God the freedom to teach us obedience in the ways that He knows are for our best, we will mature and become fully developed, lacking in nothing. Then *we* can *be His message* – an accurate reflection of His perfect, good and loving character to everyone around us. As the author of Hebrews exhorted his listeners, "Today, if you hear his voice, do not harden your hearts."[40]

Let's conclude our lesson by summarizing several additional lessons these wilderness tests can teach us about obedience.

---

40  Hebrews 4:7, quoting Psalm 95:7

**TRUTH #1: YOU CAN COMPLAIN OR YOU CAN EXPERIENCE GOD'S GRACE, BUT YOU CAN'T DO BOTH AT THE SAME TIME!**

If you are at all familiar with the exodus story, you know that Israel was constantly complaining about her circumstances. You probably also recall that their complaining did not please God. Just like Israel, my husband and I had fallen into the trap of complaint after God moved us from Ohio to Florida in November 2015. That is until God taught us a vitally important Kingdom principle about complaining.

The heat and humidity of the first Florida summer concerned us greatly and we were constantly murmuring and grumbling about it. In June 2016 we were driving from Florida to Washington D.C. for a prayer assignment the Lord had given us and we had stopped overnight in Sevierville, Tennessee. The next morning, I was sitting at a picnic table outside the hotel. It was a lovely summer morning. It was sunny but with a gentle cooling breeze, not cold, just enough to be delightfully refreshing. It was the kind of breeze you get in the north but we seemed to lack in the panhandle of Florida. I was thinking about the warm breezes in Florida that are accompanied by humidity and wondering what it was going to be like as we went further into those first summer months. In particular, I was pondering how we would ever be able to tolerate the month of August, which local people had consistently told us was the worst month of the year for its heat and humidity. As I sat there in quiet reflection, I heard the Spirit of the Lord say, "*You can complain about it or you can receive the grace to sustain you through it, but you can't do both!*"

Without hesitation, I knew the choice I would make – no more complaining! God had just made clear that His grace was the key to survival and I didn't want to miss any measure of that grace! If we do not complain about *what is*, God will release His all-sufficient grace for what *can be*!

## TRUTH #2: IT MATTERS TO GOD WHICH DIRECTION YOUR MAGNIFYING GLASS IS POINTED.

When I taught the book of Exodus verse-by-verse in women's Bible study, God repeatedly emphasized the desire of His heart for Israel in the wilderness was that she would have kept her eyes focused on Him rather than on her circumstances. In that season of teaching He gave me a wonderful teaching tool that I have used repeatedly since then. He showed me that (metaphorically) Israel had in her hands at all times her own magnifying glass. Nevertheless, it was completely up to her discretion as to which direction it was pointed. Would she use it to see the Lord more clearly in the middle of her circumstances thereby magnifying, exalting and trusting Him while waiting on His solution? Or would she point that magnifying glass on her circumstances and in so doing magnify and enlarge them? The choice belonged entirely to Israel. However, the truth is this, whatever you place under a magnifying glass will always get bigger!

Every Christ-follower holds in their hands their own God-given magnifying glass. The question for us is the same as it was for ancient Israel, "When times of trial or testing come, how will I use it? In which direction will I turn it, will I magnify my circumstances (the trial, the suffering, the testing) – OR – will I use it to magnify the Lord?" When our present circumstances become our greatest focus, we will *always* seek short-term solutions to address that present need! And when we do, we will often miss God's **best** for us. His best will invariably provide the opportunity in the midst of those pressing circumstances to see Him more clearly and to experience His provision in His perfect timing.

David, a man after God's own heart, instructs us with wisdom gained by personal experience:

> O magnify the LORD with me, And let us exalt His name together. Psalm 34:3

**TRUTH #3: GOD WILL SUPPLY US WITH DO-OVERS UNTIL WE GET IT RIGHT!**

"The Lord never reduces his standards to match the weaknesses of his people; he raises his people to the height of his standard."[41] God's goal is to make us perfect, complete and lacking nothing (James 1:2-4). The apostle Paul says it this way, "that He might present us to Himself as a glorious church without a spot or wrinkle or any other blemish, holy and without fault."[42] Because that's His goal, God will supply us with do-overs until we get it right! Several years ago, I heard a report of a "new, innovative and revolutionary" approach to teaching that permits students who fail a test to re-take the test (without penalty) to get a better grade. In fact, in this style of teaching the student can have as many "do-overs" as it takes to get a passing grade on that test. In reality, this is not "new" at all – it is a strategy that is as old as God's relationship with Israel!

During the exodus story, we see that God's lesson plan often presented a chance to replay the learning experience. Repeat lessons can have a two-fold purpose. For those who didn't learn the object lesson the first time, it is a gracious do-over – another grace-filled learning opportunity.

However, the repeated lesson can serve an entirely different purpose for those who first failed but then responded to God's rebuke with repentance. They were the ones who decidedly learned from their failure. In that case, a repeat lesson becomes a wonderful yardstick of individual growth and God's faithfulness. God loves to reveal His faithfulness and one of the ways He does is to bring us back around to the same or similar situation we confronted before. God can use the do-over as an opportunity to show us He has acknowledged our desire for change and quietly went to work on our heart. At some later point in time, He ordains circumstances that repeat or closely simulate those we encountered earlier. This time when our response lines up with His character, God can lovingly

---

41 Motyer, J. Alec, *Isaiah*, Tyndale Old Testament Commentaries (IVP Academic 1999) Isaiah 35:8-10, p. 245
42 Ephesians 5:27, my paraphrase

highlight our growth, evidencing the miraculous work He has done in us! He then invites the response of a truly devoted learner – that we praise Him for His faithfulness.

The bottom line is this: In God's sovereignly designed method of mastery-based learning we will keep suffering in the same direction until the impurities of our life in that particular area have been filtered out of us. The Bible uses the metaphor of clothing to help us understand the spiritual transformation process – biblically, clothing symbolically refers to character. There are character traits we need to "take off" and there are character traits we need to "put on." Trials (God's ordained instructive experiences) enable us to do both. The ultimate goal is to "take off" things that hinder us from being like Christ and in their place to "put on" new character qualities that reflect God's glory.

There is another truth that is emerging from the exodus story, the truth of God's Lordship, and that will be the subject of our next lesson.

**Hear What The Spirit is Saying to the Church**: *I have not changed, I am the same yesterday, today and forever. The lessons I sought to teach Israel in the wilderness are the very same lessons I desire to teach you. I have taken my Body into a season of a new wilderness so that I may tenderly teach her there to be more like me.*[43] *How will you choose to respond to my teaching?*

---

43  Ultimately the wilderness itself is a metaphor. It is a picture of a people separated from the world's ways – set apart, separated, holy unto God!

LESSON 7:

ANOTHER WORD FOR
OBEDIENCE IS LORDSHIP

"Then [Moses] said to [God], 'If Your presence does not go *with us*, do not lead us up from here....'" Exodus 33:15, italics in original

THE PRESENCE Moses was asking for in this lesson's Key Scripture was God's manifest presence – the tangible presence of God whereby He makes Himself known. It was that very presence God had promised to Moses at the burning bush when He commanded Moses to "go" with the assurance, "Certainly I will be with you."[1] Moses had learned the same lessons David would later learn. They were practical lessons that led David to proclaim that with Yahweh's help he could "advance against a troop" and with the help of his God he could "scale a wall."[2] In other words, it matters whether or not God is present because His manifest presence among His covenant people assures them of His personal involvement in their affairs. His presence declares that He is both willing and able to act on their behalf no matter what need arises. Moses understood it is *God's presence* that distinguished Israel from all the other nations on the face of the earth (Exodus 33:16).

So how is it that Moses finds himself begging the Lord to go with Israel or to not send them from the place in the wilderness where they were presently camped? Even if you didn't know the story of the golden calf, by this point in our study you could prob-

---

1  The first part of God's promise in Exodus 3:12
2  2 Samuel 22:30; Psalm 18:29

ably guess that question can be answered in two words: ***Israel's disobedience***!

In Lesson 6 we followed Israel in the early stages of her wilderness journey through the lens of the tests God had purposefully used in His ideal classroom setting. We will pick up the exodus story at the point where Israel is camped at the foot of Mt. Sinai and Moses has been called up the mountain to meet with God.

> Now when the people saw that Moses delayed to come down from the mountain, the people assembled about Aaron and said to him, "Come, make us a god who will go before us; as for this Moses, the man who brought us up from the land of Egypt, we do not know what has become of him." Aaron said to them, "Tear off the gold rings which are in the ears of your wives, your sons, and your daughters, and bring *them* to me." Then all the people tore off the gold rings which were in their ears and brought *them* to Aaron. He took *this* from their hand, and fashioned it with a graving tool and made it into a molten calf; and they said, "This is your god, O Israel, who brought you up from the land of Egypt." Now when Aaron saw *this*, he built an altar before it; and Aaron made a proclamation and said, "Tomorrow *shall* be a feast to the LORD." So the next day they rose early and offered burnt offerings, and brought peace offerings; and the people sat down to eat and to drink, and rose up to play. Then the LORD spoke to Moses, "Go down at once, for your people, whom you brought up from the land of Egypt, have corrupted *themselves*. They have quickly turned aside from the way which I commanded them. They have made for themselves a molten calf, and have worshiped it and have sacrificed to it and said, 'This is your god, O Israel, who brought you up from the land of Egypt!'" The LORD said to Moses, "I have seen this people, and behold, they are an obstinate people. Now then

let Me alone, that My anger may burn against them and that I may destroy them; and I will make of you a great nation." Exodus 32:1-10, italics in original

Now when Moses saw that the people were out of control—for Aaron had let them get out of control to be a derision among their enemies— then Moses stood in the gate of the camp, and said, "Whoever is for the LORD, *come* to me!" And all the sons of Levi gathered together to him. He said to them, "Thus says the Lord, the God of Israel, 'Every man *of you* put his sword upon his thigh, and go back and forth from gate to gate in the camp, and kill every man his brother, and every man his friend, and every man his neighbor.'" So the sons of Levi did as Moses instructed, and about three thousand men of the people fell that day.... On the next day Moses said to the people, "You yourselves have committed a great sin ...." Exodus 32:25-28,30, italics in original

And the LORD inflicted a plague on the people for what they did with the calf Aaron had made. Exodus 32:35 HCSB[3]

After Moses dealt with the irresponsible leadership of Aaron and the rebellion of the Israelites, God instructed Moses to leave that place. Yahweh will keep His promise to Abraham, Isaac and Jacob that their descendants would live in the land flowing with milk and honey. There was one caveat – from this point forward an angel will lead them without Yahweh's abiding presence (Exodus 32:34; 33:1-2) that had been continuously visible in the pillar by day and night. The people had sought a substitute for Him, Yahweh now gives them what they asked for. From this point forward,

---

3   "Most commentators have difficulty with this verse. W. C. Kaiser says the strict chronology is not always kept, and so the plague here may very well refer to the killing of the three thousand ('Exodus,' *EBC* 2:481)." *NET Bible Notes*, study note 75, Exodus 32:35

the angel will act "as a surrogate for an absent, infuriated Yahweh."[4] Moses pleaded with God. In response God relented and agreed to continue leading Israel with His presence because Moses had found favor in His sight (Exodus 33:17).

What is important for our purposes is the reason behind God's announcement that He was planning to send an angel in His place. We have been continuing to learn that obedience is a non-negotiable requirement of fellowship with God. However, there is something more to the story than simply fellowship and that is the Lordship of Yahweh. To stand in God's presence requires a heart attitude of Lordship.

If we go back in history before this incident we will be able to see exactly what the Patriarchs and Moses had understood about the Lordship of Yahweh.

> Now it came about in *the course of* those many days that the king of Egypt died. And the sons of Israel sighed because of the bondage, and they cried out; and their cry for help because of *their* bondage rose up to God. So God heard their groaning; and **God remembered His covenant with Abraham, Isaac, and Jacob**. God saw the sons of Israel, and God took notice of *them*. Exodus 2:23-25, italics in original, bold added

> Now Moses was pasturing the flock of Jethro his father-in-law, the priest of Midian; and he led the flock to the west side of the wilderness and came to Horeb, the mountain of God. The angel of the Lord appeared to him in a blazing fire from the midst of a bush ... yet the bush was not consumed. So Moses said, "I must turn aside now and see this marvelous sight, why the bush is not burned up." When the Lord saw that he turned aside to look, God called to him from the midst of the bush

---

4  Levison, John R., *The Holy Spirit Before Christianity* (Baylor University Press 2019) p. 19

and said, "Moses, Moses!" And he said, "Here I am." Then He said, "Do not come near here; remove your sandals from your feet, for the place on which you are standing is holy ground.... **I am the God of your father, the God of Abraham, the God of Isaac, and the God of Jacob.**" Then Moses hid his face, for he was afraid to look at God. Exodus 3:1-6, bold added

By identifying Himself to Moses as the "God of Abraham, Isaac and Jacob" God implicitly evoked the promises of redemption He had made to the Patriarchs. It is in the context of those redemptive promises that Abraham had first addressed God as "Lord" in Genesis 15:2,8 and indeed it is the first time in the Bible we find God being addressed in that way.[5]

> But [Abraham] said, "[Master **Lord**],[6] what can You give me, since I am childless, and the heir of my house is Eliezer of Damascus?" ... Now the word of [Yahweh] came to [Abraham]: "This one will not be your heir; instead, one who comes from your own body will be your heir." Genesis 15:2,4, HCSB, bold added

> [Yahweh] also said to [Abraham], "I am Yahweh who brought you from Ur of the Chaldeans to give you this land to possess." But [Abraham] said, "[Master **Lord**],[7] how can I know that I will possess it?" Genesis 15:7-8 HCSB, bold added

---

5 When Abraham negotiated with God to spare Sodom and Gomorrah, he addressed God as *Adonai* (Genesis 18:16-33).
6 This translation is more in keeping with the original Hebrew text. *NET Bible Notes*, study note 3, Genesis 15:2
7 This translation is more in keeping with the original Hebrew text. *NET Bible Notes*, translator's note, Genesis 15:8, referencing back to study note 3, Genesis 15:2

> **WORD STUDY**
>
> *In the Scriptures just quoted, the bold text word translated as* **Lord** *is the Hebrew word 'Adonay {ad-o-noy'} [English spelling Adonai].* The Theological Wordbook of the Old Testament *states unequivocally, "no doubt exists about the meaning of this word."[8] It is not a name, it refers to the relationship of a servant to his master.[9] Adonai recognizes Yahweh as the ruler of the entire universe. The use of Adonai always denotes submission and reverence by the one who uses it.[10]*

When God is addressed as *Adonai*, at least four characteristics of God are being called to mind:[11]

1. *God is sovereign:* God's sovereignty is based on the undeniable fact that as the creator of heaven and earth He alone has dominion over all things. As Creator, He exclusively has the highest position within the universe and ultimate say-so over the whole universe. He is "God of gods, and Lord of lords (Deuteronomy 10:17)." He is "the Lord of all the earth (Joshua 3:11; Psalm 8:1)." One of the

---

8   Harris, Archer, and Waltke, editors, *Theological Wordbook of the Old Testament* (Moody Press 1999) word #27b, p. 12
9   Sarna, Nahum M., *The JPS Torah Commentary: Genesis*, The Traditional Hebrew Text with the New JPS Translation Commentary (The Jewish Publication Society 1989) Genesis 15:2 under *O Lord God*, p. 113
10  Unger, Merrill F., *The New Unger's Bible Dictionary* (Moody Press 1988) entry for *The Lord*, p. 781
11  *Adonai-Lord-The Name of God*, Precept Austin, citing *Preacher's Outline and Sermon Bible on Adon/Adonai.* Retrieved from https://www.preceptaustin.org/adonai-lord-the_name_of_god (last accessed September 6, 2021)

very last scenes in the Bible declares the absolute sovereign power of God, "And I heard, as it were, the voice of a great multitude, as the sound of many waters and as the sound of mighty thunderings, saying, 'Alleluia! For the Lord God Omnipotent reigns (Revelation 19:6 NKJV).'"

2. *God has supreme authority:* As the Creator, He has no equal. There is no authority greater than God. He alone is the sole Judge of everything. He has the undeniable right to rule as He wills. He rules according to His own purposes and pleasure with the freedom to govern and execute justice as He alone decides (Deuteronomy 28). When God decides to do a thing, He does it and no one has the authority to stop Him.

3. *God has the right to expect submission and command obedience:* It was God who breathed life into us. He alone has the right to demand obedience and submission. God has the unchallenged entitlement to direct the activities of all humanity and expect each person to respond with appropriate actions to attain *His* purposes. The fact that I am God's total possession should result in my total submission (Isaiah 6:1, 8-11; Joshua 7:8-13). Paul warned the church at Corinth that they "were bought with a price [a precious price paid by Christ]; [therefore they should] not become slaves to men [but to Christ] (1 Corinthians 7:23 AMP)."

4. *God can provide:* God's nature is to provide for His creation. In the culture of the Bible, a "master" was always expected to provide for his servants. As Creator, God is the all-sufficient provider of all things His servants need (Genesis 15:2; Psalm 23:1; 34:10; 37:25).

Referring to God as *Adonai* suggests that Abraham was fully aware that his relationship with God was that of master-servant.[12]

---

12 Sarna, Nahum M., *The JPS Torah Commentary: Genesis*, The Traditional Hebrew Text with the New JPS Translation Commentary (The Jewish Publication Society 1989) Genesis 15:2 under *O Lord God*, p. 113

That means he understood God would supply all his needs and he was obligated to do whatever God asked him to do. Since the Bible is silent on the source of this understanding, we might wonder how Abraham would have come to this knowledge of God. I think it is likely that the answer, first and foremost, relates back to Abraham's genealogy. Genesis 11:10-26 informs us that Abraham was a descendant of Shem, Noah's second-born son who had entered the Ark. I made brief mention of this ancestry in our third lesson with a promise to explore that relationship more fully here. Because Shem, along with Japheth, had done what was honorable in providing a covering for their father (Genesis 9:23-27), the first recorded blessing of Noah was given to Shem. It is reasonable to suggest that the knowledge of Yahweh had passed down from Noah to Shem and then down through the generations to Abraham. That would explain how Abraham, living in a pagan land, among pagan gods would have recognized the voice of Yahweh and considered Him to be the one true God. Of note is that the genealogy Matthew provides in the opening of his gospel picks up where the ancestry given in Genesis 11 leaves off. By doing so, Matthew informs us that the Messiah was a descendant of Shem.

This God who revealed Himself to the Patriarchs and who made them and their descendants promises of redemption is the same God who addressed Moses at the burning bush. As we will see, Moses recognized this to be so and accordingly he referred to Yahweh in the same way in which Abraham had.

> Then Moses said to the LORD, "Please, **Lord** [*Adonai*], I have never been eloquent, neither recently nor in time past, nor since You have spoken to Your servant; for I am slow of speech and slow of tongue." The LORD said to him, "Who has made man's mouth? Or who makes *him* mute or deaf, or seeing or blind? Is it not I, [*Yahweh*]? Now then go, and I, even I, will be with your mouth, and teach you what you are to say." But he said, "Please, **Lord** [*Adonai*], now send *the*

*message* by whomever You will." Exodus 4:10-13, italics in original, bold added

By addressing Yahweh with the title *Adonai* Moses recognizes God's sovereign right and authority as Master and confesses his position as Yahweh's servant/slave. When Moses called God *Adonai*, he acknowledged that it was not his place to choose his own work. As a fully submitted servant he had to heed his Master's directives.[13] Ultimately for Moses, that means – despite his objections – there was only one viable option: to obey.

From the very outset of God's instruction to Moses the stage is set and a very specific picture begins to emerge. The call of Moses is not going to be about Moses becoming the ideal American model of rough individualism. It's not even about Moses and God as two co-equal partners. It is all about Yahweh's Lordship! That means the entire exodus story is going to be about God's uncontested sovereign rule, His supreme authority, His right to demand total submission and obedience, His unilateral privilege to discipline disobedience and His power to provide for the needs of His covenant people in the way in which He sovereignly chooses. The fact that Yahweh is the sovereign Lord is "the one fundamental statement in the theology of the Old Testament.... Everything else derives from it. Everything else leans upon it. Everything else can be understood with reference to it and only it."[14]

With this understanding, it seems only natural that the Ten Commandments clearly and unambiguously demand the absolute prohibition on polytheism and idolatry for all of Israel.

> "I am the LORD your God, who brought you out of the land of Egypt, out of the house of slavery. You shall

---

13 *Adonai-Lord-The Name of God*, Precept Austin, citing Robert Lightner comments on *Adon/Adonai*. Retrieved from https://www.preceptaustin.org/adonai-lord-the_name_of_god (last accessed July 8, 2021)

14 Smith, Gary V., *The Concept of God/The Gods As King In The Ancient Near East and the Bible*, Trinity Journal 3NS (1982) pp. 18-38, at p. 33, quoting Kohler, *Old Testament Theology* (Westminster 1957) p. 30

have no other gods before Me. You shall not make for yourself an idol, or any likeness of what is in heaven above or on the earth beneath or in the water under the earth. You shall not worship them or serve them; for I, the LORD your God, am a jealous God ...." Exodus 20:2-5a

God leaves no doubt. He alone is to be worshipped by Israel! Understandably then when Moses appealed to God to go with Israel even after their grievous sin he again addressed God as *Adonai*.

[Moses] said, "If now I have found favor in Your sight, O **Lord** [*Adonai*], I pray, let the **Lord** [*Adonai*] go along in our midst, even though the people are so obstinate, and pardon our iniquity and our sin, and take us as Your own possession." Exodus 34:9, bold added

Moses had learned what Israel did not yet understand. Obedience is not about a destination. It is not receiving instruction, knowing what to do and then meeting God at the finish line. It is about relationship. That means that a lifetime of obedience is not the picture of two old friends who arrange a time and place to meet so they can reconnect and rekindle their friendship after years of separation. It's quite the opposite. Biblical obedience pictures those two friends doing life together – walking the road of life day-in and day-out heart to heart with Yahweh leading and the faithful disciple following.

The promised presence of the Lord going with Moses and Israel was intended to be a blessing. By their very nature, God-appointed blessings are filled with hope. Biblical hope is full of confident expectation. However, hope is fueled by obeying what God has commanded and therefore it only operates in an atmosphere of obedience. As we are beginning to see, an obedient atmosphere is naturally present when the Lordship of God is honored. This concept of Lordship is so critical to biblical thought that we will use the remainder of our lesson to explore four foundational truths that flow from it.

**TRUTH #1: LORDSHIP IS FIRST AND FOREMOST ABOUT RELATIONSHIP.**

In Lesson 4 we said that from Genesis to Revelation the Bible reveals God's heart to be in relationship with us such that He is our only God and we fellowship with Him as His covenant people. Obedience is not a hoop you jump through to make God happy. Obeying God is born out of a loving relationship. A long track record of obedience in the same direction assures the uninterrupted fellowship our hearts long for. The need for daily obedience never ends because obedience was never intended to be a destination we arrive at. Obeying God has always been and forever will be about relationship.

God-honoring obedience demands that we continually exalt God and His ways above ourselves and all that we think best. Obedience means we die daily to every fleshly desire.[15] We exchange each of our own desires for the desire of God's heart because He is Lord of all or He is not Lord at all.

**TRUTH #2: LORDSHIP IS THE ONLY SOLUTION FOR SIN AND DISOBEDIENCE.**

The ancient Hebrews were a nomadic people who traveled a circuit through the wilderness, following what must have become well-worn paths from one pasture to the next, one campsite to the next and one water source to the next. Anyone leaving this path could easily become lost and wander aimlessly putting their life at risk. Using this pattern of life as a metaphor, the Bible speaks of the righteous person as the one who follows the correct path, the path (the way) of God. The righteous person (the one who does what is expected by God) is the one who fully submits himself to the Lordship of Yahweh allowing Him to direct every step of life.

---

15 The book of Jude warns against those who follow passionately after their own ungodly desires. They are described as those who "are unbelievers not having the Spirit." Jude 19 HCSB

Proverbs 14:12 warns that the wisdom of man leads to death! The Hebraic concept underlying God's commands is that they are directions God has provided for our life journey to keep us from veering off the safe path. God has a plan for us and a path marked out with His wisdom to bring us into every aspect of His blessing (Jeremiah 29:11). God's pathway contains all the provision needed at each appointed step along the way. Obedience responds to God's loving direction and prevents us from relying on what *we* think is best.

In the mind of the ancient Hebrews, Hebrew words generally paint a picture of action. The word for "sin" is *chatta'ah* {khat-taw-aw'} which pictures an archer pulling back the bow string but his arrow "misses the mark." Using the metaphor of the correct path of life, the one who sins misses the mark God set for his life by choosing to depart from the path that provides safety and blessing.

In our lessons about Adam and Eve, we learned that rejection of God's Lordship allowed the first sin blemish to occur. On the other hand, it is submission to His Lordship that removes spots and wrinkles from our hearts. Complete heartfelt submission is the only way to remove *every* spot. In fact, where God is truly *Adonai* the flesh is perfected. True Lordship means dying to all self-will so we can live a life with no separate will of our own. When we live that way, we reach God's goal for life. Jesus summed it up this way:

> Therefore you are to be perfect [*teleios*], as your heavenly Father is perfect [*teleios*]. Matthew 5:48

As noted, the word translated as perfect is the Greek word *teleios* {tel'-i-os} (from *telos* meaning goal, purpose). As a reference to people, it speaks of "fully completed growth," reaching maturity.[16] It refers to one who has reached the end (aim) or the intended goal (*telos*). When something has fully attained that for

---

16 Zodhiates, Spiros, *The Complete Word Study Dictionary: New Testament* (AMG Publishers 1992) word #5046, p. 1372; McCartney, Dan G., *James*, Baker Exegetical Commentary on the New Testament (Baker Academic 2009) James 1:4, p. 87

*The Power of Obedience*

which it has been designed by God it is *teleios* (perfect, without blemish in God's eyes).

The way in which true Christian character expresses itself is to be like God, not simply to do what we define as good. When true spiritual transformation has occurred from within, "you will exhibit divine characteristics in your life, not good human characteristics. God's life in us expresses itself as *God's* life, not as human life trying to be godly."[17] The perfection to which we are called is clearly impossible in our own power, "but with God all things are possible (Matthew 19:26, Mark 10:27)." Whatever God commands and demands as Lord, He empowers and enables Christ-followers to accomplish through the power of the Holy Spirit.

As soon as we realize through divine conviction that we have left God's designated path by missing the mark, God expects a change of heart. That heart change should lead us to change our direction by returning with firmly planted feet to the path God has appointed. This is the idea that is concretely expressed in the Hebrew verb *shuwb* {shoob} often translated as "return" or "repent." Let's consider, for example, God's instruction to Israel as recorded in Deuteronomy.

> "So it will be when all of these things have come upon you, the blessing and the curse which I have set before you, **and you call** [*shuwb*] **them** to mind in all the nations where the LORD your God has banished you, **and you return** [*shuwb*] to the LORD your God and obey Him with all your heart and soul according to all that I command you today ... then the LORD your God **will restore** [*shuwb*] you from captivity, and have compassion on you .... The LORD your God will bring you into the land which your fathers possessed .... Moreover, the LORD your God will circumcise your heart and the hearts

---

17 Chambers, Oswald, *My Utmost For His Highest* (Barbour Publishing 1935, copyright renewed 1936) The Divine Rule of Life, September 20, italics in original

of your descendants, to love the LORD your God with all your heart and all your soul, so that you may live.... And you **shall again** [*shuwb*] obey the LORD, and observe all His commandments which I command you today...."
Deuteronomy 30:1-3,5-6,8, italics in original, bold added

In Deuteronomy 30 Moses is wrapping up his instructions to the children of those whom Yahweh had led out of Egyptian captivity.[18] This second generation is about ready to be led into the Promised Land by Joshua and Moses is reminding them that their disobedience to God's commands will one day cause them to be removed from the land. However, Moses leaves them with hope! When they are captives in that foreign land and call to mind all that God had commanded them and return their hearts to Him and His commandments [*shuwb*], then God will hear and restore [*shuwb*] them. They will once again [*shuwb*] obey Him. Moses makes clear that both Israel and Yahweh "'turn,' but Israel makes the first move"![19]

### TRUTH #3: LORDSHIP GUARANTEES INTEGRITY BETWEEN OUR TALK AND OUR WALK.

The very definition of *Adonai* challenges every person who calls God "Lord" to be willing to live in a way that very publicly manifests His Lordship on the earth! In other words, God never intended us to simply declare "He is Lord" with our lips. The *only* way to proclaim "He is Lord" is with our life!

---

18  Recall that all of those who had been involved in the exodus from Egypt (except Joshua and Caleb) were cursed to die in the wilderness without setting foot in the Promised Land because they refused to go in and take the land when God commanded them to do so. In Deuteronomy 30 the second generation stands on the plains of Moab and Moses is giving them final instructions from Yahweh before he is led up to Mt. Nebo where he will die.

19  Nelson, Richard D., *Deuteronomy*, The Old Testament Library (Westminster John Knox Press 2002) I Set Before You Life and Death 30:1-20 under *A Matter of Life or Death*, [1-10], p. 347

## The Power of Obedience

In the New Testament Jesus is referred to as "Savior" about 10 times, but we find the title "Lord" used about 700 times.[20] Jesus made abundantly clear the dangerous deception of calling Him "Lord, Lord" but then refusing His Lordship.

"Not everyone who says to Me, 'Lord, Lord,' will enter the kingdom of heaven, but **he who does the will of My Father** who is in heaven *will enter*. Many will say to Me on that day, 'Lord, Lord, did we not prophesy in Your name, and in Your name cast out demons, and in Your name perform many miracles?' And then I will declare to them, '**I never knew you;** DEPART FROM ME, YOU WHO PRACTICE LAWLESSNESS.'..." Matthew 7:21-23, italics and uppercase text in original, bold added

When Jesus says, "**he who does the will of My Father**" He is drawing a razor-sharp contrast between a person who *merely professes* his obedience (lip service) with one who actually obeys *by doing* what the Father commands. The "one who does the will of My Father" describes the person who has an ongoing lifestyle that is fully submitted to *Adonai* – the one who is their master.[21] This is what true Lordship looks like in the life of the Christ-follower.

Those whom Jesus does *not* **know** are met with a formal rejection and a command to depart from Him! That is because biblically to "know" (Greek *ginōskō*) denotes much more than mere acquaintance or recognition. *Ginōskō* is similar to the Hebrew word *yada`* which we considered in Lessons 2 and 5. We concluded that one of the primary biblical uses of *yada`* means to know relationally and experientially. Likewise, *ginōskō* refers to a relational knowl-

---

20 *Matthew 7:21 Commentary*, Precept Austin. Retrieved from http://www.preceptaustin.org/matthew_721 (last accessed July 8, 2021)

21 *Adonai-Lord-The Name of God*, Precept Austin. Retrieved from www.preceptaustin.org/adonai-lord-the_name_of_god (last accessed July 8, 2021)

edge gained by experience. As a matter of fact, *ginōskō* is "often practically synonymous with love and intimacy."[22]

When Jesus says, "I never knew you" He is saying that He does not acknowledge these people as part of His true family.[23] That's because such an acknowledgment is conditioned on their family resemblance. Family resemblance can only be gained through obedience (Matthew 12:47-50).

This distinction based on obedience and disobedience is a persistent biblical truth. For example, in the New Testament we see it clearly repeated in John 14:

> Jesus answered and said to him, "If anyone loves Me, he will keep My word; and My Father will love him, and We will come to him and make Our abode with him. He who does not love Me does not keep My words; and the word which you hear is not Mine, but the Father's who sent Me...." John 14:23-24

**TRUTH #4: LORDSHIP ESTABLISHES GOD'S KINGDOM ON EARTH AS IT IS IN HEAVEN.**

Jesus' disciples asked Him to teach them how to pray properly. He taught that the first priority is to ask that His Father's name be sanctified, set apart, treated as holy. Then He taught them to request the advancement of the Father's Kingdom on earth:

> Your kingdom come. Your will be done, On earth as it is in heaven. Matthew 6:10

In the original Greek, the phrase translated as "the kingdom of God" or its equivalent "the kingdom of Heaven" refers to "God ruling as King." The Kingdom denotes the sphere of God's Kingship (His Kingly dominion) over those who permit Him to rule in

---

22  Watson, J.D., *A Hebrew Word for the Day: Key Words from the Old Testament* (AMG Reference 2010) p. 68
23  France, R. T., *The Gospel of Matthew*, New International Commentary on the New Testament (Eerdmans 2007) Matthew 7:23, p. 295

their hearts. Whenever/wherever God's will is being done on earth, His Kingdom is advancing.

When Jesus announced that the Kingdom of Heaven was at hand (Matthew 4:17), He was saying, "God's promised Kingly reign [on earth] is beginning."[24] The essence of the coming of God's Kingship and Lordship is that His followers obey His commands so that His purpose can be fulfilled.[25]

Throughout the New Testament God's Kingship is in one sense already manifest on earth. However, it awaits a future "fullness" – a concept most scholars refer to as "already, but not yet." We are presently experiencing the *foretaste* of the Kingdom while we pray for the *full taste* which is yet to come.

As scholar R. T. France points out, praying the prayer that Jesus taught His disciples to pray means you are committed to honor God's name, accept His kingship and do His will.[26] It's time for God's Lordship to arise in our hearts! If you have never truly made Jesus Lord of your life, are you willing to be a true *all-in* follower not merely a sidelines fan? Are you willing to enter into relationship with Him as your *Adonai*?

A simple prayer of Lordship looks something like this: "God I know *about* you, but I don't truly know you. I want to know you by experience. I choose to lay down the reins I have held tightly on my own life and I ask you to pick them up as my *Adonai* – Lord. I will go anywhere You send me and do anything You ask so that I may know You – truly know You. Amen."

---

24 France, R. T., *The Gospel of Matthew*, New International Commentary on the New Testament (Eerdmans 2007) Matthew 3:2, p. 102
25 France, R. T., *The Gospel of Matthew*, New International Commentary on the New Testament (Eerdmans 2007) Matthew 6:10, p. 247
26 France, R. T., *The Gospel of Matthew*, New International Commentary on the New Testament (Eerdmans 2007) Matthew 6:10, p. 247

***Hear What The Spirit is Saying to the Church***: *Do you know that My desire is to bless you, but I can only release blessing where I am honored as Lord. I cannot bless disobedience, because disobedience is not for your best. Lordship is the only guarantee for blessing.*

# Lesson 8:

## God's Discipline

"My child, do not despise discipline from the LORD, and do not loathe his rebuke. For the LORD disciplines those he loves, just as a father disciplines the son in whom he delights."
Proverbs 3:11-12 NET

IN OUR LAST LESSON we looked at the fact that God expected Israel to willingly submit to His Lordship and obey His commands. We saw that Israel's disobedience left them in a vulnerable position. When Moses came down the mountain and saw Israel worshipping the golden calf, he shattered the stone tablets with God's commandments written on them. For Moses to break those tablets would have been a familiar custom in the culture of the Old Testament. It was common practice in the ancient Near East to record the stipulations of a treaty/covenant on tablets made out of clay, stone, or metal.[1] In that culture breaking the tablets would indicate that the covenant agreement between the parties had been violated.[2]

To ceremoniously and literally break the tablets that contained the terms of the written covenant provided a very visual demonstration of the consequences of Israel's sin. That sin had shattered her relationship with Yahweh. On her own Israel had no way to fix it! And yet only Yahweh's Presence distinguishes them from all other

---

1  Sarna, Nahum M., *Exploring Exodus: The Origins of Biblical Israel* (Schocken Books 1996) p. 208
2  Sarna, Nahum M., *Exploring Exodus: The Origins of Biblical Israel* (Schocken Books 1996) p. 219

nations of the world.[3] It is His presence with Israel that gives proof that Moses and Israel have found favor with Yahweh. "No people no matter how religious they are and for whatever reasons, can be a people of God without the Presence of God."[4] In the absence of Yahweh's presence, Israel will cease to exist as a people of God.

The biblical truth is that we enjoy God's Presence (fellowship with Him) when we are obedient. As we saw in our last lesson, God had implicitly withdrawn His plan to abide among the people in the Tabernacle and announced that He Himself would not accompany a rebellious people on the remainder of their journey. All of Moses' efforts in Exodus 33-34 are focused on ending this resulting alienation so that God's direct Presence among the people would once again be possible. Only by His grace does Yahweh choose to renew His covenant relationship with Israel. Just as He had done with Adam and Eve, He, Himself, reinitiated the relationship Israel had shattered by their sin.[5] Ultimately the sacrifice of Christ as the perfect Passover Lamb will make possible a restoration of *our* broken relationship with God; even so, the enjoyment of His Presence is still conditioned on our obedience.

King David demonstrated his understanding of God's Obedience-Presence Principle when he wrote:

> The arrogant cannot stand in your presence. You hate all who do wrong. Psalm 5:5 NIV

It will be helpful to our understanding to take a closer look at two of the words David used in Psalm 5:5 – the first is "wrong" and the second is "hate."

---

3   Durham, John I., *Word Biblical Commentary: Exodus*, Volume 3 (Word Books 1987) Exodus 33:16 under *Comment*, p. 447
4   Durham, John I., *Word Biblical Commentary: Exodus*, Volume 3 (Word Books 1987) Exodus 33:16 under *Comment*, p. 448
5   Genesis 3:8-11,21; Exodus 34:10-28

## Word Study

*In Psalm 5:5 the Hebrew noun translated as* **wrong** *is 'aven {aw-ven'} which is frequently rendered "evil," "iniquity," or "wicked."*[6]

*Biblical scholar Gleason Archer points out that, "Evil does not really exist in the abstract (except as a theoretical idea) ..."*[7] *Archer's point is that we can only recognize "evil" in terms of a person's evil nature or by their wicked deeds when they functionally do the work of Satan, whom the Bible refers to as "the evil one."*

*A heart that devises evil ['aven] plans is listed in Proverbs 6:18 as one of the six things that Yahweh detests.*

*'Aven* is one of the words used in the Old Testament to define sin.[8] *'Aven* "stresses the planning and expression of deception and points to the painful aftermath of sin."[9] In Isaiah 55:7 *'aven* is used broadly to refer to "people from every aspect of life" whose feet are *not* on the path God has set.[10] In Psalm 66:18 the psalmist acknowledges that Yahweh will not listen to the prayer of the person who harbors *'aven* in his heart.

---

6  Harris, Archer, and Waltke, editors, *Theological Wordbook of the Old Testament* (Moody Press 1999) word #48a, p. 23
7  Archer, Gleason L., *Encyclopedia of Bible Difficulties* (Zondervan 1982) Psalms under *Do not Psalms 5:5 and 11:5 contradict the teaching that God loves the sinner but hates the sin?* p. 242
8  Thompson, J. A., *The Book of Jeremiah*, The New International Commentary of The Old Testament (Eerdmans 1980) Jeremiah 4:14, p. 225
9  Harris, Archer, and Waltke, editors, *Theological Wordbook of the Old Testament* (Moody Press 1999) word #48a, p. 24
10 Motyer, J. Alec, *The Prophecy of Isaiah: An Introduction & Commentary* (InterVarsity Press 1993) Isaiah 55:7, p. 457

Our second word in Psalm 5:5 is the word "hate." In Lesson 1 we learned that God's need to separate Himself from Adam and Eve after their disobedience was a result of the truth that He *hates* sin. In that lesson, we considered the Hebrew word *sane'* which is the word King David used in Psalm 5:5. We will use a Word Study to refresh our memory of what it means to "hate" evil.

> **WORD STUDY**
>
> *The Hebrew verb* **sane'** *{saw-nay'} is translated as* **hate** *in Psalm 5:5. Sane' refers to what God rejects.[11] It implies that which cannot be reconciled, opposing values that are impossible to harmonize.[12]*
>
> *Sane' denotes the absence of preference for something, distancing oneself, actually treating someone as an adversary because of irreconcilable differences. The hated person or thing is detestable.[13]*

In our English language "hate" is defined as "intense hostility and aversion usually deriving from fear, anger, or sense of injury."[14] The difference between our Western understanding of *hate* and the Hebrew understanding of *sane'* is primarily a distinction between focusing on an emotion versus focusing on an action. In the English language "hate" is thought of in terms of an intense negative emotion, whereas in Hebrew "hate" is about lack of preference and the

---

11  Block, Daniel I., *For the Glory of God: Recovering A Biblical Theology of Worship* (Baker Academic 2014) p. 95

12  Hill, Gary, *The Discovery Bible*, HELPS Ministries, Inc., [H]11p (SN 8130) *śānē'*

13  Harris, Archer, and Waltke, editors, *Theological Wordbook of the Old Testament* (Moody Press 1999) word #2272, p. 880

14  *Merriam-Webster.com Dictionary*, entry for *hate*. Retrieved from https://www.merriam-webster.com/dictionary/hate?msclkid=eb20be6aa84311e-c9bff49bde176134b (last accessed March 20, 2022)

distancing action that results. In the Bible hatred describes God's responsive action to the evil that has taken place. He separates Himself from those who do evil.

Using the definitions from our Word Studies, we could paraphrase Psalm 5:5 as follows:

> Those who engage in wicked acts are foolish and cannot stand in God's presence; God desires to have no contact or relationship with those who choose to live their life on their own path rather than the pathway He prescribes.

Isaiah gives us another clear example of God's Obedience-Presence Principle in action. The book of Isaiah opens with God's indictment against Israel for her sin.

> Therefore the Lord God of hosts, The Mighty One of Israel, declares, "Ah, I will be relieved of **My adversaries** And avenge Myself on **My foes**. I will also turn My hand against you, And will smelt away your dross as with lye and will remove all your alloy...." Isaiah 1:24-25, bold added

When God refers to "My adversaries ... My foes," He is referring to Israel – His covenant people! God considered Israel His *enemy* because of her sin. As we have seen, this is the very essence of the definition of *sane'* (hate).

According to King David and the prophet Isaiah, the modern-day church perverts the truth when we soften God's reaction to sin! You have no doubt heard it said, "God hates the sin, but loves the sinner." It is something I have repeated over the years. However, the sobering truth is that is *not* exactly what God's Word says![15] The truth is that He judges sin and holds accountable the one who perverts His justice and righteousness.

---

15   Watson, J.D., *A Hebrew Word for the Day: Key Words from the Old Testament* (AMG Reference 2010) August 28 Hate, *sane'*, p. 241, citing for example, Psalm 5:5: Psalm 11:5; Hosea 9:15

In his discussion of Isaiah Chapter 1, scholar J. Alec Motyer bluntly warns:[16]

> Any [simplistic] statement that God always hates the sin but loves the sinner needs to be countered by Isaiah's insistence that those who transgress are [*God's*] *foes* and [*God's*] *enemies*. They have made themselves the adversaries of the helpless ([Isaiah 1:]23), *therefore* the sovereign Lord holds them as his enemies.

Unrighteous conduct is completely incompatible with the reality that God is holy, holy, holy (Isaiah 6:3). In fact, *The Complete WordStudy Dictionary of the Old Testament* identifies the verb *sane'* as the antonym of *'ahab* – the Hebrew verb that is typically translated as "love."[17] Whereas love draws and unites, hate separates and keeps distant.[18]

As we have said, God does not initiate hate for anyone He has created. It is His nature to love them, but in His holiness (basically defined as His separateness from the world and its ways) He cannot be in the presence of sin. Therefore, His reaction to sin and to the one who commits the sin is the same. He sets Himself apart from sin and must distance Himself from the one who sins. This truth equips us with an understanding of why the sacrificial system was so vital to Israel's existence as God's covenant people and why Jesus had to shed His blood on the cross. It also explains why God told Moses that He would *not* accompany Israel from the wilderness to the Promised Land.[19]

Lest we too quickly conclude this is Old Testament teaching that was changed by Christ's sacrificial death, let's consider James 4:4 which in essence reaches the same conclusion:

---

16 Motyer, J. Alec, *The Prophecy of Isaiah: An Introduction & Commentary* (InterVarsity Press 1993) Isaiah 1:24, p. 49, italics in original
17 Baker and Carpenter, *The Complete WordStudy Dictionary of the Old Testament* (AMG Publishers 2003) word #8130, p. 1175
18 Harris, Archer, and Waltke, editors, *Theological Wordbook of the Old Testament* (Moody Press 1999) word #2272, p. 880
19 Exodus 33:3-5

You adulteresses, do you not know that friendship with the world is hostility toward God? Therefore whoever wishes to be a friend of the world makes himself **an enemy of God**. James 4:4, bold added

James identifies anyone and everyone who chooses to be a "friend of the world" as an *enemy of God*. James is merely pointing out God's "divinely-assigned or appointed consequences ... of a [lingering] friendship with the world."[20] By now we should recognize that in biblical understanding being regarded by God as an "enemy" refers to someone God desires to distance Himself from. That person's feet are not walking on the path God ordained, they are walking on a pathway that opposes Him and His ways. Contrasted with these people are those the Bible identifies as *the upright*. They are the ones who do *not* deviate from God's path.[21]

The Lordship of God gives Him the sovereign right to mold and shape our relationship with Him according to *His* chosen design. He is the Potter, we are the clay.[22] "[S]o are all in the hand of their maker, to be given whatever [form] he decides."[23] In the natural a potter uses a variety of tools to form and shape the clay he is working with. Likewise, God, as the Master Potter of all creation, has His own chosen tools that are revealed in Scripture. One of the first tools we see Him put into practice is His divine discipline. As we read further into Chapter 1 of Isaiah, we see that God's purpose for treating Israel as an enemy is so that He can purify her. By removing her dross, her nature will be renewed and

---

20 McKnight, Scot, *The Letter of James*, New International Commentary on the New Testament (Eerdmans 2011) James 4:4-6, p. 335
21 Waltke, Bruce K., *The Book of Proverbs: Chapters 1-15*, The New International Commentary on the Old Testament (Eerdmans 2004) Proverbs 2:7, p. 225
22 We find the Potter/clay metaphor in both the Old and New Testament. See for example: Isaiah 29:16; 45:9; 64:8; Jeremiah 31:9; Romans 9:20
23 Keck, Leander E., *Romans*, Abingdon New Testament Commentaries (Abingdon Press 2005) God's Freedom to Act ([Romans] 9:19-29), p. 236, quoting Sir 33:13

she will be able to once again host God's presence and fulfill her ordained purpose.[24]

Let's take a moment to go back and refresh our memory about God's ultimate goal for His creation. Doing so will help us keep a proper perspective as we learn about God's discipline.

In Lesson 6, we said, God's ways are carefully calculated to lead His covenant people to the destiny He has in mind for them – a restored Garden of Eden with everlasting fellowship, a Kingdom over which He sovereignly rules! God calls His people not only to *bring* His message but to *be* His message through their obedience to His instructions. That's because when Christ-followers are obedient they have a magnetic appeal to a world that is watching.[25] The predominant biblical model of evangelism is that other people are *not* in large part reconciled to God by organized outreach efforts as by God's redeemed people becoming walking billboards who put His true nature and character on display through their obedient lifestyle. This attracts others to God's growing Kingdom. In other words, God's Kingdom on earth simply cannot grow without our obedience. Unless we live an obedient lifestyle, a lost and dying world cannot come to know the true nature of God! Said more bluntly – our disobedience cheats the world out of coming in contact with God's character.

When we rightly understand God's plan, it is easy to see why those who ignore God's ways and maintain friendship with the world become His enemy! In light of this truth, how are we to understand our Key Scripture for this lesson which refers to God's discipline in the context of His love? The short answer is that He is repulsed by sin, but He disciplines in the love of a perfect Father.

As we will see, His discipline is vitally important to Kingdom growth because God disciplines us for our good, so that we may share His holiness.[26] We will devote the remainder of our lesson

---

24 Isaiah 1:25-27
25 Motyer, J. Alec, *The Prophecy of Isaiah: An Introduction & Commentary* (InterVarsity Press 1993) Isaiah 2:5, p. 55
26 Hebrews 12:9-10

*The Power of Obedience*

to understanding divine discipline. A good place to begin is by returning to the exodus narrative and the incident which led God to announce that He was removing His presence from Israel.

You will recall that as Moses was meeting on the mountain with God, Israel was at the foot of the mountain worshipping the golden calf Aaron had made. Suddenly God instructed Moses,

> ... "Go down at once! For your people you brought up from the land of Egypt have acted corruptly. They have quickly turned from the way I commanded them; they have made for themselves an image of a calf. They have bowed down to it, sacrificed to it, and said, 'Israel, this is your God, who brought you up from the land of Egypt.'" Exodus 32:7-8 HCSB

In the original Hebrew text, there is an urgency in God's command. When He refers to Israel as having acted "corruptly," He is saying they have been marred by sin.[27] Notice that He does exactly what we would expect Him to do – He distances Himself from the people. Although God typically refers to Israel as "*My* people whom *I have brought out* of Egypt," here He identifies them as "*the* people *Moses brought out* of Egypt." God has disowned them because of their sin – in other words, at that moment in time they are being treated like His "enemy." We find the reason He has done so in His description of their actions: "they have quickly **turned from** the way [*derek*] I commanded them." The NASB uses the phrase "they have turned aside" to translate the Hebrew word *cuwr* {soor}. It is a verb meaning "to turn away, to change direction." In the original Hebrew text, the verb tense reflects that not only did they turn aside, they are still disobedient at the point God is

---

27 Hebrew word *shachath* {shaw-khath'} means "to spoil, to ruin, to destroy, to pervert, to corrupt ...." Baker and Carpenter, *The Complete WordStudy Dictionary of the Old Testament* (AMG Publishers 2003) word #7843, p. 1124

speaking to Moses.[28] What have they turned aside from? The *derek* [way] God has commanded.

Recall that *derek* literally means a road or a path, but it is often used figuratively to refer to the unwavering and uncompromising lifestyle (usually referred to as "way") God prescribes in His commandments. When *cuwr* is used in its literal sense it refers to leaving the road a person was traveling on or departing from the course they were originally following. In its figurative use, it refers to turning aside from God through disobedience, deserting Him in your heart, or falling away from proper worship.[29] Given this understanding, we might expect God's discipline to have something to do with steering the disobedient back onto the right path. In fact, that's precisely what we are going to see in our study of divine discipline!

Our Key Scripture for this lesson is only one of many places in the Bible that describe the nature of God's discipline. Other similar Scriptures include:

> Think about it: Just as a parent disciplines a child, the LORD your God disciplines you for your own good. Deuteronomy 8:5 NLT

> Blessed [with wisdom and prosperity] is the man whom You discipline *and* instruct, O LORD, And whom You teach from Your law. Psalm 94:12 AMP, italics in original

> I know, O LORD, that Your judgments are fair, And that in faithfulness You have disciplined me. Psalm 119:75 AMP

> [F]or the Lord disciplines the one He loves and punishes every son He receives. Hebrews 12:6 HCSB

---

28 *NET Bible Notes*, translator's note 25, Exodus 32:8
29 Johnston, Gordon H., "Exodus," in *The Bible Knowledge Word Study, Genesis – Deuteronomy*, edited by Eugene H. Merrill (Victor 2003) Exodus 32:8 under *They turned away quickly from the way*, p. 239

*The Power of Obedience*

> Those whom I love, I rebuke and discipline. So be earnest and repent. Revelation 3:19 NIV

As we can see, the Bible contains a very consistent message about God's discipline throughout both the Old and the New Testaments. Taking a closer look at our Key Scripture for this lesson will help us rightly key in on the purpose behind divine discipline.

> My son, do not reject the **discipline** of the LORD Or loathe His **reproof**, For whom the LORD loves He **reproves**, Even as a father *corrects* the son in whom he delights. Proverbs 3:11-12, italics in original, bold added

I have highlighted in bold three words we want to study further: "discipline," "reproof" and "reproves." As we noted above, God's discipline is all about redirection – graciously rerouting our feet when they have veered off the correct path.

## WORD STUDY

*In our Key Scripture, the word translated as:*
**Discipline** *is the Hebrew noun musar {moo-sawr'} which generally refers to education and instruction (primarily oral) that redirects the person to a God-centered way of life.*[30] *It denotes a father's correction for the purpose of character development.*[31]
**Reproves** *is the Hebrew verb yakach {yaw-kahh'}. It refers primarily to deciding, judging, proving, correcting in the context of a lawsuit (covenant accusation).*[32] *In the*

---

30 Harris, Archer, and Waltke, editors, *Theological Wordbook of the Old Testament* (Moody Press 1999) word #877b, pp. 386-387
31 Parsons, John J., *The Blessing of Musar, Hebrew4Christians.* Retrieved from https://www.hebrew4christians.com /Meditations/Musar/musar.html (last accessed July 8, 2021)
32 Harris, Archer, and Waltke, editors, *Theological Wordbook of the Old Testament* (Moody Press 1999) word #865, p. 377

> *Old Testament (especially in the writings of the prophets), God's complaint/corrective action regarding Israel is often presented as a covenant lawsuit[33] with God as both plaintiff and Judge and Israel as the defendant. Even in its judicial context, the focus of the verb yakach remains on education and course correction.[34]*
>
> **Reproof** *is the Hebrew word tokachath {to-kakh'-ath}[35] which refers to "the need to set things right."[36] The primary focus of tokachath is on "correcting some wrong."[37]*

There are several word pictures inherent in the three Hebrew verbs in our Word Study. The first one is found in the word *musar* which comes from a Hebrew word meaning "to make straight and right."[38] Musar refers, for example, to a father who instructs his submitted child in order to "quell his innate waywardness" and shape his character.[39] As a perfect Father, God's goal in discipline is

---

33 German scholar Hermann Gunkel is credited with identifying the literary form of the prophetic lawsuit; however, the phrase "covenant lawsuit" is credited to Herbert B. Huffmon, *The Covenant Lawsuit in the Prophets,* JBL 78 (1959) pp. 285–295 as cited in Davidson, Richard M., *The Divine Covenant Lawsuit Motif in Canonical Perspective*, Journal of the Adventist Theological Society, 21/1-2 (2010) pp. 45-84, at p. 47. Retrieved from http://archive.atsjats.org/Davidson_-_Covenant_Lawsuit_Motif.pdf (last accessed September 9, 2021)
34 Harris, Archer, and Waltke, editors, *Theological Wordbook of the Old Testament* (Moody Press 1999) word #865, p. 377
35 Also transliterated as: *towkechah* {to-kay-khaw'}
36 Waltke, Bruce K., *The Book of Proverbs: Chapters 1-15*, The New International Commentary on the Old Testament (Eerdmans 2004) Proverbs 1:2-6, p. 175
37 Baker and Carpenter, *The Complete WordStudy Dictionary of the Old Testament* (AMG Publishers 2003) word #8433, p. 1217
38 *Spirit Filled Life Bible* (Thomas Nelson 1991) W*ord Wealth [Proverbs] 3:6 direct, yashar*, p. 888
39 Waltke, Bruce K., *The Book of Proverbs: Chapters 1-15*, The New International Commentary on the Old Testament (Eerdmans 2004) Proverbs 1:2-6, p. 175

*The Power of Obedience*

to straighten the path for those who have made it crooked. God's way (*derek*) – the determination and exercise of His divine will – reflects His holy character.[40] His discipline aims to bring conviction enabling the one who has been disobedient to recognize the point at which his feet have wandered off God's ordained path and to be correctively guided back onto God's best pathway of life – His right and straight path.

Whereas *musar* often pictures the discipline of a father, our second word picture is taken from ancient legal proceedings. The related words *yakach* and *tokachath* are found in the language of covenant lawsuits that result from breaches of ancient Near Eastern treaties between nations.[41] There is a sense in which God's rebuke and discipline involve legal action in a divine courtroom setting. God is the most qualified one to initiate the lawsuit as the plaintiff. He is also the ideal judge with perfect knowledge as well as the perfect plan to make all things right. Not only is He absolutely holy, set apart from the world's way, but He is also always flawlessly righteous. He has set the standard for right living that pleases Him and accomplishes His purposes. To that end, He is always able to judge rightly and justly. God's wisdom is the source of life in all its fullness. He is not only the wise Judge He is our Redeemer. Therefore, every form of divine discipline is carefully calculated to lead to a transformed God-centered way of life.

Our Key Scripture not only helps us properly understand God's discipline, it also provides us with clear instruction about how God wants us to respond to His discipline. Let's look again at Proverbs 3:11:

---

40 *Holman Christian Standard Bible*, Study Bible edition (Holman Bible Publishers 2010) study note Psalm 77:13, p. 955
41 Much scholarly work has been done demonstrating the parallels between Yahweh's covenant relationship with Israel and similarly worded treaties between a more powerful king and one or more lesser kings. It is thought that cultural background provided an easy reference for Israel who was just getting to know Yahweh. However, while God used the literary framework from the pagan nations that surrounded Israel, His ultimate purpose was to distinguish Himself from what the people already knew.

My child, do not despise discipline from the LORD, and do not loathe his rebuke. Proverbs 3:11 NET

Solomon counsels us not to despise discipline or loathe God's rebuke. Another Word Study will be beneficial here.

### WORD STUDY

*In our Key Scripture the word translated as* **despise** *is the strong Hebrew verb ma'ac or maas {maw-as'} which is usually rendered "to reject."[42] It can also mean "to despise, to abhor, to refuse."[43] In the context of our Key Scripture, maas speaks of a person who refuses to obey God or accept His authority.[44] In fact, it denotes "to want nothing to do with" God's discipline.[45]*

**Loathe** *is a translation of the Hebrew verb quwts {koots} which refers to "an irritating abhorrence."[46] It can also refer to "emotional nausea" or "sickening dread."[47]*

---

42 Mounce, William D., editor, *Complete Expository Dictionary of Old & New Testament Words* (Zondervan 2006) entry for *Despise*, p. 175
43 Baker and Carpenter, *The Complete WordStudy Dictionary of the Old Testament* (AMG Publishers 2003) word #3988, p. 562
44 Baker and Carpenter, *The Complete WordStudy Dictionary of the Old Testament* (AMG Publishers 2003) word #3988, p. 562
45 Waltke, Bruce K., *The Book of Proverbs: Chapters 1-15*, The New International Commentary on the Old Testament (Eerdmans 2004) Proverbs 3:11, p. 249
46 Harris, Archer, and Waltke, editors, *Theological Wordbook of the Old Testament* (Moody Press 1999) word #2002, p. 794
47 Hill, Gary, *The Discovery Bible*, HELPS Ministries, Inc., [H]11m (SN 6973) *qûṣ*, citing BDB

Because no instruction can succeed if not met with a proper attitude,[48] Solomon wisely addresses the heart attitude that is required for God to accomplish His objective. In biblical language a person's heart informs their behavior.[49] A proper attitude refrains from complaint and embraces God's course correction with thankfulness recognizing that it is always for our best.

> The responsibility to respond to instruction lies squarely on the [disciple's] shoulders; he must listen to it ... accept it ... love it ... prize it ... not let go of it .... Once accepted, discipline springs from the power of internalized wisdom, not from sporadic "New Year's resolutions." It is a matter of inward spirit, not of a coerced will and [subservient] compliance.[50]

God does not discipline us to harm us, His purpose is to bless us with His skillful guidance to properly shape our character. Our Key Scripture is a centerpiece for understanding divine discipline not only in the Old Testament but also in the New Testament. The author of Hebrews quotes from Proverbs 3:12 when admonishing his audience to respond properly to God's formative discipline.

> ... **"My son, do not scorn** ["disregard," "think little of"][51] **the Lord's discipline or give up when he *corrects* you. For the Lord disciplines the one he loves and chas-**

---

48 Waltke, Bruce K., *The Book of Proverbs: Chapters 1-15*, The New International Commentary on the Old Testament (Eerdmans 2004) Proverbs 3:11-12, p. 249
49 Waltke, Bruce K., *The Book of Proverbs: Chapters 1-15*, The New International Commentary on the Old Testament (Eerdmans 2004) Theology under *C. Revelation, Inspiration, and Tradition, 1. Definitions of "Wisdom" and of "Knowledge,"* p. 77
50 Waltke, Bruce K., *The Book of Proverbs: Chapters 1-15*, The New International Commentary on the Old Testament (Eerdmans 2004) Proverbs 1:2-6, p. 176
51 *NET Bible Notes*, translator's note 4, Hebrews 12:5

**tises every son he accepts** [quoted from LXX]."[52] Endure your suffering as discipline; God is treating you as sons. For what son is there that a father does not discipline? But if you do not experience discipline, something all sons have shared in, then you are illegitimate and are not sons. Hebrews 12:5-8 NET, bold in original, italics added

First, take note that it is the one God *loves* who receives His correction. The fact that God disciplines us so we can enjoy His fellowship and blessings is actually proof of His love. C. S. Lewis has concluded that when we complain about discipline, which might include suffering, we are not asking for *more* love, we are actually asking God to love us *less*![53]

In this Scripture quote from Hebrews 12, I have highlighted in italics the word "corrects." In the original Greek, it is the verb *elencho* {el-eng'-kho} which implies a person's sin is exposed for the purpose of correction.[54] When we look at the Greek translation of our Key Scripture for this lesson, we see that this same Greek word *elencho* is used to translate the word "rebuke" [Hebrew *tokachath*]:

> My child, do not despise discipline from the LORD, and do not loathe his **rebuke** [*elencho*]. Proverbs 3:11 NET, bold added

In the New Testament, we find the Greek verb *elencho* used in the same way:

> Those whom I love, I **reprove** [*elencho*] and discipline; therefore be zealous and repent. Revelation 3:19, bold added

---

52 The LXX is the Greek translation of the Old Testament, also known as The Septuagint.
53 Waltke, Bruce K., *The Book of Proverbs: Chapters 1-15,* The New International Commentary on the Old Testament (Eerdmans 2004) Proverbs 3:12, p. 250, citing C. S. Lewis, *The Problem of Pain* (Geoffrey Bles and Centenary 1940) pp. 30-33
54 *NET Bible Notes,* translator's note 5, Hebrews 12:5

## The Power of Obedience

Clearly the connection in both the Old and the New Testament is between God's judgment and His loving discipline for the purpose of avoiding the coming judgment of the world. This truth is summarized by Paul in his letter to the Corinthians:

> But when we are judged, we are disciplined by the Lord so that we will not be condemned along with the world. 1 Corinthians 11:32

In earlier classical Greek *elencho* (also transliterated as *elegcho*) refers to shaming or disgracing another.[55] Here, as in Lesson 2, we need to carefully avoid our natural tendency to impose our modern Western culture and values on the biblical text. As we learned in our second lesson, a common understanding of "shame" in our culture is that it is "an intensely painful feeling or experience of believing that we are flawed and therefore unworthy of love and belonging."[56] In our Western culture, shame operates as a tool in the hands of our adversary to silence our voice and alienate us from everyone including God. If we are not intentional about distinguishing our modern understanding of shame from that which was culturally known and accepted in the world of the Bible, we will inadvertently read the biblical text with our interpretation of shame in mind.

God's plan is for every disciple to develop normative behavior as a Christ-follower. In God's Kingdom, shame refers to His judgment that behavior modification is necessary. When understood within its biblical framework shame is intended to motivate a Christ-follower to change his course of action.

You may recall that in Lesson 2 we discussed the difference between Adam's nakedness before sin where he felt no shame and

---

[55] *Titus 1:9 Commentary*, Precept Austin, quoting Vincent, M. R., *Word Studies In The New Testament*, Vol. 2, pp. 1-102. Retrieved from https://www.preceptaustin.org/titus_19 (last accessed February 4, 2022)

[56] Brown, Brené, *Shame vs. Guilt*, brenebrown.com, January 15, 2013. Retrieved from https://brenebrown.com/articles/2013/01/15/shame-v-guilt/ (last accessed February 8, 2022)

his nakedness linked with his awareness of shame after sin. For those who love God, His discipline is the way He brings their disobedience to light by revealing the sin that had been hidden. He permits "shame or disgrace" as a **rebuke** to compel the person to see and to admit their error. As we've been pointing out, God's purpose in highlighting sin is to encourage repentance and self-correction. With this understanding, it becomes clear to us why the Bible points out that Adam felt no shame *before* his sin but knew shame *after* sin. It also helps us understand why the covering God made was placed over Adam and Eve and not over their shame. As soon as Adam's *sin* is covered, the shame is removed.

One of God's great gifts to us is the power of choice. When we have not chosen wisely and He disciplines us, the Bible makes abundantly clear it is a demonstration of His Fatherly love for us.[57] A human father corrects a child who is beginning to deviate from his instruction to develop responsible character within the child. For the same reason, God lovingly corrects us as His children to form His character within us. The absence of God's correction would be indicative of His rejection, not His love.[58] Do you recall the conclusion reached by C. S. Lewis that "when we complain of [God's discipline] we are not asking for more love, but for less"?[59] Let those words sink in for a moment – to complain about God's discipline actually asks God to love us *less*, not more!

God's plan has always been to reveal His glory *through* obedient people, not merely *to* them. That in and of itself is a most amazing blessing associated with our obedience. However, God's heart is to pour out an abundance of blessing on His covenant people. So, let's conclude this lesson by considering some of the

---

57 See for example: Job 5:17; Proverbs 3:11; cf. Hebrews 12:5,6
58 Waltke, Bruce K., *The Book of Proverbs: Chapters 1-15*, The New International Commentary on the Old Testament (Eerdmans 2004) Proverbs 3:12, p. 250, citing W. Lane, *Discipline*, in ISBE, 1:948
59 Waltke, Bruce K., *The Book of Proverbs: Chapters 1-15*, The New International Commentary on the Old Testament (Eerdmans 2004) Proverbs 3:12, p. 250, quoting C. S. Lewis, *The Problem of Pain* (Geoffrey Bles and Centenary 1940) pp. 30-33

*The Power of Obedience* 157

other remarkable dividends that are associated with the only proper response to God's discipline – repentance followed by obedience.[60]

- God's love for us will be evident (Hebrews 12:6; Revelation 3:19)
- We will be blessed (Psalm 94:12)
- We will have a greater revelation of God (Job 42:5,12; James 5:11)
- We will grow into maturity, becoming who God intends us to be (James 1:2-4)
- We will receive the crown of life (James 1:12)
- What is hidden in our heart will be made known to us (Deuteronomy 8:2)
- It will prove to be for our good in the end (Deuteronomy 8:16)
- It will provide proof that we are God's legitimate sons and eternal heirs (Hebrews 12:6-8)
- We will know the way of life and be protected from hidden pitfalls (Proverbs 6:23)
- Foolishness will be removed from our heart (Proverbs 22:15)
- We will share God's holiness, being conformed to His character (Hebrews 12:10)
- We will live according to the way God expects us to live, in well-being and wholeness in our relationship with God and with fellow Christ-followers[61] (Hebrews 12:11)
- We will avoid being condemned along with the world (1 Corinthians 11:32)
- We will receive honor (Proverbs 13:18)

---

60 This list is my edited version of the list found in *Hebrews 12:5-6 Commentary*, Precept Austin. Retrieved from https://www.preceptaustin.org/hebrews_125-6 (last accessed July 8, 2021)
61 Cockerill, Gareth Lee, *The Epistle to the Hebrews*, New International Commentary on the New Testament (Eerdmans 2012) Hebrews 12:11, p. 628

- We will be made wiser than our enemies (Psalm 119:98, Proverbs 19:20)
- It helps us learn God's statutes by experience; His law will be written on our heart, enabling us to obey (Psalm 119:71; Hebrews 10:15-18)
- We will be more likely to keep God's Word and less likely to wander off His path (Psalm 119:67)
- It demonstrates that we love knowledge (not the type of knowledge that comes from reading books, but experiential knowledge of the Living God) (Proverbs 12:1)
- It will help develop our faith, resulting in praise, glory and honor at Christ's return (1 Peter 1:7)

To sum it up, the reception of God's formative instruction brings life, wisdom, honor and the favor of the Lord. However, rejection of His discipline results in death, poverty and judgment.[62]

The story is told of a person who received a repair bill for $10,000. He was shocked because the repair had taken less than 5 minutes. When the customer inquired about the extraordinarily high bill for something that took so little time, the repairman provided this detailed explanation: "Tapping with a hammer $2.00; Knowing where to tap $9,998.00."[63] As the Master Potter, God is infinite in wisdom and He always knows precisely where to tap the clay! When we rightly respond to God's correction in our life, we will learn to trust in His character and His promises and be properly aligned with His plans and purposes.

**Hear What The Spirit is Saying to the Church**: *I do not discipline in anger, I discipline in perfected love. The desire of my heart is to bless. Oh that my people would rightly respond to my rebuke so that I may bless them in abundance.*

---

62  Proverbs 4:13; 5:23; 8:33; 13:18
63  Snopes Staff, *The Handyman's Invoice: The Bill of a Famed Fix-It Man Detailed the Difference Between Value of Work and Value of Knowledge*, published April 17, 2001. Retrieved from https://www.snopes.com/fact-check/know-where-man/ (last accessed July 8, 2021)

LESSON 9:

# THE ATTITUDE OF THE HEART, THE FOCUS OF THE EYES, AND THE DIRECTION OF THE FEET

"Enter through the narrow gate.... How narrow is the gate and difficult the road that leads to life, and few find it...." Matthew 7:13-14 HCSB

IN OUR STUDY we have been recognizing that there is a life path God desires us to walk on and when our feet are firmly planted on *that* path, He calls it obedience. In our Key Scripture for this lesson, Jesus refers to this path of obedience as "the difficult road that leads to life" and He cautions that the entryway to that road is through a narrow gate. Because the primary purpose for a gate was to grant entry, in biblical thought a gate was used figuratively to refer to "the entrance, introduction, or means of acquiring a thing."[1]

As was His custom, Jesus was likely using that which would have been a familiar scene as a backdrop to His teaching. Ancient cities in His day were surrounded by walls. At one or more points there was a breach in the wall providing entry into the city through some sort of gate. Some of those gates enabled entry to the city's great boulevards, they were broad and could accommodate a large multitude of people. On the other hand, other gates served more

---

1 Ryken, Wilhoit, and Longman III, editors, *Dictionary of Biblical Imagery* (Intervarsity Press 1998) entry for *Gate*, p. 322; Clarke, Adam, *Commentary on the Whole Bible*, Matthew 7:14. Retrieved from Hill, Gary, *The Discovery Bible*, HELPS Ministries, Inc.

private purposes. They would have been narrow by comparison and much fewer people would have used them.[2]

The word translated as "narrow" in the phrase "narrow gate" is the Greek word *stenos* {sten-os'}. It comes from a root meaning "to groan," as groaning from being under pressure. It is used figuratively to represent a restriction or constriction. *Stenos* pictures obstacles that are standing close to each other.[3] The use of this word suggests that Jesus is describing an entry to a way of life that is hard as opposed to the naturally preferred easy way.[4]

When Jesus mentioned the "difficult road," He was referring to a pattern of behavior that describes a person's lifestyle.[5] The "narrow gate" refers to the beginning of a new disciple's life as a Christ-follower. The "difficult road" refers to the faithful continuation of that life of discipleship. Some translators retained the use of the "narrow" metaphor and rather than describing the road as difficult, rendered it as "the narrow way" that leads to life.[6] To say that the "way" is narrow pictures a path that is literally pressed or hemmed in between walls or rocks. It depicts the pathway in a narrow mountain gorge.[7] W.E. Vine's commentary concludes that "the gate which provides the entrance to eternal life (is) nar-

---

[2] Barnes, Albert, *Barnes' Notes on the New Testament*, Matthew 7:13. Retrieved from Hill, Gary, *The Discovery Bible*, HELPS Ministries, Inc.

[3] *Luke 13:22-30 Commentary*, Precept Austin. Retrieved from https://www.preceptaustin.org /luke_1322-30_commentary (last accessed July 8, 2021)

[4] Bromiley, Geoffrey W., *Theological Dictionary of the New Testament*, Abridged in One Volume (Eerdmans 1985) entry for *stenos*, under C. *The NT*, p. 1077

[5] Lowery, David K., "Matthew," in *The Bible Knowledge Word Study The Gospels*, edited by Eugene H. Merrill (Victor 2006) Matthew 7:13 under *Way*, p. 61

[6] See for example NASB 1995, "Enter through the **narrow gate** …. For the gate is small and the **way is narrow that leads to life**, and there are few who find it." Matthew 7:13-14, bold added

[7] Ellicott, Charles John, *Ellicott's Commentary for English Readers*, Matthew 7:14. Retrieved from Hill, Gary, *The Discovery Bible*, HELPS Ministries, Inc.

row because it runs counter to natural inclinations, and "the way" [thereafter] is similarly characterized."[8]

In His reference to the road being "difficult" Jesus used a form of the Greek word *thlibo* {thlee'-bo}. A leading Greek Lexicon lists three glosses (words or phrases proposed as possible translations of a particular Greek word) for this word: "to press or crowd close against, to cause something to be constricted or narrow, to cause to be troubled."[9] *Thlibo* can refer to pressing or squashing,[10] such as squeezing grapes to remove the juice. Figuratively it is used to refer to pressuring trouble, affliction, or distress.[11] Not only is the gate hard to get through, but Jesus warns the way itself will be constricted and full of trouble. In other words, Jesus alerts those who want to be His disciples that the entire path is going to be as hard as the first step.[12] Entering into discipleship "involves a revolution in all our purposes and plans for life, and a surrender of all that is dear to natural inclination, while all that follows is but a repetition of the first great act of self-sacrifice."[13]

---

8    *Luke 13:22-30 Commentary*, Precept Austin, quoting *Vine*. Retrieved from https://www.preceptaustin.org/luke_1322-30_commentary (last accessed September 9, 2021)

9    Mounce, Bill, *Narrow gate* (Matt 7:13-14), Monday With Mounce, referring to *A Greek-English Lexicon of the New Testament and Other Early Christian Literature*, 3rd edition by Walter Bauer, edited by Frederick William Danker (*BDAG*). Retrieved from https://www.billmounce.com/monday-with-mounce/"narrow-gate"-matt-7-13-14 (last accessed September 9, 2021)

10   Bromiley, Geoffrey W., *Theological Dictionary of the New Testament*, Abridged in One Volume (Eerdmans 1985) entry for *thlibo* under *A. thlibo, thlipsis in Secular Greek*, p. 334

11   *Matthew 7:13-14 Commentary*, Precept Austin. Retrieved from http://www.preceptaustin.org/matthew_713-14 (last accessed July 8, 2021)

12   Jamieson, Fausset, and Brown, *Commentary Critical and Explanatory on the Whole Bible*, Matthew 7:14. Retrieved from Hill, Gary, *The Discovery Bible*, HELPS Ministries, Inc.

13   Jamieson, Fausset, and Brown, *Commentary Critical and Explanatory on the Whole Bible*, Matthew 7:14. Retrieved from Hill, Gary, *The Discovery Bible*, HELPS Ministries, Inc.

Jesus no doubt puzzled Pilate when He declared that His, "Kingdom is not of this world (John 18:36)." His way is dramatically different from the way of the world. We are called to be a holy people, separate and distinct from the world. That means we enter through the "narrow" gate rather than the "broad" gate. Thereafter we continue on a difficult road not a trouble free one. A way of life lived in common with other Christ-followers that is truly different from the world is far from easy and straightforward. It is lived against the grain of the advanced modern world. It is by design counter-cultural. Jesus never hid the truth that His disciples will stand out from the majority of the society in which they live. Nor was He secretive about the reality that those obvious differences may subject them to hardship and persecution.

Failure to make an intentional choice to enter the narrow gate and walk on the difficult/narrow path will guarantee that you will walk on the broad path. Pastor Kyle Idleman tells the story of a friend who heard the gospel one evening, believed what he heard and was saved that night.[14] The friend told Idelman that was 10 years ago and "looking back the only problem was that he did not die that night." Idelman's friend confessed he had spent about a decade of his life not understanding that he was also called to follow Jesus. The friend then said, "I wish that man who led me to Christ would have told me that death starts now!" What he meant was that he *believed* the gospel message when he heard it, but he didn't apply it to his life.

The appeal of the broad way is how easy it is to walk and the abundance of companions to be found along the way. The fact that "everybody does it" is no proof that what they are doing is right in God's eyes. Quite the contrary is true! God's people have always been a remnant, a small minority in this world. The reason is obvious: the way of the disciple's life is narrow, lonely and costly. It is possible to walk on the broad way and hold on to the baggage containing our sin and worldliness. However, if we enter the "nar-

---

14  Idleman, Kyle, *Not A Fan* (City On A Hill Studio 2016) Video Segment #4, bury the dead

row" way, we must die to ourselves and allow the Holy Spirit to totally transform us from the inside out. That requires hard work!

For most of us, the activity of walking is so natural that it is likely second only to breathing as the most taken-for-granted thing we do. When we walk on a broad smooth surface, such as the floor in our home, we can easily walk and multi-task other activities at the same time. For example, we walk and talk on the phone. We walk and twist open the cap on a bottle of water at the same time, perhaps even take a few sips as we keep walking. We walk and sing along to music playing in the background.[15]

From experience we recognize that walking is done much of the time without intentional thought. However, when we walk on a *narrow* surface the brain needs to direct all of its focus to the activity of walking. God designed our bodies in such a way that vision and balance are highly integrated in the brain.[16] Maintaining balance while walking on something narrow requires us to fix our focus on a particular spot or object to give our brain a constant, unmoving reference point.[17] As long as we maintain that static

---

15   One thing we are not able to do is walk on two different floors or in two different directions on the same floor at the same time. This is my own version of a metaphor about the truth that we cannot walk on two different paths at the same time.

16   UC Davis Health News, *Diminished balance found in those with poor vision*, Science News, June 6, 2013, citing research by Jeffrey R. Willis, an ophthalmology resident at UC Davis Health System Eye Center. Retrieved from https://www.sciencedaily.com/releases/2013/06/130606190827.htm (last accessed July 8, 2021)

17   *Why Focusing on Something Helps Maintain Balance*, Science ABC, posted July 17, 2015, updated February 3, 2017. Retrieved from https://www.scienceabc.com/sports/why-focussing-on-something-helps-in-maintaining-balance.html (last accessed July 8, 2021). To maintain balance and navigate space in our physical world, we must organize and integrate information from the visual (eyes), proprioceptive (information perceived through our muscles and joints to tell us where we are in space) and vestibular (inner ears sensing motion, equilibrium and spatial awareness) systems. A deficiency in any of these three vitals systems can impact us dramatically. Davis, Nathan, OD, *The Connection Between Vision & Balance*, VEDA Life Rebalanced, December 23, 2016. Retrieved from

visual reference point it is possible to walk upright on a narrow surface without falling.[18]

God's design of the human body is absolutely amazing. What is also amazing is that the functioning of the human body provides an enlightening illustration for how to walk successfully on the narrow road that leads to life. Just as actually walking on something narrow depends on the focus of our eyes, our spiritual vision directly impacts our ability to walk on the narrow road of discipleship. In fact, the Bible provides us with some very clear instructions about the connection between our eyes and the direction of our feet. Solomon, based on the wisdom God gave him, instructed his son:

> Let your eyes look directly ahead And let your gaze be fixed straight in front of you. Watch the path of your feet And all your ways will be established. Do not turn to the right nor to the left; Turn your foot from evil. Proverbs 4:25-27

Using the metaphor of a straight path, Solomon emphasizes the attitude of the heart, the focus of the eyes and the direction of the feet. The phrase "let your eyes look" means to fix your eyes upon something or to look steadily in one direction.[19] "Straight" is a metaphor commonly used to picture correct behavior.[20] Of course correct behavior is that which is obedient to God's commands. The reference to "the right and to the left" is a common figure of

---

https://vestibular.org/sites/default/files/page_files/Documents/Vision%20and%20Balance_21.pdf (last accessed July 8, 2021)

18  *Why Focusing on Something Helps Maintain Balance*, Science ABC, posted July 17, 2015, updated February 3, 2017. Retrieved from https://www.scienceabc.com/sports/why-focussing-on-something-helps-in-maintaining-balance.html (last accessed July 8, 2021)

19  "The idea that the eyes should look directly forward suggests resolution about remaining in the right way." *ESV Study Bible* (Crossway Books 2008) study note Proverbs 4:25, p. 1142, bold omitted

20  Berlin and Brettler, editors, *The Jewish Study Bible: Featuring The Jewish Publication Society Tanakh Translation* (Oxford University Press 2004) study note Proverbs 4:20-27, p. 1455

*The Power of Obedience* 165

speech referring to any type of moral deviation from that which is correct.[21] Admonishment not to turn to the right or the left speaks of complete obedience, *every* step must decidedly follow the way of obedience.[22]

Solomon is demanding "an extreme separation from the wrong way and an extreme commitment to the right path."[23] He unquestionably leaves no third option available. There is nothing in between the wrong path and the right path, no grey areas! "The eyes must give undivided attention to the right path, and the foot must not deviate from it."[24] This is God's divine recipe for establishing a person's way as firm and secure. The fact that the original Hebrew reflects the passive voice is indictive that God is the one who establishes that security for the one who is obedient.[25]

Where the eyes look and the feet walk go hand in hand, they are indivisible actions. If we return to the Genesis narrative of Adam and Eve's sin we see an example of this connection. The first step in the direction of that sin was when Eve *looked* at the forbidden fruit. What her eyes fixed upon metaphorically directed the path on which her feet walked. Once she focused her eyes on that which was forbidden, she did that which was forbidden.

The psalmist likewise observed the connection between his heart – his eyes – and his feet.

---

21 Waltke, Bruce K., *The Book of Proverbs: Chapters 1-15*, The New International Commentary on the Old Testament (Eerdmans 2004) Proverbs 4:25, p. 301
22 McConville, J. G., *Deuteronomy*, Apollos Old Testament Commentary 5 (IVP Academic 2002) Deuteronomy 5:32-33, pp. 133-134
23 Waltke, Bruce K., *The Book of Proverbs: Chapters 1-15*, The New International Commentary on the Old Testament (Eerdmans 2004) Proverbs 4:25, p. 301
24 Waltke, Bruce K., *The Book of Proverbs: Chapters 1-15*, The New International Commentary on the Old Testament (Eerdmans 2004) Proverbs 4:25, p. 300
25 *Holman Christian Standard Bible*, Study Bible edition (Holman Bible Publishers 2010) study note Proverbs 4:25-27, p. 1037

> Teach me your decrees, O LORD; I will keep them to the end. Give me understanding and I will obey your instructions; I will put them into practice with all my heart. Make me walk along the path of your commands, for that is where my happiness is found. Give me an eagerness for your laws rather than a love for money! Turn my eyes from worthless things, and give me life through your word. Psalm 119:33-37 NLT

Employing an ancient metaphor, another psalmist determined to focus his eyes on the place where he expected his help to come from.

> I will lift up my eyes to the mountains; from where shall my help come? My help *comes* from the LORD, who made heaven and earth. He will not allow your foot to slip …. Psalm 121:1-3, italics in original

Naturally, the psalmist addressed his concerns about protection, guidance and blessing to Yahweh (Psalm 121:3-8). In the culture of the Old Testament, the mountains were thought to be the place where the gods had their abode. Since a mountain was considered to be the meeting point of heaven and earth, it was thought that it was on the mountain heights where a god would reveal himself to man.[26] In the case of Psalm 121, the psalmist was anticipating that Yahweh would reveal His need-meeting provision there so he determined (metaphorically) to keep his eyes focused in that direction. By doing so, he was fixing his eyes on Yahweh.

We find a similar focus of the eyes commanded in the New Testament. The author of Hebrews uses a metaphor familiar in Paul's writings which compares the life of discipleship to running a race. Through this author, God makes clear that the key to finishing the race of discipleship under the New Covenant is for every Christ-follower to steadfastly fix their eyes on Jesus.

---

26 Sarna, Nahum M., *Understanding Genesis Through Rabbinic Tradition and Modern Scholarship* (The Jewish Theological Seminary 2015) p. 75

## The Power of Obedience

> ... let us also lay aside every encumbrance and the sin which so easily entangles us, and let us run with endurance the race that is set before us, fixing our eyes on Jesus, the **author** and **perfecter** of faith .... Hebrews 12:1-2, bold added

We'll jump right into a Word Study which will once again permit us to capture what has been lost in translation. We will look at the word "author" and the word "perfecter" which I have placed in bold text above.

### Word Study

*In Hebrews 12:2 the word translated as **author** is the Greek word archegos {ar-khay-gos'}. It refers to someone who pioneers a new path for others to follow.[27] Jesus pioneered a new way for His followers so they could reach their ultimate destiny – the end goal of the Father's will.*

***Perfecter** is a translation of the Greek word teleiotes {tel-i-o-tace'}. It belongs to a word group that refers to completion or reaching an intended goal.[28]*

In our 21st century Western culture, we think of an "author" as a person who writes some sort of literary work such as a novel or a poem. But *archegos* is a "term which was used for both human and divine heroes, [like] founders of schools or those who cut a path forward for their followers and whose exploits for humanity

---

27  Keener, Craig S., *The IVP Bible Background Commentary: New Testament* (Intervarsity Press 1993) Hebrews 2:10, p. 654
28  Zodhiates, Spiros, *The Complete Word Study Dictionary: New Testament* (AMG Publishers 1992) word #5051, p. 1375

were rewarded by exaltation."[29] As a true pioneer, Jesus has gone before us. He has cleared a pathway for our life of faith so we may complete the race we have begun and reach the intended goal.

Not long ago my husband and I were seeking God's direction on a matter, determined not to move forward until we were both in agreement we had received wisdom from the Lord. Days and even weeks passed by and we had no clear, consistent answer to our prayers. As the decision deadline approached, I finally prayed and asked the Lord why we were not able to hear His voice on this matter. His answer was that my feet were not on the same path as His! He proceeded to explain that my eyes were focused on the wrong thing and that my feet followed my eyes leading me off the narrow path. I quickly confessed and repented and then God revealed this Kingdom principle:

> Your feet will always follow your eyes – what your eye is focused on will direct the path you walk. Unless your eyes are fixed on God you cannot walk on the path He is walking on; it simply cannot be. However, if we fix our heart on Him, our eyes will follow our heart – then our feet will follow our eyes. The line of our vision establishes the path upon which we walk.

Our heart sets the line of vision for our eyes. Our eyesight sets the course for our feet to walk. Because that is universally true, it is worth our while to think about what a faithfully obedient heart looks like to God.

Let's start with the basics. Planning to obey is not the same thing as obedience. My good "intention" is simply a transaction that occurs in my brain. Those thoughts that I have might be a valuable starting place, but to qualify as obedience will require follow through with action that puts feet to my intention.

---

29  Keener, Craig S., *The IVP Bible Background Commentary: New Testament* (Intervarsity Press 1993) Hebrews 2:10, p. 654. *Archegos* is used 4 times in the New Testament: Acts 3:15 and 5:31; Hebrews 2:10 and 12:2

"Not everyone who calls out to me, 'Lord! Lord!' will enter the Kingdom of Heaven. Only those who *actually do* the will of my Father in heaven will enter...." Matthew 7:21 NLT, italics added

Even when I actually do what I purposed to do, not every act of obedience is equally pleasing to God. The type of obedience my actions express depends on the condition of my heart. As I have reflected on this matter there are several types of obedience I have taken note of in my own life. I have noticed levels of obedience that are consistent enough for me to have labeled them:

1. reluctant obedience
2. delayed obedience
3. willing obedience
4. desired (desire-based) obedience

*Important note*: While the descriptions represent concepts found in the Bible these are **not** terms/labels that are actually used in the Bible. I am using them just for teaching purposes to distinguish one from the other.

We will spend the rest of this lesson considering each type. However, let me say right up front that I have learned that *desire-based* obedience is the most powerful and most pleasing type of obedience to God. Desire is a want (a yearning) that is so strong that it changes your behavior.[30]

### Reluctant Obedience Says: "I will do what you asked, but I don't want to do it."

*Example of Reluctant Obedience:* Gideon released all the fighting men who were reluctant to go to battle because of fear (Judges 7:2-3). As leaders, both Gideon (Judges 6) and Moses (Exodus 3) could be considered examples of reluctant obedience.

---

30  Pastor David Palmisano, *Centerline*, Sermon Calvary Chapel Melbourne, October 31, 2021

## Some Characteristics of Reluctant Obedience

- A hesitation or holding back because of unwillingness, lack of confidence, lack of courage, or other reasons.
- Evidences lack of trust in God.
- Before obeying, reluctant obedience usually rehearses *all* the reasons why what God has asked won't work and/or why we are not the most qualified person to do it!
- Is often accompanied by a complaining spirit.
- Can easily transition into conditional obedience which says, "I will obey as long as _____ (you fill in the blank)."

## Risks Associated with Reluctant Obedience

- Reluctant obedience leaves a gap for the enemy to come in. We will typically find ourselves in great spiritual warfare over the matter because of our disinclined, hesitant heart attitude.
- We can be easily persuaded to give up when we encounter obstacles on the path.
- If we have placed limitations on our obedience by setting conditions and those conditions are not met, we will be at great risk of backsliding into rebellious disobedience.
- What is in our heart will eventually be revealed in our words ("out of the overflow of the heart, the mouth speaks Luke 6:45)." Reluctance to obey that is secretly harbored in our heart will often hold on to a heart attitude that at the first sign of difficulty will be quick to say something like: "I knew this would not work!" "I never wanted to do it anyway!" "This wasn't *my* idea!"
- If reluctance is strong enough, the response to obstacles in the path of obedience may be voiced in a complaint that accuses God of wrongdoing.

## DELAYED OBEDIENCE INITIALLY SAYS: "I *WILL NOT* DO WHAT YOU ASKED," BUT EVENTUALLY REPENTS AND AGREES, "I *WILL* DO IT."

*Example of Delayed Obedience:* Jonah 1-2 reveals Jonah's initial refusal to do what God asked. God's discipline (spending three days in the belly of a great fish) resulted in delayed obedience (Jonah 3-4).

### *Some Characteristics of Delayed Obedience*

Jesus told His disciples a parable about two sons who were asked by their father to go out and work in the vineyard. His parable provides us with a picture of what delayed obedience looks like.

> "But what do you think? A man had two sons, and he came to the first and said, 'Son, go work today in the vineyard.' And he answered, 'I will not'; but afterward he regretted it and went. The man came to the second and said the same thing; and he answered, 'I *will*, sir'; but he did not go. Which of the two did the will of his father?" They said, "The first." Jesus said to them, "Truly I say to you that the tax collectors and prostitutes will get into the kingdom of God before you. For John came to you in the way of righteousness and you did not believe him; but the tax collectors and prostitutes did believe him; and you, seeing *this*, did not even feel remorse afterward so as to believe him...." Matthew 21:28-32, italics in original

### *Risks Associated with Delayed Obedience*

- The initial reluctance or refusal to obey may lead to God's discipline.
- God always walks in perfect time; therefore, the obedience that is best for us is on-time obedience. Delayed obedience may cause us to miss God's best timing.

- Esther provides us with another biblical example of someone who struggled to obey what God had commanded. Amid her hesitation, Mordecai gave her this warning, "For if you remain silent at this time, relief and deliverance will arise for the Jews from another place and you and your father's house will perish (Esther 4:14a)." Obeying what God has asked us to do is a serious matter. Hesitation could cause us to lose that Kingdom assignment at the risk of great personal loss! Another Christ-follower may be given the assignment and reap the benefit of their obedience. Warning: God is not obligated to wait around until we decide we are ready to obey!
- I have learned from personal experience that God will overlook us for assignments if we have a wrong heart attitude about obedience. In May 2014 my closest friend and one of my most faithful prayer partners told me that God had given her a prayer assignment that concerned expanding my teaching borders. That caught me by surprise, I had never known of God giving one of my prayer partners an assignment I knew nothing about. Sometime later I inquired of the Lord, asking Him why He gave that prayer assignment to my friend and not to me? He answered that I would not have prayed it with the right heart attitude. My initial defensive response was disbelief. However, as I thought it through I knew God was right! My lack of desire for what He planned disqualified me for that prayer assignment. I was content right where I was at that time and learned that contentment, under those circumstances, can become the enemy of desire.[31]
- The delay of unwillingness between instruction and obedience leaves a gap for the enemy to cause confusion as well as offer doubt that you really heard God. The result will be increased spiritual warfare. In general, delay causes obedience to be more difficult than it would have initially been.

---

31  Personal Journal May 03, 2014; Personal Journal November 29, 2019

*The Power of Obedience*

- Before we move on, we need to recognize the reality that often times our delay and reluctance to obey are the result of fear of failure. The type of fear I am referring to is the anxiety associated with questions such as, "What if I get it wrong? What if I make a mistake?" Fear can hold us captive as we wait for assurance that may never come. The best antidote for that type of apprehension is the truth that God does not measure us by our mistakes, He measures us by our obedience.[32]

**WILLING OBEDIENCE SAYS: "I AM WILLING TO DO WHAT YOU ASK BECAUSE *YOU* HAVE ASKED IT." ON BALANCE, AN ATTITUDE OF WILLING OBEDIENCE IS MORE INCLINED TO OBEY THAN TO DISOBEY.**

*Example of Willing Obedience:* Israel in the wilderness period after leaving Egypt (see for example Exodus 16-17; Numbers 10-11,20-21).

*Some Characteristics of Willing Obedience*

- If you are willing to do something, you do it when God asks you, even if you do not want to.
- This type of obedience is **not** 100% wholehearted; therefore, willing obedience stops short of acknowledging that what God has asked is *good* and for our best.[33]
- Like reluctant obedience, obedience based on our willingness to do what God asks is often conditional obedience: "I will obey as long as _____ happens (or doesn't happen)." If the condition I set is not met, I will find myself struggling to continue in my obedience.

---

32  Revelation God gave me early one Sunday morning in January 2022 when I was preoccupied with mistakes I had made in a manuscript I had released for printing!

33  Personal Journal December 28, 2019

## Risks Associated with Willing Obedience

- Willing-based obedience can easily hold on to preferred self-will on the matter, always hoping God changes His mind. As a result, willing-based obedience is prepared to let the chips fall where they may. It will often be insufficient to motivate us to battle our way through obstacles.[34]
- We are called to love the Lord with **all** our heart, mind, soul and strength. That type of love unhindered will result in whole-hearted-sold-out-all-in obedience evidencing no will of our own that is not totally aligned and committed to the Lordship of God.
- When we place conditions on obeying God, He may allow "testing" (trials) to expose the incongruity that is in our hearts.[35] Let me share the illustration God gave me recently when I was preparing to teach some ministry leaders about obedience. He gave me the picture of a *piñata*. As you may know, the contents of a *piñata* remain hidden until someone hits it with a stick in just the right place. At that point, everything inside the *piñata* comes spilling out onto the ground.
- When our heart attitude does not align with whole-hearted obedience it is just like that *piñata*, holding in unseen thoughts and attitudes. God's testing will put the *piñata* stick in someone's hands. When that stick connects with our heart in just the right place, what is inside of us explodes out of our mouth revealing what was hidden in our heart. Now what used to be invisibly and safely tucked away inside your heart is suddenly out in the open for others to see. At that moment wrong heart attitudes empower words that flow freely from our mouth. That's because spontaneous reactions can't be faked – they are the real deal. "It is much easier to *act* like a Christian than it is to *react*

---

34  Personal Journal November 29, 2019
35  Personal Journal February 4, 2020

like one!"³⁶ Our actions reveal things about our true character, but our *reactions* reveal even more. "Most of us are good actors, but it's far more difficult to fake a reaction."³⁷

> Search me, O God, and know my heart; Try me and know my anxious thoughts; And see if there be any hurtful way in me, And lead me in the everlasting way. Psalm 139:23-24

- Willingness can give way to what I'll call martyrdom-obedience. We are obeying because God asked. However, in our martyrdom the "sacrifice" we are asked to make to obey (i.e., the cost of obedience) is not only highlighted but it is also proclaimed to anyone and everyone who will listen. In other words, we want everyone around us to know that our obedience is costing us something! This type of obedience is not reflective of "all-in" obedience. It puts the spotlight on us rather than on glorifying God.³⁸
- Willing obedience can allow room for double-mindedness – keeping one foot in the "I really don't want to do this" position and one foot in the "I am willing to do it because you asked." This type of double mindedness is characteristic of Israel's wilderness years. When all was going well, according to their self-set barometer, they were content to worship and obey Yahweh. However, as soon as they faced hardship or suffering as a test of their faith they quickly fell into rebellious grumbling and accusation against God. What God desired for them was to firmly plant both feet on the path with whole-hearted commitment. He wanted them to allow Him to have His way. He wanted their heart

---

36 Batterson, Mark, *All In: You Are One Decision Away From a Totally Different Life* (Zondervan 2013) p. 153
37 Batterson, Mark, *All In: You Are One Decision Away From a Totally Different Life* (Zondervan 2013) p. 69
38 Personal Journal December 22, 2019

*176 The Attitude of the Heart, The Focus of the Eyes, and The Direction of the Feet*

to change to passionate desire, trusting that which He had planned was for their best.[39]

**DESIRE-BASED OBEDIENCE SAYS: "LORD, I AM PLEASED TO DO WHAT YOU ASK BECAUSE THE DESIRE OF YOUR HEART HAS BECOME THE DESIRE OF MY HEART."**

As a reminder, we are defining "desire" as a want (a yearning) that is so strong it changes your behavior. Desire gives birth to *invested stewardship* of that which God is asking you to do.[40]

*Example of Desire-based Obedience:* Jesus! Everything about His life and ministry evidence desire-based obedience. On one specific occasion, Luke explicitly records the desire Jesus held in His heart to obey His Father's will. The occasion was the last Passover meal Jesus planned to eat with His disciples.

> And [Jesus] said to [His disciples], "I have **earnestly desired** to eat this Passover with you before I suffer; for I say to you, I shall never again eat it until it is fulfilled in the kingdom of God." Luke 22:15-16, bold added

A Word Study will help us more fully understand the type of enthusiastic[41] desire Jesus was speaking about.

## WORD STUDY

*In Luke 22:15 the phrase "earnestly desired" is a translation of two related Greek words.* **Earnestly** *is the Greek*

---

39 Personal Journal November 29 2019
40 "Invested stewardship" is a phrase that became lodged in my heart when I was in the midst of my own challenging desire-based obedience. Personal Journal January 22, 2022
41 *NET Bible Notes*, translator's note 40, Luke 22:15 "This phrase … serves to underline Jesus' enthusiasm for holding this meal (BDF §198.6)."

> noun *epithumia {ep-ee-thoo-mee'-ah}. It denotes passionate excitement.*[42]
>
> **Desired** *is the Greek verb epithumeo {ep-ee-thoo-meh'-o}. It means "set the heart upon" referring to affections that are directed toward something.*[43]
>
> *This phrase is variously translated as: eagerly desired, very eager, earnestly desired, fervently desired, with desire I have desired.*[44]

Jesus does not want His disciples to miss the point. The phrase "earnestly desired" is more literally translated as "with desire I desire."[45] In the original Greek text of this verse, it would be easy to see that the first words Jesus spoke to His disciples about the matter were the words "with desire." In our Western culture, we often emphasize words in written text using underlines, italics, or bold font. Or when speaking, we use voice inflection to emphasize a word or a phrase. However, in Greek and Hebrew, positioning words at the very beginning of a sentence (even if that disrupts the more common flow of the words spoken) is a common way to emphasize the most important thought in the sentence. What is

---

42  Renner, Rick, *Sparkling Gems from the Greek* (Harrison House Publishers 2003) September 16, p. 690

43  *Titus 3:3 Commentary*, Precept Austin. Retrieved from https://www.preceptaustin.org/titus_33#lusts%20epithumia (last accessed September 10, 2021); Zodhiates, Spiros, *The Complete Word Study Dictionary: New Testament* (AMG Publishers 1992) word #1937, p. 627

44  Luke 22:15: "And he said to them, I have eagerly desired to eat this Passover with you before I suffer (NIV)." / "Jesus said, 'I have been very eager to eat this Passover meal with you before my suffering begins (NLT).'" / "And he said to them, 'I have earnestly desired to eat this Passover with you before I suffer (ESV).'" / "Then He said to them, 'I have fervently desired to eat this Passover with you before I suffer (HCSB).'" / "And he said unto them, 'With desire I have desired to eat this passover with you before I suffer (ASV).'"

45  *Young's Literal Translation*, Luke 22:15

being underscored here is that Jesus does not merely have a desire to obey, He has a *longing* to do what the Father had asked of Him.[46]

Jesus wanted to be certain His disciples understood that the intense desire of His heart was to please His Father and do His will. Jesus was not sitting down to His last Passover meal with them in reluctance; He was fully aligned with His Father. He recognized that the fullness of time had come for *this* Passover meal to take place and initiate all that would transpire over the coming days related to His death-burial-resurrection. He knew *this* particular Passover meal was a necessary step along the path that would ultimately fulfill His Father's redemptive plan.

Jesus was being driven by an inward passionate desire to do His Father's will. There was no reluctance or unwillingness on His part – the desires of His Father's heart had become the desires of His heart. Being fully submitted to the Father's plan released the full unhindered power of Holy Spirit to operate in Him and through Him. Therefore, the Holy Spirit was free to empower, equip and enable every ounce of obedience necessary to completely fulfill the mission for which Jesus had come. In fact, we could say that operating in desire-based obedience *supercharged* the power of Holy Spirit enabling Jesus to become the perfect once-for-all Passover Lamb of God![47]

Another biblical example of desire-based obedience is seen in the life of the Apostle Paul. His letter to the Philippians describes the passion with which he pursued the Kingdom assignment he had received from Christ.

> Not that I have already obtained *it* or have already become perfect, but I press on so that I may lay hold of that for which also I was laid hold of by Christ Jesus. Brethren, I do not regard myself as having laid hold of *it* yet; but one thing *I do*: forgetting what *lies* behind and

---

46  *NET Bible Notes*, translator's note 40, Luke 22:15, citing BDF §198.6
47  Personal Journal November 29, 2019, "I tell you by adding *desire* to obedience you supercharge the power of Holy Spirit."

reaching forward to what *lies* ahead, I press on toward the goal for the prize of the upward call of God in Christ Jesus. Philippians 3:12-14, italics in original

Undoubtedly Paul was thinking about the very type of goal-driven desire that was behind his own obedience when he instructed Timothy about those who aspire/desire to become an overseer in the church.

It is a trustworthy statement: if any man **aspires** to the office of overseer, it is a fine work he **desires** *to do*. 1 Timothy 3:1, italics in original, bold added

A Word Study will help us more fully understand what type of desire Paul said was most appropriate for ministry.

### WORD STUDY

*In 1 Timothy 3:1 the Greek word translated as **aspires** is the word oregomai {or-eg'-om-ahee}. It describes a longing, a strong inclination or burning ambition to achieve something.*[48] *Oregomai pictures being fixed on the object of desire so that one's whole being is "stretched forward" to grasp it. He is not satisfied until he has it in hand.*[49]

***Desires** is a translation of the Greek word epithumeo {ep-ee-thoo-meh'-o}. As we learned in the Word Study on page 177, it means "set the heart upon" referring to affections that are directed toward something.*

---

[48] Renner, Rick, *Sparkling Gems from the Greek Volume II* (Harrison House Publishers 2016) November 20, p. 1052
[49] Renner, Rick, *Sparkling Gems from the Greek Volume II* (Harrison House Publishers 2016) November 20, p. 1052

John MacArthur provides the following explanation for Paul's use of these two words.[50]

> The first [*oregomai*] means "to reach out after." It describes external action, not internal motive. The second [*epithumeo*] means "a strong passion," and refers to an inward desire. Taken together, these two words aptly describe the type of man who belongs in the ministry—one who outwardly pursues it because he is driven by a strong internal desire.

The point is that desire is a passionate drive toward an intended goal. When focused desire floods our heart that yearning zeal draws us toward the goal. We will have much more to say about this in our next lesson.

*Some Characteristics of Desire-based Obedience*

- A willingness to obey is not the same as desire. Desire means we fix our heart firmly on that which God has called us to do.[51] Desire will often make a difference between our success and our failure in reaching the goal God has set for us.[52] Desire motivates and supplies energetic power to overcome obstacles to reach that goal.[53]
- Because desire-based obedience establishes the matter in your heart, it brings your heart into such perfect alignment with God that you agree that what He has asked you to do is "good." It evidences an undivided heart. In fact, desire-based obedience is notable in that it **cannot** operate in a divided heart! It is the type of obedience that

---

50 MacArthur, John, *The MacArthur Study Bible* (Thomas Nelson 2006) study note 1 Timothy 3:1 under *It is a trustworthy statement*, p. 1833
51 Personal Journal November 29, 2019
52 Personal Journal December 4, 2019
53 Renner, Rick, *Sparkling Gems from the Greek Volume II* (Harrison House Publishers 2016) November 20, p. 1052

demonstrates that I have obeyed the command to love God with *all* my heart.
- Because it is out of the mouth that the heart speaks, the words I speak will reveal whether my obedience is merely *willing* obedience or whether it is *desired* obedience. When my heart is fully aligned with the desires of God's heart my mouth will only speak words that evidence desire-based obedience. If my words reflect reluctance or complaint about the matter, I am *not* walking in desired obedience.
- What pleases God is whole-hearted devotion that proclaims by word and action, "Because God has asked, I am eager to obey. His desire has become my desire." That is the type of obedience that displays whole-hearted devotion and pleases God – it is *all-in* devotion that fully worships God.[54] Obedience fueled by desire expresses the internalization of God's law that characterizes the New Covenant. When testing comes, desire-based obedience is the only type of obedience capable of revealing that what is on the inside of us is the same as what we are portraying on the outside.
- One of the most common words to describe a "disciple" of Christ in the New Testament is the Greek word *doulos* {doo'-los}. The most accurate translation is bondservant – one who sells himself into slavery to another. In a spiritual sense, it refers to our discipleship in terms of becoming a slave of God.[55] According to the *Theological Dictionary of the New Testament*, the word denotes compulsory service. In other words, one who is "saved by the blood of the Lamb" *owes* Him their service. The *doulos* belongs to his master. He is so intensely obligated and *desirous to do the master's will* that his own will is completely occupied with the will of the master. One who serves in the capacity of a *doulos* understands himself to be in a permanent relation

---

54 Personal Journal December 22, 2019
55 *NET Bible Notes*, translator's note 175, Revelation 1:1

of servitude. A *doulos* is not permitted to resign to go to work for another employer.[56] In short, the very definition of a *doulos*, a disciple of Christ, is that he is inwardly motivated by an eager obligation to do God's will. A *doulos* will always engage in invested stewardship of his master's business!

- Here is an example of how desire works: One morning about 3 hours after going to bed, the Holy Spirit awakened me out of very deep sleep. I had a hard time getting my eyes to open to look at the clock – it was 1:00 a.m. Once open it was a challenge to keep my eyes open, but I had a sense that I was purposely awakened to get up and spend quiet time with the Lord. After fighting sleep for the next 10 minutes I finally cried out to God to release the grace I needed to do what He was calling me to do. I have learned in the past that God's grace is *always* available to do that which He asks us to do. He will always empower our obedience. That morning I experienced an example of just how desire works in God's Kingdom. Because I chose to "desire" that which God desired for me, I asked for the grace I needed to fulfill that desire. That is exactly how desire works as a spiritual principle – desire releases power to obey. God had given me an experience so I could understand this spiritual truth of His Kingdom. Only through desire was I enabled to become awake sufficiently to seek God's grace. I trusted His grace would empower me and enable me to do what I needed to do to fulfill that desire.[57] As I came to my office and sat down in the quiet place typical of such early morning times spent with the Lord I realized He had

---

56 Zodhiates, Spiros, *The Complete Word Study Dictionary: New Testament* (AMG Publishers 1992) word #1401, p. 483; *Spirit Filled Life Bible* (Thomas Nelson, 1991) study note Romans 1:1 under *Bondservant*, p. 1686
57 Personal Journal December 4, 2019

something to speak to my heart that morning and I was glad that I had chosen to desire what He desired for me.[58]

As we conclude this lesson, my prayer is that we will join the psalmist and wholeheartedly proclaim:

> I thought about my ways and turned my feet toward your instruction. Psalm 119:59 CJB

> I will hurry, without delay, to obey your commands. Psalm 119:60 NLT

**Hear What The Spirit is Saying to the Church**: *In the days ahead, as My Kingdom advances on earth, desire will make a difference often times between success and failure. Desire will drive pursuit of those things I desire for My Bride.*[59]

---

58   Personal Journal December 4, 2019
59   Personal Journal December 4, 2019

LESSON 10:

THE POWER OF
DESIRE-BASED
OBEDIENCE

 "Praise the LORD! How blessed is the one who obeys the LORD, who takes great delight in keeping his commands." Psalm 112:1 NET

IN OUR LAST lesson we considered various types of obedience: reluctant, delayed, willing and desire-based. From those descriptions, we can set up an obedience continuum beginning with delayed or reluctant obedience on one end of the scale and desire-based obedience on the other end. While willing obedience is good, we noted that desire-based obedience is the very essence of one who calls himself a disciple of Christ! Passionate desire for the things God desires is the highest level of obedience. It is the most pleasing to God and the type of obedience that releases the most equipping and enabling power.[1]

**LET'S ADD A FEW MORE CHARACTERISTICS OF DESIRE-BASED OBEDIENCE**

- Desire-based obedience elevates obedience to the level of longing and passion. *Willingness* refers to being inclined or favorably disposed to. On the other hand, *desire* implies deep-seated inclination or aim, a strong feeling of wanting to have something or see something happen. Desire refers

---

1   Personal Journal November 29, 2109

to resolutely setting our hearts upon something.[2] The inward determination and resolve that naturally accompany desire will always push us further and drive us harder to reach the goal than mere willingness.[3]

- It is a spiritual principle of God's Kingdom that desire releases power.[4] This is the only type of obedience that fuels the tenacity to press forward refusing to quit no matter what the cost.[5] This type of determined drive is often necessary to fulfill the assignment God has given us and cross the finish line with the right heart attitude. In our last lesson, we referred to that type of inward drive as *invested stewardship.*

- Desire supplies the all-important inward motivation to overcome when there are obstacles between us and the intended goal. Other forms of obedience will likely view obstacles as stumbling blocks or blockades. Desire sees those obstacles like a hurdle in a track and field event. As a skilled hurdler, the one walking in desire-based obedience will take a long, gliding stride over each hurdle. They will be proficient at getting their feet back on the ground quickly after clearing each hurdle. Then, they will continue running with consistent strides so they can clear the next obstacle just as smoothly as the last. Desire will view this hurdles course as a sprint race to the finish line with a few overcomable obstacles along the way.[6]

---

2 Refer to Word Study of *epithumeo* in Lesson 9
3 Personal Journal December 6, 2019
4 Personal Journal December 4, 2019
5 Renner, Rick, *Sparkling Gems from the Greek Volume II* (Harrison House Publishers 2016) November 19, p. 1054
6 My husband ran track and field in high school and was trained in the hurdles event. He noted that to be a successful hurdler you need to plan your steps, adjusting your stride as you approach every hurdle in order to clear it as efficiently as possible without slowing down your sprint pace.

- Desire-based obedience means we are of one mind and purpose with God. We are simultaneously doing what we want *and* what God wants.
- The heart that desires the things God desires creates the *ideal* dwelling place for Him. As He dwells in that heart, He will fully accomplish His perfect will without hindrance.[7]

In summary, desire-based obedience gives Holy Spirit the permission He is waiting for to accomplish God's perfect will, God's perfect way and in God's perfect timing. In all things God asks us to do, He asks that we allow the desire of *His* heart to flood *our* hearts. He will release His desires to us if we are open to receiving them. When you add desire to obedience, it is like supercharging the power of Holy Spirit.[8] God's desire released into our heart gives Holy Spirit permission to supply full-throttle power and energy. Jesus undoubtedly understood this Kingdom principle and set His heart to desire that which His Father desired for Him.

Desire-based obedience not only supercharges obedience with divine supernatural power it supercharges your heart attitude alignment with God's truth. It is much more difficult for Satan to successfully tempt a heart that is deeply intertwined with God's heart because of desire-based obedience. When you truly desire that which God desires for you there is no demonic power that can overcome you. You *will* be victorious![9]

Let's turn our attention toward understanding why this type of power is so vital to our obedience. In Lesson 9 we considered the related words *epithumeo* (verb) and *epithumia* (noun) noting this word group refers to a strong passionate desire that draws a person toward a particular thing upon which they are focused. When we studied these words, we looked at them in the context of the desire Jesus expressed for eating that last Passover meal with His disciples. However, the fact is that in the Greek language these words can also be used in a *negative* sense. They can refer to lustful desires and

---

7   Personal Journal June 29, 2019
8   Personal Journal November 29, 2109
9   Personal Journal December 28, 2019

cravings that can drive the flesh toward sin. Paul writes about this reality in a number of his epistles. We'll begin with what he wrote to the church at Ephesus when he pointed out:

> [Jews and Gentiles alike] all formerly lived in the **lusts** [*epithumia*] of our flesh [*sarx*], indulging the **desires** [*thelema*] of the flesh [*sarx*] and of the mind, and were by nature children of wrath, even as the rest. Ephesians 2:3, bold added

To clarify what he meant, Paul's letter contained a list of behaviors typical of those that originate from the flesh nature and are consistent with worldly ways. Those enumerated behaviors can be generally categorized as: 1) a perversion of sexual practices, 2) a perversion of religious practices, 3) anti-social conduct and 4) personal sins such as envy and drunkenness.[10] When Paul refers to the "flesh" he is not referencing a part of the physical self. He is referring to a spiritual power that can govern life.[11] He describes the ones who practice sin as being by nature "children of wrath (Ephesians 2:3)."[12] Paul's understanding is that sin takes up residence and operates in the flesh. He viewed the power of sin to be

---

10  See Ephesians 5:19-21; Arnold, Clinton E., "Ephesians," in *Zondervan Illustrated Bible Backgrounds Commentary*, Vol. 3, edited by Clinton E. Arnold (Zondervan 2002) The acts of the sinful nature ([Ephesians] 5:19-21), p. 292

11  Typical Rabbinic teaching from Jewish rabbis is that every person has two inclinations or desires. One is a good inclination or desire (*yetser tov*) and the other desire pulls in the opposite direction toward evil (*yetser ra'*). Arnold, Clinton E., "Ephesians," in *Zondervan Illustrated Bible Backgrounds Commentary*, Vol. 3, edited by Clinton E. Arnold (Zondervan 2002) The acts of the sinful nature ([Ephesians] 5:19-21), p. 292

12  "Children of wrath is a Semitic idiom which may mean either 'people characterized by wrath' or 'people destined for wrath.'" *NET Bible Notes*, study note 14, Ephesians 2:3

## The Power of Obedience

stronger than the mere power of self-will.[13] Therefore Paul taught that the flesh has no power against sin without Christ.[14]

In Ephesians 2:3 the word "lusts," highlighted in bold text in the quote above, is our now familiar word *epithumia*. We have said it conveys the idea of a passionate focused longing toward reaching a particular goal. When used in a negative sense, as in Ephesians 2:3, the word denotes craving, coveting or lusting.[15] The word "desires," which is also in bold in our Ephesians 2:3 quote, is a translation of *thelema* {thel'-ay-mah}. It is a word that is often used biblically to refer to God's will. Here, however, Paul uses *thelema* to denote the result of a person expressing their own will.[16] Paul is pointing out that "the flesh has a mind of its own. And if allowed to do so, the flesh will become obsessed with a fleshly temptation."[17]

Every follower of Christ has an old nature from his physical birth (our old man, Romans 6:6) and a new nature from his spiritual birth (the new man, Colossians 3:10). The New Testament contrasts these two conflicting natures. If Paul's only statement about our flesh nature was Ephesians 2:3 we might think that for the Christ-follower our old flesh nature has ended and been totally replaced by our new nature, our born-again, born-from-above nature. However, Ephesians 2:3 is not Paul's exclusive teaching on the flesh nature.

Paul thoroughly understood that the battle with flesh was not merely something left in the dust of the past for Christ-followers.

---

13  Keck, Leander E., *Romans*, Abingdon New Testament Commentaries (Abingdon Press 2005) The Conflicted Self ([Romans] 7:13-25), p. 193
14  Keck, Leander E., *Romans*, Abingdon New Testament Commentaries (Abingdon Press 2005) The Conflicted Self ([Romans] 7:13-25), pp. 189-194; Liberation by the Resident Spirit ([Romans] 8:1-30), p. 194; The Power of the Spirit ([Romans] 8:1-17), pp. 194-202
15  Mounce, Bill, *Bill Mounce Greek Dictionary*, entry for ἐπιθυμία [epithumia], BillMounce.com. Retrieved from https://www.billmounce.com/greek-dictionary/epithumia (last accessed September 11, 2021)
16  Zodhiates, Spiros, T*he Complete Word Study Dictionary: New Testament* (AMG Publishers 1992) word #2307, p. 721
17  Renner, Rick, *Sparkling Gems from the Greek* (Harrison House Publishers 2003) July 13, p. 490

In his letter to the Galatians, he made it unmistakably clear that for the one who chooses to follow Christ this battle of opposing desires is a lifelong war! Let's look, for example, at Galatians 5:17. We'll consider it from two different translations.

> For the flesh **sets its desire** [*epithumeo*] against the Spirit, and the Spirit against the flesh [*sarx*]; for these are in opposition to one another, so that you may not do the things that you please. Galatians 5:17 NASB 1995, bold added

> The sinful nature wants to do evil, which is just the opposite of what the Spirit wants. And the Spirit gives us desires that are the opposite of what the sinful nature desires. These two forces are constantly fighting each other, so you are not free to carry out your good intentions. Galatians 5:17 NLT

It is important to rightly understand Paul's three uses of the word "flesh" in Ephesians 2:3 and Galatians 5:17.

### WORD STUDY

*The word **flesh** in Ephesians 2:3 and Galatians 5:17 is a translation of the Greek word* sarx *{sarx} which is used frequently in the New Testament (147 times).*

*In a literal sense,* sarx *refers to the physical body (flesh and blood). However, most often Paul uses* sarx *in a negative sense to refer to that which is "human and earthly ... and as people trust in* sarx *in this sense, it becomes a power that opposes the working of the Spirit .... A life oriented to [the flesh] serves [the flesh] and carries out its thinking."*[18]

---

18 Bromiley, Geoffrey W., *Theological Dictionary of the New Testament*, Abridged in One Volume (Eerdmans 1985) entry for *sarx* under *6. Sarx as the Subject*

*The Power of Obedience*

Paul instructed Christ-followers that the flesh "sets its desire" against the Spirit. The phrase "sets its desire" is highlighted in bold in the Galatians 5:17 NASB 1995 quote on page 190. It is once again a translation of the Greek word *epithumeo*. If we were to look at the original Greek text, the verb tense would put us on notice that Paul was referring to an inward battle that is ongoing, continual and habitual. It is something that is always present.[19] In that the flesh is bent toward self and not the things of God, it produces what J. I. Packer calls "anti-God energy."[20] Wisdom dictates that we *not* ignore the power the flesh can assert in our life.

Paul was writing to other *Christ-followers* when he warned that the flesh can set its desire ("focused passion")[21] in such a way as to oppose what the Holy Spirit wants to do in us and through us. The result is we don't do what we want to do (Galatians 5:17 NASB 1995). We are not free to carry out our good intentions (Galatians 5:17 NLT). In other words, Paul knew that the enemy, if permitted, will set up his headquarters for wrongful lusts and desires in a person's flesh. Satan knows very well that a person is enslaved to whatever overcomes him.[22] The Bible teaches us that we must *die* to the flesh to live (Romans 8:13). Dying to self, or the flesh, is an intentional decision we make. It is an act of obedience to God and this type of *dying* requires the power of the Holy Spirit. When we walk by the Spirit we do not gratify the desires of our flesh.[23]

As I was reflecting on Galatians 5:17 and the battle between our flesh and the Holy Spirit I had an image of ancient battle lines being drawn and knew that those battle lines in some way pic-

---

*of Sin*, p. 1005, indicating that it is in this sense that Paul uses the word in Galatians 5:17

19  Hill, Gary, *The Discovery Bible*, HELPS Ministries, Inc., explanation of *Greek Present tense*
20  *Galatians 5:16 Commentary*, Precept Austin. Retrieved from https://www.preceptaustin.org/galatians_516 (last accessed July 8, 2021)
21  Hill, Gary, *The Discovery Bible*, HELPS Ministries, Inc., [G]1937 *epithyméō*
22  2 Peter 2:19 ESV
23  Galatians 5:16

tured this spiritual battle that takes place in every Christ-follower. Let's set our context by considering how ancient warfare typically unfolded. To do so, I'm turning to an online source called, *War History Online*, and in particular, a 2015 article titled, *Being a Footsoldier in Ancient Battles: A Frontline View of Victory.*[24]

While all ancient battles could have elements of uniqueness, they were often fought in organized formations. These formations consisting of line unity and cohesion were vital to victory. The two sides would stand about 5-10 feet apart facing each other. That space in between the two opposing armies would be "no man's land."

As lines were established, those who were veteran soldiers had a distinct advantage. They could more easily remain calm because their past experience had taught them how to survive the battle and exploit the enemy. With the lines facing each other, eventually one or more men from one line would charge out into "no man's land" in some way to attack their opponents. These attacks were often sudden and quick followed by a hasty retreat back into the safety of their own line. Early charges by one side or the other were primarily aimed at causing confusion. Optimally these early charges would trigger the enemy's retreat before a full-scale battle began.

Battles were often won when one side was able to take full court advantage of a gap that occurred in the opposing line. The gap would be advantageously exploited by the opposing army who would work to widen it. At the point it became wide enough, the "no man's land" would actually turn into a type of funnel for the aggressively advancing line. The aggressor, energized by the pursuit of victory, would keep pressing forward. The opening in the opposing line would keep enlarging and as it did it continued to divide the enemy army until victory was finally achieved.

---

24  Mclaughlin, William, *Being a Footsoldier in Ancient Battles; A Frontline View of Victory,* War History Online, December 1, 2015. Retrieved from https://www.warhistoryonline.com/ancient-history/ancient-battles-frontline-viewvictory-m.html (last accessed July 8, 2021)

With this general background, we can better picture narratives from the Old Testament which take place on the battlefield. For example, the story of David and Goliath tells us that battle lines were being drawn each day by both the Philistines and Israel's army.

> So David got up early in the morning, left the flock with someone to keep it, loaded up, and set out as Jesse had instructed him. He arrived at the perimeter of the camp as the army was marching out to its battle formation shouting their battle cry. Israel and the Philistines **lined up in battle formation facing each other**. David left his supplies in the care of the quartermaster and **ran to the battle line**.... [S]uddenly the champion named Goliath, the Philistine from Gath, came forward from the Philistine battle line and shouted his usual words, which David heard. 1 Samuel 17:20-23 HCSB, bold added

We know from the story that young David, carrying only his slingshot, courageously advanced toward the well-armed Philistine giant. The rest is history as they say!

Galatians 5:17 seems to paint a picture for us of two opposing spirits lined up in battle formation facing each other. One spirit is our flesh and the other is Holy Spirit in us. We are going to learn in this lesson that desire-based obedience reorders the battlefield altogether because it completely removes the opposition! That's because, as we have noted, obedience that flows out of our heart's desire is the only type of obedience that enables us to simultaneously do what *we* want to do while doing what *God* wants.

In Genesis, we learn that the serpent's strategy was to tempt Eve through her desire for what she did not have (Genesis 3:6). Appealing to our flesh through our desires is a strategy that is often successful. As a result, Satan continues to use it. That means desire-based obedience is our best defense! Let me explain. When the desires of our heart are actually God's desires, the enemy's temptations are no match for God's power to accomplish His own will. That is why Jesus could not be successfully tempted by Satan – His desires were 100% based on His Father's will. He only did what His Father told Him to do! Because in His flesh Jesus had no desire of His own, the enemy could not entice Him to sin! When Satan did tempt Jesus, He simply quoted His Father's word!

In his devotional book, *Sparkling Gems*, Rick Renner provides some of the clearest descriptions of how the devil works that I've ever encountered. Renner describes Satan's tenacity of repeatedly assaulting our minds and emotions until he successfully penetrates our thought life.[25] His goal is to rule over us. In fact, Peter describes Satan as a lion seeking whom he may devour (1 Peter 5:8).

As Satan wins battles, he gains authority to operate on earth and expand his kingdom. So, he will work monotonously to wear down our resistance.

Jesus knew Satan's strategy and cautioned the three disciples who were with Him in Gethsemane that, "… the spirit is willing, but the flesh is weak." In other words, good intentions are not enough to withstand an enemy assault against weak flesh. Because that's true, Jesus counseled them to stand guard in prayer. He knew something more was needed than man's own plans and hopes to resist an enemy like Satan. Jesus not only had divine wisdom, He knew from personal experience that if Satan does not succeed at first, he will change his approach and try again. With virtual unending patience, our adversary will wait hoping we will let down our guard permitting him the victory on his next assault.[26] He seeks to gain access to our thoughts so he can flood our minds with lies. Remember Jesus called that his native language (John 8:44). Once he finds an entry point, the strategy of the evil one is to layer lie upon lie in a person's mind so that he can construct a mental stronghold. Wherever a stronghold is in place it will allow Satan to influence and essentially manipulate the person in that

---

25  Renner, Rick, *Sparkling Gems from the Greek* (Harrison House Publishers 2003) November 5, p. 839
26  Renner, Rick, *Sparkling Gems from the Greek Volume II* (Harrison House Publishers 2016) July 13, p. 643

area of thought and behavior.[27] As a result, that person ends up functionally doing work which benefits the kingdom of darkness.

There is power in obedience – a supernatural power that is reserved for those who obey. The only power the enemy has over a Holy Spirit-filled Christ-follower is when he can convince us to believe his lies and come into agreement with his desires. The outcome of the battle between the desires of our flesh and the desires of the Holy Spirit is determined by our alignment with God. Desire-based obedience simply means *aligning perfectly* with God's will, His plan and His purpose. That means I allow the revelation of His will to take firm root in me. I permit it to find a home in my heart and then I allow Him to accomplish in me and through me His good and perfect will. *Every* time I choose to obey God, the Holy Spirit wins the battle and the enemy stands defeated!

As we've been learning, in desire-based obedience, the desires of God's heart have become the desires of our hearts. Rather than our flesh lined up *against* God's will, we have put to death the desires of our flesh and we are completely lined up *with* Holy Spirit. That's why I said desire-based obedience reorders the battlefield by completely removing the opposition! It bears repeating that obedience that flows out of our heart's desire is the only type of obedience that enables us to simultaneously do what *we* want to do while doing what *God* wants. God will *always* release sufficient grace to equip, enable and empower us to accomplish His will. In fact, our obedience ensures God's enabling grace and desire-based obedience guarantees that grace will be released at the highest level.[28]

We will conclude this lesson by considering several Scriptures that provide promises and instruction related to desire-based obedience. We'll begin with the declaration of our Key Scripture for this lesson that the one who *delightfully obeys* God's commands is blessed.

---

27  Renner, Rick, *Sparkling Gems from the Greek* (Harrison House Publishers 2003) August 18, p. 604 and December 10, p. 942
28  Personal Journal June 15, 2020

Praise the LORD! How **blessed** is the one who obeys the LORD, who takes great **delight** in keeping His commands. Psalm 112:1 NET, bold added

Two of the words in the above-quoted Scripture are highlighted in bold: blessed and delight. Both words merit further study.

> ## WORD STUDY
>
> In our Key Scripture the word **blessed** is the Hebrew word 'esher {eh'-sher}. It conveys a deep sense of well-being, "an inward contentedness not affected by circumstances."[29]
>
> 'Esher is related to 'ashar a verb that means to go or be straight or to advance forward. In its figurative use, 'ashar refers to following a straight path in your heart or in your understanding.[30]

Note that to be "blessed" refers to having a deep sense of well-being. On the other hand, spiritual death refers to the *loss* of well-being! The state of blessedness then is the very opposite of spiritual death. It is abundant life rooted in moral, mental and physical well-being in the way in which God alone can provide.

The fact that the noun *'esher* derives from the verb *'ashar* means it carries the distinction of blessedness which is "to be envied with desire."[31] This type of blessing follows from action a person

---

29 *Psalm 1:1 Commentary*, Precept Austin. Retrieved from https://www.preceptaustin.org/psalm_1_commentary (last accessed July 8, 2021); Watson, J.D., *A Hebrew Word for the Day: Key Words from the Old Testament* (AMG Reference 2010) February 27 Blessed *'ešer*, p. 58

30 Baker and Carpenter, *The Complete WordStudy Dictionary of the Old Testament* (AMG Publishers 2003) word #833, p. 108

31 Harris, Archer, and Waltke, editors, *Theological Wordbook of the Old Testament* (Moody Press 1999) word #183, #183a, p. 80

has taken.[32] The resulting blessing leads others to be envious or jealous with a desire for that same type of blessing. For example, "to be envied with desire is the man who trusts in the Lord."[33] Using this definition in our Key Scripture we could say, "To be envied with desire is the man who obeys the Lord." Obedience results when that desirous envy of the blessed person motivates the envious person to do the same thing the blessed person had done.

As we will see from our next Word Study the Hebrew word "delight" is another way to express obedience that flows out of desire. In other words, another name for desire-based obedience is delight-based obedience.

## Word Study

*In our Key Scripture the word* **delight** *is the Hebrew verb ḥāpēṣ also transliterated as* chafets *{khaw-fates'}. It means "to take pleasure in; to be bent or inclined toward; to cherish; to be favorably disposed toward someone; to love and* **desire.**"[34] *This verb refers to a person's favorable disposition toward engaging in delight, it flows out of what they value most.*[35]

*The Hebrew language has other words that can be translated as "desire." What distinguishes ḥāpēṣ from those other words is: 1) the intensity of the emotional delight is stronger when the word ḥāpēṣ is used and 2) the fact*

---

32 Harris, Archer, and Waltke, editors, *Theological Wordbook of the Old Testament* (Moody Press 1999) word #183, #183a, p. 80
33 Harris, Archer, and Waltke, editors, *Theological Wordbook of the Old Testament* (Moody Press 1999) word #183, #183a, p. 80
34 *Spirit Filled Life Bible* (Thomas Nelson 1991) *Word Wealth [Psalm] 112:1 delights, chafets*, p. 852
35 Hill, Gary, *The Discovery Bible*, HELPS Ministries, Inc., [H]10e, quoting TWOT (2, 554) and R. Girdlestone

> *ḥāpēṣ denotes that the object of delight has intrinsic qualities making it desirable.*[36]

Dr. David Jeremiah noted that when he traced the word "delight" through the Old Testament he was surprised to learn that the majority of its uses are in relationship to the Word of God and most often the reference is to delight in God's Word.[37] He concluded that, "There is a profound relationship between delighting in the Lord and delighting in His Word." When your fixed focus is on delighting in the Lord then "everything else is brought into perspective."[38]

In Lesson 9 we considered the importance of having focused eyesight to remain on the path of obedience. In a physical sense, research has shown that the impact of vision on our lives is much more profound than the ability to perceive clear images through our eyes. Scientists generally think that between half to two-thirds of the brain is used for visual processing.[39] That means when our eyes are open, most of the electrical activity of the brain is devoted to vision. Our vision is so powerful it can overrule information gained from the other senses.[40] What is true in the physical is also true in the spiritual. When our spiritual eyesight is delightfully

---

36 Harris, Archer, and Waltke, editors, *Theological Wordbook of the Old Testament* (Moody Press 1999) word #712, p. 310
37 The psalmists delighted in God's will as expressed in His law (Psalm 40:8); delighted in His statutes (Psalm 119:16); delighted in His commands (Psalm 119:35) and delighted in His precepts and law (Psalm 119:69–70,77,92,174)
38 *Delight Yourself in the Lord*, Precept Austin, citing Dr. David Jeremiah. Retrieved from https://www.preceptaustin.org /delight_yourself_in_the_lord (last accessed July 8, 2021)
39 Davis, Nathan, OD, *The Connection Between Vision & Balance*, December 23, 2016. Retrieved from https://vestibular.org/sites/default/files/page files/Documents/Vision%20and%20Balance_21.pdf (last accessed September 16, 2021)
40 Davis, Nathan, OD, *The Connection Between Vision & Balance*, December 23, 2016. Retrieved from https://vestibular.org/sites/default/files/

focused on God and His Word (His commands) we can successfully overrule information/temptation from fleshly desires.

King David may well have understood this Kingdom principle when he wrote these words in Psalm 37:

> **Delight** yourself in the LORD; And He will give you the desires of your heart. Psalm 37:4, bold added

Our flesh nature is quick to jump to the promise of receiving the desires of our heart. However, as Warren Wiersbe points out, "this is not a promise for people who want '*things*.'"[41] This promise is reserved for those who truly want "more of God" Himself.[42] In the Hebrew text there is a close affiliation between the phrase "delight yourself in the LORD" and the phrase "desires of your heart."[43] The connection involves God's pre-set, non-negotiable order. Delighting in the Lord is a condition that must be met first. The fulfillment of the promise that God "will give you the desires of your heart" follows. Only when the condition is satisfied can the promise be fulfilled.

To properly understand the condition and the promise of Psalm 37:4 we need to know the meaning of the word "delight" (the basis of the condition). King David used a different Hebrew word here for "delight" than the one we discussed above in Psalm 112:1.

---

page files/Documents/Vision%20and%20Balance_21.pdf (last accessed September 16, 2021)

41 *Delight Yourself in the Lord*, Precept Austin, citing Wiersbe, Warren, *Bible Exposition Commentary – Be Worshipful* (Psalms 1-89). Retrieved from https://www.preceptaustin.org /delight_yourself in_the_lord (last accessed September 16, 2021)

42 *Delight Yourself in the Lord*, Precept Austin, citing Wiersbe, Warren, *Bible Exposition Commentary – Be Worshipful (Psalms 1-89)*. Retrieved from https://www.preceptaustin.org /delight_yourself in_the_lord (last accessed September 16, 2021)

43 *Delight Yourself in the Lord*, Precept Austin, quoting Douglas Carew. Retrieved from https://www.preceptaustin.org /delight_yourself_in_the_lord (last accessed July 8, 2021)

> **WORD STUDY**
>
> *The word **delight** which I have highlighted in bold text in Psalm 37:4 is the Hebrew verb `anag {aw-nag'}. It only has a few uses in the Old Testament. `Anag comes from a root that means "to be brought up in luxury, to be pampered."*[44]
> *Its core meaning describes enjoying what is exquisite, i.e. of rare surpassing quality.*[45] *It implies the fact that what you delight in is desirable.*[46]

David was referring to satisfaction in his heart that came from delighting himself in Yahweh.[47] The *NET Bible* suggests David's use of the Hebrew *'anag* can be understood as expressing the joy he found in his relationship with Yahweh.[48] The idea behind this kind of "delight" is of a preoccupation with God Himself.[49] Ac-

---

44 *Delight Yourself in the Lord*, Precept Austin, citing Wiersbe, Warren, *Bible Exposition Commentary – Be Worshipful (Psalms 1-89)*. Retrieved from https://www.preceptaustin.org /delight_yourself in_the_lord (last accessed July 8, 2021)
45 Hill, Gary, *The Discovery Bible*, HELPS Ministries, Inc., [H]45g (SN 6026) *'ānag*
46 *Delight Yourself in the Lord*, Precept Austin, citing Douglas Carew. Retrieved from https://www.preceptaustin. org /delight_yourself_in_the_ lord (last accessed July 8, 2021)
47 Scholar J. Alec Motyer concludes that the phrase *"your soul will delight"* denotes a satisfaction of [the person's] heart." Motyer, J. Alec, *The Prophecy of Isaiah: An Introduction & Commentary* (InterVarsity Press 1993) Isaiah 55:2, p. 453, italics in original
48 *NET Bible Notes*, translator's note 37, Isaiah 58:14, indicating a similar understanding from the original Hebrew text in Psalm 37:4
49 Kidner, Derek, *Psalms 1-72: An Introduction and Commentary*, Tyndale Old Testament Commentaries (IVP Academic 1973) Psalm 37:1-11 under *The quiet spirit*, p. 167

cordingly, delight speaks of the abundance of the blessings we have in the Lord *Himself* not what He gives us. "If we truly delight in the Lord, then the chief desire of our heart will be to know Him better so we can delight in Him even more, and the Lord will satisfy that desire!"[50]

The desire/delight of God's heart is what we refer to as "His will." The point of Psalm 37:4 is not to give God lip service to get from Him what *we* want. It is to find our ultimate delight/pleasure/satisfaction in God. When we do, He plants *His* will in our hearts so that our will merges with His will. Then He gladly gives us *those* desires.

We will close this lesson with one more instructive Scripture.

> The steps of a **man** are from the LORD, and he establishes him in whose way he delights. Psalm 37:23 RSV, bold added

In the original Hebrew text, the phrase "from the Lord" is emphatic.[51] In this context the psalmist is stressing the contrast between a man's steps that are directed by God versus a man's self-directed steps. The word "man" highlighted in bold is the Hebrew word *geber* {gheh'-ber} – one of three Hebrew words properly translated as "man." In Psalm 37:23, *gerber* refers to a strong man or warrior who prevails over another because his path in life is made firm or secure by God.[52]

With this understanding, we could say, "When God is the One who establishes the steps of a person, that person is strong enough to prevail over the enemy." A man in perfect step with God excels in

---

50  *Delight Yourself in the Lord*, Precept Austin, citing Wiersbe, Warren, *Bible Exposition Commentary – Be Worshipful (Psalms 1-89)*, bold omitted from original. Retrieved from https://www.preceptaustin.org /delight_yourself_in_the_lord (last accessed July 8, 2021)

51  Kidner, Derek, *Psalms 1-72: An Introduction and Commentary*, Tyndale Old Testament Commentaries (IVP Academic 1973) Psalm 37:23,24. Cast down, but not destroyed, p. 170

52  Harris, Archer, and Waltke, editors, *Theological Wordbook of the Old Testament* (Moody Press 1999) word #310a, pp. 148-149

obedience and wins spiritual battles. The psalmist declares that God delights (*ḥāpēṣ*) in that type of man![53] Our Word Study on *ḥāpēṣ* informs us that: 1) there is strong intensity in God's emotional delight and 2) the man who permits God to establish his steps has intrinsic qualities that makes him desirable to God!

**Hear What The Spirit is Saying to the Church**: *I look at the heart. The man after my own heart is the man who desires what I desire – the man who chooses to advance my will, not his own. To that one, I come and make my will known.*[54]

---

[53] Most commentators would agree with Jewish tradition that concludes Psalm 37:23 teaches God delights in those who obey Him. Chaim & Laura, *Word Study Delight Chaphets* חפץ, December 22, 2014 Devotional, Chaim Bentorah's Daily Word Study. Retrieved from https://www.chaimbentorah.com /2014/12/word-study-delight-chaphets-חפץ/ (last accessed July 8, 2021)

[54] Personal Journal August 1, 2019

LESSON 11:

## CULTIVATING A HEART OF DESIRE-BASED OBEDIENCE

 "For God is working in you, giving you the desire and the power to do what pleases him." Philippians 2:13 NLT

BECAUSE IT IS the most pleasing to God, as well as the absolute best protection against Satan's schemes, it is important to cultivate obedience based on desire in these end times![1] That will be our focus in this lesson. To begin with, I want to return to something that I noted in Lesson 2. There we said that even though Adam and Eve's sin was the result of the serpent's deception and they could not fully anticipate all the consequences, God still held them accountable for their disobedience! The truth that God's covenant people have the responsibility of discernment permeates the biblical story. As another example, let's consider Jeremiah 14:15-16 and its context.

> So the LORD said to [Jeremiah], "Do not pray for the welfare of this people. When they fast, I am not going to listen to their cry; and when they offer burnt offering and grain offering, I am not going to accept them. Rather I am going to make an end of them by the sword, famine and pestilence." Jeremiah 14:11-12

---

1   Personal Journal December 6, 2019

God announced His judgment on His covenant people with finality. However, Jeremiah knew they had been deceived by false prophets. He appealed to God contending that it would be unfair to judge the people so harshly. From Jeremiah's perspective, the fault was with those false prophets who told the people everything was just fine and there was no reason for concern. As a matter of fact, those false prophets had accused Jeremiah of being the false prophet! Let's read the words Jeremiah spoke to Yahweh on behalf of his countrymen.

> But, "Ah, Lord GOD!" [Jeremiah] said, "Look, the prophets are telling them, 'You will not see the sword nor will you have famine, but I will give you lasting peace in this place.'" Jeremiah 14:13

Now listen to God's reply:

> Then the LORD said to [Jeremiah], "The prophets are prophesying falsehood in My name. I have neither sent them nor commanded them nor spoken to them; they are prophesying to you a false vision, divination, futility and the deception of their own minds. Therefore thus says the LORD ... those prophets shall meet their end! The people also to whom they are prophesying will be thrown out into the streets of Jerusalem because of the famine and the sword; and there will be no one to bury them—*neither* them, *nor* their wives, nor their sons, nor their daughters—for I will pour out their *own* wickedness on them." Jeremiah 14:14-16, italics in original

Clearly, God did not concur with Jeremiah's plea for mercy. The fact that false prophets had led Israel astray and reassured the people there was no need for repentance was *not* an acceptable excuse. That brings us face to face with a sobering truth of Scripture. Every person who is in covenant relationship with God is responsible for discerning false prophets from true prophets – truth from lie.

In the Old Testament, a prophet was "a proclaimer or expounder of divine matters or concerns that could not ordinarily be known except by special revelation."[2] Among the prophets, any message that undermined Yahweh's authority or attempted in any way to impair Israel's obedience to His commands should have stood out like a sore thumb so-to-speak. In fact, the dead giveaway that a prophet was a *false* prophet was his attempt to lead God's covenant people into a violation of that covenant.[3] Any type of covenant breach adversely affected Israel's relationship with God. As a result, the words of that prophet should have prompted immediate and decisive rejection![4]

Lest we assume that was the *Old* Testament and God's standards of discernment were changed by the cross, let's turn to the book of Revelation. The entirety of the vision John recorded while he was in exile on the Isle of Patmos is in the form of a warning to the church! The narrative largely unfolds in the context of two opposing worldviews – that of Babylon and that which informed the lives of the true Bride of Christ. In Revelation, Babylon is the world system ruled by the antichrist spirit with its false worship system.[5] Babylon uses her power to favor the worldly-focused earth dwellers and persecute the followers of Christ. Babylon lies and deceives and distorts the truth. Revelation promises that those who

---

2  Lowery, David K., "Matthew," in *The Bible Knowledge Word Study The Gospels*, edited by Eugene H. Merrill (Victor 2006) Matthew 11:9 under *Prophet*, p. 72, quoting *BDAG*, 890; *BAGD*, 723

3  Thompson, J. A., *The Book of Jeremiah*, The New International Commentary of The Old Testament (Eerdmans 1980) Jeremiah 14:15-16, p. 383

4  Thompson, J. A., *The Book of Jeremiah*, The New International Commentary of The Old Testament (Eerdmans 1980) Jeremiah 14:15-16, p. 383

5  Babylon is a biblical symbol that describes any human institution which demands allegiance to its idolatrous definitions of good and evil. Mackie, Tim and Collins, Jon, *Way of the Exile*, BibleProject Video. Retrieved from https://www.bing.com/search?q=The+Way+of+Exile+youtube. com&form=ANSNB1&refig=62fcd9a2c4984840b1d315873d4bac-7d&pc=U531&ntref=1 (last accessed March 20, 2022)

discern God's truth, overcome the lies and live faithfully for Christ are given the crown of life. In the language of honor and shame, crowning someone is a physical demonstration of honor being conferred upon them.[6] On the other hand, Babylon and all of her followers (the earth dwellers) are judged with a judgment that sounds very similar to the one God pronounced on His unfaithful covenant people in Jeremiah's day.

God does not change. The truth of the Old Testament applies to us today! God expects you and me to know the truth well enough that we can discern the enemy's lies. Practicing the truth is the best way to learn God's truth. However, we can't practice what we don't know. We expose ourselves to God's truth every time we read His Word. We practice truth by whole-heartedly submitting ourselves to what we read. There are no shortcuts here. Plain and simple, a Christ-follower who does not regularly spend time in God's Word leaves himself vulnerable to the enemy's lies.

The biblical motif of obedience conveys nothing short of total surrender to the will of God. Abraham is held up as the premier example of the type of obedience that God requires of His covenant people. God's demand for totally surrendered obedience is not purely arbitrary. Obedience plays a fundamental role in our proper relationship with God. As we have been learning, obedience is how God is able to retain fellowship, reveal His nature and character and release blessing. In fact, Jesus said it this way, "When you seek the Father's Kingdom, He *delights* in blessing you."[7]

The key is that God asks us to seek His Kingdom, His will on earth as it is in heaven, with *all* our hearts.[8] God always knows what is best for us. He knows that in that type of totally surrendered heart there is nothing left over – nothing remains that does not seek to obey Him. Stated differently, the heart that is totally consumed with obedience has no separate will of its own. Total-

---

6   deSilva, David A., *Hope of Glory: Honor Discourse and New Testament Interpretation* (Wipf & Stock 1999) p. 13
7   Luke 12:31-32 HCSB, my paraphrase
8   Deuteronomy 4:29, Jeremiah 29:13

ly committed whole-hearted devotion allows the desires of God's heart to replace every other desire. The result will be unbroken fellowship with God and out of that fellowship will flow blessings.

Sounds easy enough, but if we are completely honest we will admit that our fallen flesh nature does not naturally gravitate toward God. Our natural tendency is *not* to delight in God's ways. As we noted in our last lesson, unredeemed flesh inclines to lean in a direction *away* from God. Therefore, we must depend on the Holy Spirit to give us the desire and the power to lay down our independently assertive will and replace it with God's will. The good news of the gospel is that this is the very thing God delights in doing!

Our Key Scripture for this lesson comes from the apostle Paul's letter to the Philippians. I quoted the verse from the New Living Translation at the beginning of our lesson. Let's look at it in two more translations:

> [F]or it is God who works in you, both to will and to work for his good pleasure. Philippians 2:13 ESV

> [F]or the one bringing forth in you both the desire and the effort – for the sake of his good pleasure – is God. Philippians 2:13 NET

Paul lived an obedient life. He no doubt had personal familiarity with what he wrote to the church at Philippi. He knew the grace of God and could testify firsthand how *God* is the One who does all the heavy lifting. Paul knew his job was to remain in a position to receive that grace and as a result accomplish all God called him to do.

As we continue in our study I want to turn our attention to the NASB 1995, a more literal translation, of our Key Scripture:

> [F]or it is God who is at work in you, both to will and to work for *His* good pleasure. Philippians 2:13, italics in original

Using this translation of Philippians 2:13 will set the framework for a few Word Studies and explanations enabling us to better understand what Paul was communicating. Our study will be aided by a commentary-type approach so we can consider Paul's exhortation phrase by phrase.

*[F]or it is God who is at work:* The first thing we want to note in our Key Scripture is *who* is at work. Paul emphasizes God's essential role highlighting the truth that He alone supplies all the working power![9] We need to be quick here to add that Paul is *not* saying that God's power eliminates our responsibility to work hard. Let's push ahead in our study to bring clarity to this balance between our work and God's power.

A Word Study is our best starting point to consider the idea of God being at work.

### WORD STUDY

*In our Key Scripture the Greek verb energeo {en-erg-eh'-o} is used twice; first translated as* **at work** *and secondly as* **to work**. *In the New Testament, energeo almost always describes supernatural energizing activity attributed to God.*[10]

*The related noun energeia emphasizes inner strength that is supplied by God.*[11]

---

9   *Philippians 2:13 Commentary*, Precept Austin. Retrieved from https://www.preceptaustin.org/philippians_213 (last accessed July 8, 2021)
10  *Philippians 2:13 Commentary*, Precept Austin. Retrieved from https://www.preceptaustin.org/philippians_213 (last accessed July 8, 2021)
11  *Colossians 1:29 Commentary*, Precept Austin, citing *New American Commentary*. Retrieved from http://www.preceptaustin.org/colossians_129 (last accessed July 8, 2021)

> *Energeo* denotes active energy (divine power) that produces an effect. It is distinguishable from potential power denoted by the word *dynamis*.[12]

*Energeo* is energy in operation that produces an outcome. A good analogy is an electrical current flowing through a wire to illuminate a light bulb.[13] Or as scholar Lynn Cohick offers, we can think of *energeia* as the energy produced when a stick of dynamite explodes.[14] Before the wick is lit the dynamite only has potential power, however when it explodes that hidden power is made visible. Paul says through the indwelling Holy Spirit, God supernaturally supplies a consistent source of effective, energetic power to the Christ-follower. As we will see, God-given energy provides us with the necessary will and power for supernatural obedience.[15]

**to will (NASB) - *giving you the desire* (NLT):** In a lesson that considers not only the *need* for a heart filled with desire-based obedience, but seeks to understand *how* to cultivate that type of obedience this is a key biblical truth to understand. Let's see what Paul meant when he referred to "desire."

## Word Study

*In our Key Scripture the Greek word thelo {thel'-o} is translated as* **to will** *in the NASB and it is translated as*

---

12  Hill, Gary, *The Discovery Bible*, HELPS Ministries, Inc., [G]1754 *energéō*, citing Abbott-Smith; Zodhiates, Spiros, *The Complete Word Study Dictionary: New Testament* (AMG Publishers 1992) word #1754, p. 589

13  Hill, Gary, *The Discovery Bible*, HELPS Ministries, Inc., [G]1754 *energéō*

14  Cohick, Linn H., *The Letter To The Ephesians*, The New International Commentary of the New Testament (Eerdmans 2020) a. Prayer for the Ephesians ([Ephesians] 1:15-19 under *[Ephesians] 17-19*, p. 121

15  *Philippians 2:13 Commentary*, Precept Austin. Retrieved from https://www.preceptaustin.org/philippians_213 (last accessed July 8, 2021)

> **desire** in the NLT. *Thelo* implies an active preference and purpose. It denotes thoughtful, purpose-driven choice, not merely emotional desire or impulse.[16]
> *Thelo* denotes choice that pushes all the way to action.[17]

Warren Wiersbe refers to the life of a Christ-follower as "a process of 'ins and outs.' God works in, and we work out."[18] We see that *in and out process* in Philippians 2:13. "God works in humans, producing the desire to fulfill God's will and the power to achieve it. Paul admonishes the Philippians 'to work out' what God in his grace 'worked in.'"[19]

God places His desire in us and with the power He provides, we press forward to the action that is required to fulfill that desire. As we have noted, Paul was a student of the Old Testament. His teaching to the church at Philippi most certainly came out of his own personal experience, but his grasp of this truth was bolstered by revelation recorded in the Old Testament. Let's turn to Haggai Chapter 1 and you will see what I mean.

> So the LORD **stirred up** the spirit of Zerubbabel ... governor of Judah, and the spirit of Joshua ... the high priest, and the spirit of all the remnant of the people; and

---

16 Zodhiates, Spiros, *The Complete Word Study Dictionary: New Testament* (AMG Publishers 1992) word #2309, pp. 727-728; *Philippians 2:13 Commentary*, Precept Austin. Retrieved from https://www.preceptaustin.org/philippians_213 (last accessed July 8, 2021)
17 Zodhiates, Spiros, *The Complete Word Study Dictionary: New Testament* (AMG Publishers 1992) word #2309, pp. 727-728
18 *Philippians 2:13 Commentary*, Precept Austin, quoting Warren Wiersbe, *Bible Exposition Commentary* (Victory 1989). Retrieved from https://www.preceptaustin.org/philippians_213 (last accessed July 8, 2021)
19 Garland, David E., "Philippians," in *The Expositor's Bible Commentary: Ephesians – Philemon*, Vol. 12, Revised Edition, edited by Longman III and Garland (Zondervan Academic 2006) Philippians 2:13, p. 225, citing Müller, 91

*The Power of Obedience* 211

they came and worked on the house of the LORD of hosts, their God. Haggai 1:14, bold added

"Stirred up" (highlighted in bold text on page 210) is a translation of the Hebrew verb `uwr` {oor}. The *ESV Study Bible* explains the verb this way, "God awakens in the people an intense desire" to do the work He commanded.[20] At a time in Israel's history when they were overwhelmed by the task of rebuilding the Jerusalem temple, Haggai makes clear that it was *God* who supplied the necessary desire. He initiated their obedience by giving them His desire and ability which then motivated their action.[21]

In our Key Scripture, the Greek verb *thelo* leads to a similar result. As noted in our Word Study, *thelo* pushes all the way to action. That inward motivation is a key way in which *desired* obedience differs from *willing* obedience. (*This is a good place to remind you that these obedience labels are not found in the Bible, I have developed them and am using them for the sake of discussion in this study.*)

Willing obedience often waits on God with an attitude that is lackadaisical, apathetic, indifferent, lacking concern as to the completion of that which God has commanded. The resulting attitude is whatever will be, will be. *Que sera, sera.* On the other hand, desire-based obedience is a "resolute willingness"[22] that delights in

---

20  *ESV Study Bible* (Crossway Books 2008) study note Haggai 1:14 under *the Lord stirred up the spirit*, p. 1745; This same truth of God stirring up desire to initiate action is also found, for example, in Zechariah 9:13. Meyers and Meyers, *Haggai, Zechariah 9-14: A New Translation with Introduction and Commentary*, The Anchor Bible Vol 25B (Doubleday 1987) Zechariah 9:13 under *rouse ... against*, p. 147

21  *NET Bible Notes*, study note 28, Haggai 1:14; Meyers and Meyers, *Haggai, Zechariah 1-8: A New Translation with Introduction and Commentary*, The Anchor Bible Vol 25B (Doubleday 1987) Haggai 1:14 under *roused the spirit*, p. 35

22  Bromiley, Geoffrey W., *Theological Dictionary of the New Testament*, Abridged in One Volume (Eerdmans 1985) entry for *thelo* under *A. The Common Greek Meaning of (e)thelo*, p. 319

God's will. That desire then motivates all the follow-through necessary to ensure that, once initiated, obedience crosses the finish line.

Paul plainly states that we do not initiate that type of desire. It is only possible when God places *His* desire in our hearts! A genuine determination to do God's will, as well as the power to obey it, always originates with God. The desire to do what is pleasing to God develops in the heart of every Christ-follower who fully and unconditionally submits to the work of the Holy Spirit.

*for His good pleasure (NASB) - to do what pleases Him (NLT):* In our Key Scripture the Greek word *eudokia* {yoo-dok-ee'-ah} is translated as pleasure. At its core meaning *eudokia* conveys the idea of what seems good or beneficial to someone.[23] In Paul's writings, *eudokia* most often refers to God's good pleasure or benevolent will.[24]

The Kingdom of God is exactly that – it is *God's* Kingdom, not ours! Of necessity that means God's Kingdom advances according to what pleases Him – what He deems good and beneficial. Chuck Swindoll points out:[25]

> As [God] pours His power into us, we do the things that bring Him pleasure. Take special note that *His* pleasures (not ours), *His* will (not ours), *His* glory (not ours) are what make life meaningful.

For His will to be done on earth as it is in Heaven demands that we submit our will to His so completely and unconditionally that we listen to His voice and do what He says. Paul calls this being *led by the Spirit of God*. By that, he means we are being "'controlled by' or 'determined by' or 'governed by' the [Holy] Spir-

---

23 Hill, Gary *The Discovery Bible*, HELPS Ministries, Inc., Cognate: [G]2107 *eudokia*
24 Bromiley, Geoffrey W., *Theological Dictionary of the New Testament*, Abridged in One Volume (Eerdmans 1985) entry for *eudokia* under *E. eduokia in the NT*, p. 274
25 *Philippians 2:13 Commentary*, Precept Austin, quoting Chuck Swindoll, italics added. Retrieved from https://www.preceptaustin.org/philippians_213 (last accessed July 8, 2021)

*The Power of Obedience* 213

it."[26] When Paul talked about being "led" by the Spirit in Romans 8:14, the Greek verb he used is *ago* {ag'-o}. It is the root for *agon*.[27] What is insightful about that connection is *agon* {ag-one'} refers to "*an intense conflict*" of some kind, including one involving the human will.[28]

In Romans 8:1-17 Paul describes the conflict every Christ-follower faces between flesh and Holy Spirit. Paul recognizes that sin is a power stronger than the human will (on its own) to obey God.[29] On the other hand, submission to the Spirit always results in obedience because God's Spirit *always* obeys God's will. In other words, those who habitually allow the Spirit to govern their lives are *not* driven by the desires of their flesh, their decisions are controlled by what pleases God.

The question is, "What does it take for a Christ-follower to be controlled by or led by the Holy Spirit?" Simply put, we allow Holy Spirit to be fully and freely who He is. As a Christ-follower you have all of the Holy Spirit, but that does not *automatically* mean Holy Spirit has all of you![30] For Him to be fully enabled to do all that God desires, demands we allow Him to be fully in charge! Because the Spirit knows the mind of Christ and knows

---

26   Schreiner, Thomas R., *Romans*, Baker Exegetical Commentary on the New Testament, 2nd edition (Baker Academic 1998, 2018) Romans 8:14, p. 416
27   The form of the verb *ago* Paul used in the original Greek "is significant; it suggests that the Spirit is the primary agent in Christian obedience, that it is his work in believers that accounts for their obedience." Schreiner, Thomas R., *Romans*, Baker Exegetical Commentary on the New Testament, 2nd edition (Baker Academic 1998, 2018) Romans 8:14, p. 416, citations omitted
28   Renner, Rick, *Sparkling Gems from the Greek Volume II* (Harrison House Publishers 2016) June 9, p. 548, italics in original
29   Keck, Leander E., *Romans*, Abingdon New Testament Commentaries (Abingdon Press 2005) The Power of the Spirit ([Romans] 8:1-17), p. 194
30   Shirer, Priscilla, *Discerning the Voice of God: How to Recognize When God Speaks* (LifeWay Press 2006) DVD Session 2, The Holy Spirit

the Father's will, when He is given free rein He is perfectly aligned and empowered to accomplish God's will.

As we have noted, the Bible recognizes the battle that exists between the desires of our flesh and the desires of God. However, it is a battle we are entirely capable of winning. The key is to be so driven by the desires of God's heart that we have no independent will of our own. When that happens the wants of our heart mirror God's. That means the answer we seek to every prayer and every circumstance is whatever will bring Him the most glory.

The only way that happens in the life of a Spirit-filled Christ-follower is that we refrain from turning down the volume knob when Holy Spirit is speaking and we refuse to turn down the power knob when He is acting! We allow Holy Spirit the freedom to lead and we obediently follow. That will ensure that God will accomplish His good and pleasing will through us.

On the other hand, when Christ-followers choose self-will over God's will, we can expect God's purposeful discipline. Let's return to the potter/clay imagery we discussed in Lesson 8. The metaphor found in Jeremiah 18 portrays God as a Master Potter and His covenant people as lumps of clay in His skillful hands. It provides a helpful metaphor to instruct us about God's discipline.

Jeremiah 18:1-12 points out that the quality of the clay that lies on the Potter's wheel determines what the Potter is able to do with that clay. Only when the lump is *obedient* clay, can the Potter's original intention be fulfilled.[31] Our disobedience renders us unsuitable to be the vessel God had sovereignly designed for His purposes.

God's discipline is a picture of Him as the Master Potter sitting at His Potter's wheel working with a lump of clay that is not serving its intended function. Through divine discipline, He will skillfully

---

31 Thompson, J. A., *The Book of Jeremiah*, The New International Commentary of The Old Testament (Eerdmans 1980) Jeremiah 18:1-3, p. 433

*The Power of Obedience*

reshape that clay.[32] As He does, Isaiah warns the clay has no right whatsoever to question God's authority to do so![33]

> "Woe to the one who argues with his Maker—one clay pot among many. Does clay say to the one forming it, 'What are you making?' ..." Isaiah 45:9 HCSB

Reshaping the clay is God's way of providing for a do-over. God intends to energize those newly shaped lumps of clay to obey and serve Him! The truth of the matter is that it is always for our best to be cooperative clay in God's skillful hands.

We have said that to become mature in our faith, we want to allow God to move us from obedience based on *willingness* to obedience that is driven by *desire*. The last question we want to address in this lesson is, "How do we cultivate a heart of desire-based obedience?" We will finish out our lesson by considering the truth that we become what we behold.

All humans have been created to be reflecting beings.[34] While we were uniquely fashioned by God to reflect Him, we will in fact reflect whatever we are devoted to, whatever we value the most. By His creative design, we always resemble what we revere (worship). Because it's in our nature to bear the image of something, it is impossible to be neutral on this matter. We either reflect the Creator (because we worship Him) or something in creation (because we have given our worship to it).[35]

In 2 Corinthians 3:18, Paul exhorts Christ-followers to "behold" the image of God Himself because it is the only way we can become like Him! Beholding requires a fixed and determined gaze – *setting our face like flint* with intentional resolve to see God and

---

32 Thompson, J. A., *The Book of Jeremiah*, The New International Commentary of The Old Testament (Eerdmans 1980) Jeremiah 18:1-3, p. 433
33 Motyer, J. Alec, *The Prophecy of Isaiah: An Introduction & Commentary* (InterVarsity Press 1993) Isaiah 45:9-11, p. 361
34 Beale, G. K., *We Become What We Worship* (IVP Academic 2008) p. 22
35 Beale, G. K., *We Become What We Worship* (IVP Academic 2008) pp. 16, 22

become like Him.[36] As we fix our gaze on His image, we behold His glory. In other words, we see Him as He truly is.

So, the question naturally arises, how do we behold God as He really is? I'd like to suggest several disciplines that bring us into closer relationship with God. The starting place is to be in God's Word daily, reading it with a humble, teachable spirit.

When reporting on the results of their 2011 *Transformational Discipleship* study, LifeWay Research concluded that reading and studying the Bible are the activities that have the *most impact* on growth towards spiritual maturity. The report found that even though that discipline is so basic to discipleship there are "numerous churchgoers who are not reading the Bible regularly."[37] The study concluded that a Christ-follower "simply won't grow if [they] don't know God and spend time in God's Word.... Bible engagement points people toward maturity and maturing Christians have practices that correspond to Bible reading."[38]

---

36 The phrase "I have set My face like flint" is used in Isaiah 50:7 to describe the resolute determination the Messiah would have for doing God's will. "So sure was He of the Lord God's help that He resolutely determined to remain unswayed by whatever hardship might await Him." MacArthur, John, *The MacArthur Study Bible* (Thomas Nelson 2006) study note Isaiah 50:7 under *set My face like flint*, p. 1012. Luke tells us that Jesus fulfilled this Messianic prophecy: *"When the days drew near for [Jesus] to be taken up, he set his face to go to Jerusalem."* Luke 9:51 ESV

37 Ranking, Russ, *Bible Engagement in Churchgoers' Hearts, Not Always Practiced*. Retrieved from https://www.lifeway.com/en/articles/research-survey-bible-engagement-churchgoers (last accessed July 8, 2021)

38 Ranking, Russ, *Bible Engagement in Churchgoers' Hearts, Not Always Practiced*. Retrieved from https://www.lifeway.com/en/articles/research-survey-bible-engagement-churchgoers (last accessed July 8, 2021). The LifeWay research team discovered 8 factors that are at work in the lives of Believers who are progressing in spiritual maturity. Lifeway calls them the attributes of discipleship: 1) Bible engagement; 2) obeying God and denying self; 3) serving God and others; 4) sharing Christ; 5) exercising faith; 6) seeking God; 7) building relationships and 8) transparency. Lifeway, *Transformational Research Identifies Eight Attributes of Growing Disciples,* Communications Staff, January 01, 2014. Retrieved

I love the suggestion one author made:[39]

> Instead of watching a Netflix movie tonight, why don't you set aside a couple of uninterrupted hours and ask God's Spirit to unveil the words of [one of the] Gospel[s] as you read through it in one sitting (or two sittings over successive nights). A good movie might have given you temporal joy, but a good book [of the Bible] will give you eternal transformation!

I recently heard Carol Kent speak at a Women's Retreat. She told of a time when she was in college and a Chapel speaker challenged the students to choose one book of the Bible and read it over and over for an entire month. The speaker guaranteed that by the end of that month they *would* be transformed by what they read. Carol said she undertook the challenge, could personally attest to its transforming power and admonished each of her listeners to accept the same challenge.

Regularly reading God's Word with an open heart is the most important place to begin, but there's more. From my own experience, other effective spiritual disciplines that provide meaningful opportunities for transformational growth to occur include: meditating on God's Word; praying His Word; studying His Word to mature from milk to meat; believing His Word by faith; quickly agreeing with God's discipline; confessing sin; asking for forgiveness and obeying His Word by intentionally putting His commands into practice in increasing measure. Additional disciplines include fasting as directed and guided by the Holy Spirit; serving others in agape love and obedient, cheerful stewardship of your time, talent and treasure. Worshipping Him and being in regular fellowship with others who practice these disciplines are imperatives in the life of every Christ-follower. We were created for fellowship. There are

---

from https://www.lifeway.com/en/articles/transformational-research-attributes-of-growing-disciples (last accessed March 25, 2022)

39 *John 1:1 Commentary,* Precept Austin. Retrieved from http://www.preceptaustin.org/john_11_commentary (last accessed July 8, 2021)

no lone rangers in God's Kingdom! Remember the enemy prowls around like a roaring lion seeking whom he may devour and lone rangers are his easiest prey.[40]

Our hearts are constantly being formed and fashioned into the image of whatever we focus on. A. W. Tozer is credited with comparing this process to that of an old film camera.[41] Images on cameras used to be imbedded and stored on a piece of film. The process of capturing the photographed image on the film involved focusing the camera lens on the object and holding the camera shutter open. Basically, once the camera shutter was open two things affected the picture: 1) the amount and type of light and 2) the length of time the camera shutter remained open. Spiritually speaking the same two factors determine the images that get imbedded and stored in our hearts. First, the heart image that gets imbedded is determined by whether the object we focus on honors the Kingdom of Light or the kingdom of darkness. Second, how long the shutter of our heart is open towards that object determines the degree of heart impact.[42] In short, what we are focused on and how long we fix our eyes on it will determine how it impacts our heart.

Because this is true, developing the regular habit of spiritual discipline is imperative in the life of *every* disciple. We cannot occasionally come to the Word of God for a few leftover crumbs; we cannot refuse to sit in His Presence daily; we cannot ignore His commands by living life on our own terms and expect to become

---

40  1 Peter 5:8
41  Synder, John, *Beholding and Becoming: Christ-Focused Sanctification*, Series: Looking Unto Jesus, Behold Your God Radio broadcast September 24, 2014. Retrieved from http://beholdyourgod.org/resource/beholding-and-becoming-christ-focused-sanctification/ (original access 2017, webpage no longer available)
42  Synder, John, *Beholding and Becoming: Christ-Focused Sanctification*, Series: Looking Unto Jesus, Behold Your God Radio broadcast September 24, 2014. Retrieved from http://beholdyourgod.org/resource/beholding-and-becoming-christ-focused-sanctification/ (original access 2017, webpage no longer available)

more like Him! There will be a very direct correlation between how long the shutter of our heart is open towards God and the degree of impact on our heart. That's why we are commanded to love Him with **all** of our heart, mind, soul and strength. Nothing less transforms us into the image of Christ. My responsibility is to nurture a heart attitude of desire, then God will release the desires of His heart into my heart and will supercharge my obedience through unhindered Holy Spirit power.

Several years ago, a good friend of ours shocked us with the announcement that he had just been diagnosed with a form of leukemia. His treatment plan called for a bone marrow transplant. Thankfully one of his brothers was a match and agreed to go through the process of the donation. Today our friend is in remission and doing well thanks to the successful, prayer-saturated transplant. I share that story because I believe it is a picture of how the desires of God's heart become the desires of our hearts. The image I have of that bone marrow transplant procedure would make trained medical personnel laugh heartily. Even though somewhat child-like in its imagery, I'll share it here because I think it provides a good analogy for God's strategy of replacing our own desires with the ones that originate in His heart.

I imagine two hospital beds side-by-side. The bone marrow donor is lying in one bed and the recipient in the other. I imagine a single clear tube which is the sole connecting point between the two. When the procedure begins, healthy bone marrow from the donor flows unhindered through that clear tube directly to the recipient. As it does, the recipient's unhealthy bone marrow is increasingly displaced by the donor's healthy bone marrow. By the end of the procedure, all that remains in the recipient is the donor's bone marrow.

Now imagine with me that God is in the first hospital bed and you are in the second one. What connects the two of you is the Holy Spirit. What flows from God to you is His desires and as they do they displace your fleshly desires until all that remains in your heart are God's desires.

As we delight ourselves in the Lord He reshapes our heart so that the desires of *His* heart become the desires of *our* heart. That's true heart transformation and it is a death knell to the power of the kingdom of darkness.

Our last lesson in the study will look at the end result of God's power at work in and through our obedience.

**Hear What The Spirit is Saying to the Church**: *Unless My people develop a heart of desire-based obedience I am not able to fulfill the purpose for which I created them.*

LESSON 12:

USHERING IN
THE NEW HEAVEN
AND NEW EARTH

 "For all creation is waiting eagerly for that future day when God will reveal who his children really are. Against its will, all creation was subjected to God's curse. But with eager hope, the creation looks forward to the day when it will join God's children in glorious freedom from death and decay. For we know that all creation has been groaning as in the pains of childbirth right up to the present time." Romans 8:19-22 NLT

AS ODD AS it may sound to our Western ears, the purpose of the New Testament is not to inform us how to get to heaven. "The New Testament is designed to draw us into the story of God's plan to rescue the world from chaos and idolatry and to launch His new transformative creation."[1] The end result of God's plan is captured in the biblical phrase "new heaven and earth." Our last lesson seeks to understand how that "new heaven and earth" becomes a reality *on earth*.

The ancient understanding of the universe was captured in the phrase "heaven and earth" which was a reference to all of creation.[2]

---

1   Wright, N.T., "Beginning New Testament Study, and a Conversation in Jerusalem," in *The New Testament in Its World*, Podcast EP1 (Zondervan Academic). Retrieved from https://zondervanacademic.com/pages/new-testament-in-its-world#podcast (last accessed September 17, 2021)
2   Ryken, Wilhoit, and Longman III, editors, *Dictionary of Biblical Imagery* (Intervarsity Press 1998) entry for *World*, p. 967; Motyer, J. Alec, *The Prophecy of Isaiah: An Introduction & Commentary* (InterVarsity Press 1993) Isaiah 65:17, p. 529

From our Key Scripture for this lesson, we learn that ever since sin entered God's created order the totality of His creation has been sighing and groaning.[3] In the beginning, God proclaimed the world He had created was good. However, creation has not been able to fulfill the purpose for which it was fashioned by God. In Romans 8:19-22, Paul explains that this was not by its own choice. The created world was subjected to death and decay as a result of Adam's sin. Because creation has been longing to be set free, it has been groaning ever since.

While sin leads to captivity, obedience results in the freedom God has desired for His creation. In Romans 8:21, Paul explains that the entire captive universe eagerly yearns for the day when it will be liberated from frustration, suffering and oppression. Paul's description pictures the full realization of the new heavens and new earth when, according to John's words in Revelation, "no longer will there be any curse (Revelation 22:3)."

> Paul envisions the day when "the children of God fully share in God's glory—his divine life and all that characterizes it—then they will be restored to their role of exercising God-like dominion over creation."... He envisions a future salvation that will engulf the entire cosmos and reverse and transcend the consequences of the fall.... We await a new creation ... which doesn't mean the annihilation of this world and the creation of a new world. Instead, the present world will be transformed and purified of all evil.[4]

---

3   "Groaning" is a translation of the Greek word *sustenazo* {soos-ten-ad'-zo} which is a compound word. The Greek word *"sun"* refers to that which is done together + *"stenazo"* refers to groaning or sighing. The compound word means to groan or sigh together. Zodhiates, Spiros, *The Complete Word Study Dictionary: New Testament* (AMG Publishers 1992) word #4959, p. 1349

4   Schreiner, Thomas R., *Romans*, Baker Exegetical Commentary on the New Testament, 2nd edition (Baker Academic 1998, 2018) Romans 8:20-21, pp. 428-429, citations omitted

## The Power of Obedience

When the sin-curse is lifted, all creation will be restored to the purity of the Eden-like reflection of God's glory. Paul's thought in Romans 8:21 falls right in line with ancient Jewish literature. Those authors spoke of a new heaven and earth that would fulfill the original purpose of creation.[5]

According to the Bible, the renewal of God's physical creation is inseparably connected to the redemption of His covenant people.[6] Every person who is *in Christ* is a new creation and the first fruits of the full renewal yet to come.[7] I'm using the phrase "in Christ" in a positional sense – referring to being in proper relationship with Christ resulting in our redeemed status. The completed work of redemption anticipates the reversal of the curse on creation. When at last the weight of sin is removed, all of nature will explode in glory and God will be rightfully reigning as the unchallenged King of the universe.

Both the Old Testament and the New Testament explicitly declare that the Kingdom of God is the centerpiece of the gospel, the Good News. Jesus assured those who inquired that the work of ushering in the Kingdom of God had begun through Him.[8] An obedient people who have declared God to be their King permits Him to dwell among them as their God.[9] Even so, we only live in the foretaste of the age to come while at the same time remaining in the present evil age. When the age to come is in its fullest measure,

---

5   See for example: Isaiah 65:17; 66:22; 1 Enoch 45.4-5; 2 Baruch 31.5-32.6; 2 Esdras [4 Ezra] 7:11,30-32,75. Schreiner, Thomas R., *Romans*, Baker Exegetical Commentary on the New Testament, 2nd edition (Baker Academic 1998, 2018) Romans 8:22, p. 429

6   Schreiner, Thomas R., *Romans*, Baker Exegetical Commentary on the New Testament, 2nd edition (Baker Academic 1998, 2018) Romans 8:22, p. 429, citing Isaiah 11:6-9; 43:19-21; 55:12-13; Ezekiel 34:25-31; Hosea 2:18; Zechariah 8:12

7   2 Corinthians 5:17; Matera, Frank J., *II Corinthians* (Westminster John Knox Press 2003) 2 Corinthians 5:16-17, pp. 135-137; See also: Ephesians 2:15, 4:24

8   Matthew 11:2-6; Luke 7:18-23; 17:20-21

9   Jeremiah 31:33; Ezekiel 11:20, 37:27; 2 Corinthians 6:16; Hebrews 8:10; Revelation 21:7

those who have been faithful to God will be living in the completely consummated new heaven and new earth.

God's eternal Kingdom on earth will reach its fullness at the second coming of Christ. In between His first and second coming Jesus gave His disciples work to do. He expects us to advance His Kingdom on earth as it is in heaven. As we do that work, we are ushering in the new creation – the new heaven and earth. In other words, it is the body of Christ who "serves as the agent of life and renewal to a world that languishes under the curse of sin and death."[10]

There are many different ways we could approach the goal we have for this lesson. The one I feel led to use draws a direct correlation between what we commonly call "The Great Commission" and the advancement of the Kingdom of God. Let's begin by looking at the last recorded command Jesus gave His disciples before He ascended into heaven. Based on the authority He had been given, Jesus commanded His followers to:

> "… Go, therefore, and make disciples of all nations, baptizing them in the name of the Father and of the Son and of the Holy Spirit, **teaching them to observe everything I have commanded you….**" Matthew 28:19-20 HCSB, bold added

Notice that Jesus didn't just say, "Make disciples by baptizing people." He said the assignment is to "make disciples" and then He explained how to do that: 1) by baptizing them *and* 2) by teaching them to observe everything He has commanded. In short, the mission of the church is to make Kingdom disciples – true obedient *talmidim*.

Before we proceed further, I want to park here for a moment and quote from the Preface to this study where I explain the use of the plural Hebrew word *talmidim* – translated as disciples.

---

[10] Block, Daniel I., *The Book of Ezekiel: Chapters 25-48*, The New International Commentary on the Old Testament (Eerdmans 1998) Ezekiel 47:8-12 under *Theological Implications*, p. 702

By the time of Jesus, discipleship was well-established within the Jewish culture. All the great sages, rabbis and the teachers of the Torah had *talmidim* (disciples). A *talmid* (a disciple) was on a pilgrimage that was far more than an intellectual pursuit. The *talmid's* goal was to be *like* the rabbi – he wanted to assimilate the essence of who the rabbi was into his own life. This was radical discipleship – it was a complete re-making of the one who was being discipled so as to become like his rabbi in knowledge, wisdom and ethical behavior.

In other words, the *talmid's* deepest desire was to follow his rabbi so closely that he would start to think and act just like his rabbi. Jesus summed up the goal of discipleship this way: *"every disciple fully trained will be like his teacher."*[11] A *talmid's* behavior would be a reflection on their teacher's reputation – either positively or negatively.[12] That means perseverance was a standard requirement for every *talmid*.[13] Once a *talmid* was fully trained, he would become a teacher and he would disciple *talmidim* of his own. What Jesus had begun by making *talmidim* of His first followers, the body of Christ now does as they make new *talmidim* of Jesus. We see the apostle Paul following this established rabbinic pattern when he says, *"Imitate me, as I also imitate Christ. Now I praise you because you always remember me and keep the traditions just as I delivered them to you."*[14]

Next, let's undertake two Word Studies to be sure we understand the commission Jesus has given us as His *talmidim*. The first

---

11  Luke 6:40
12  Keener, Craig S., *The Gospel Of John: A Commentary*, Volume Two (Hendrickson Publishers 2003) John 13:34-35, citing e.g., Aeschines Timarchus 171-173 among others, pp. 926-927
13  Keener, Craig S., *The Gospel Of John: A Commentary*, Volume Two (Hendrickson Publishers 2003) John 13:34-35, p. 926
14  1 Corinthians 11:1-2

word we will consider is the word "observe" and then we'll study the word "commanded."

> **WORD STUDY**
>
> *In the Great Commission the word translated as **observe** is the Greek word tereo {tay-reh'-o} which refers to guarding some precious thing in your possession.*
>
> *Tereo denoted a soldier who fulfilled his duty by being steadfastly faithful on his assigned watch no matter how many or what type of assaults he had to endure.*[15]
>
> *Used in a figurative sense, tereo refers to obeying, observing, performing a duty watchfully and vigilantly.*[16]

When you receive Jesus as Lord and Savior, you are born from above as a new creation now having a new life, new desires, new values, a new direction and the indwelling power of the Holy Spirit. To "keep" the word of God or His commands is to walk faithfully with God on the narrow road of discipleship by consistently refusing compromise in the face of temptation. As individual *talmid* do this, they collectively (as the church) become a visible and viable alternative to the systems of the world in this evil age.

In the original Greek the command in Matthew 28:20 to *tereo* pictures ongoing, continual, habitual action. Enabled by the Holy Spirit, obedient Christ-followers demonstrate *tereo* in their walk with Christ by diligently obeying all of His commands.[17] Those

---

15  Renner, Rick, *Sparkling Gems from the Greek* (Harrison House Publishers 2003) May 3, p. 303
16  Zodhiates, Spiros, *The Complete Word Study Dictionary: New Testament* (AMG Publishers 1992) word #5083, p. 1380
17  Hill, Gary, *The Discovery Bible*, HELPS Ministries, Inc., [G]5083 *tēréō*. Thankfully John reminds us as "little children" that when we miss the

*The Power of Obedience*

who *tereo* His commands walk in holy fear of being disobedient.[18] That doesn't mean they are afraid of God. (See Lesson 3 Word Study on fear – *yare* '). Holy fear essentially refers to worshipfully submitting to God's revealed will out of a sense of reverent awe and respect.[19] Those who fear the Lord are able to enjoy intimate fellowship with Him (Proverbs 3:32). The author of Hebrews acknowledges that the prayers of Jesus were heard because He feared His Father.[20]

Disciples are to be taught to obey God's commands as a continuous life-long habit. What we commonly call "the great commission" reinstates God's instruction to Adam and Eve to, "Be fruitful and multiply. Fill the earth and govern it. Reign over [that which God has created] (Genesis 1:28 NLT)."[21] It is through the fulfillment of this reinstated mandate to "fill, govern and reign over" that the new creation Christ began will be successfully consummated at His second coming.[22]

---

mark, confess and repent Jesus is an advocate with the Father on our behalf.

18  *1 John 2:1-6 Commentary*, Precept Austin, citing Wuest, *Word Studies In The Greek New Testament*, Volume 1-3 (Eerdman Publishing Company 1973). Retrieved from www.preceptaustin.org/1john_21-6_commentary (last accessed July 8, 2021). The Bible does not place the love of God and the fear of God in tension with each other. In biblical understanding they rightfully coexist. Levenson, Jon D., *The Love of God: Divine Gift, Human Gratitude, and Mutual Faithfulness in Judaism* (Princeton University Press 2016) p. 31

19  Waltke, Bruce K., *The Book of Proverbs: Chapters 1-15*, The New International Commentary on the Old Testament (Eerdmans 2004) Introduction, p. 65

20  Hebrews 5:7 KJV; other translations render the Greek word *eulabeia* {yoo-lab'-i-ah} as devotion (NET); reverence (CSB); godliness (CJB); piety (NAS 1977)

21  Beale, G. K., *A New Testament Biblical Theology* (Baker Academic 2011) p. 423

22  The biblical concept of "dominion mandate" causes alarm in some Christian circles, even going so far as to be labeled a heresy. However, the ordinary meaning of the words in Genesis 1:28 "actually form two commands: reproduce and rule.... [I]n ruling [Adam and Eve] will serve

Now let's consider the word "commanded."

> ### WORD STUDY
>
> In the Great Commission the word translated as **commanded** is the Greek verb entellomai {en-tel'-lom-ahee} which means to enjoin, charge or give commandments.
>
> In the first century, the related noun entole referred to the command of an official such as a king or to a teacher's instruction.[23]
>
> In the Greek translation of the Bible, entole translates the Hebrew word mitzvah.

Did you happen to catch the fact that Jesus uses a word which in an ordinary sense referred to the command of a King? For citizens of God's Kingdom salvation does *not* mean life without obligation. Christ has given us freedom; however, that freedom *demands* a certain code of conduct – the narrow path of righteousness. Biblical righteousness has at its very core the notion of conforming to a standard. One who is considered righteous does what is expected according to covenant obligations. When you behave in the way God expects in your relationship with Him and others He considers you to be righteous.[24] From a Jewish perspec-

---

as God's vice-regents on earth. They together, the human race collectively, have the responsibility of seeing to the welfare of that which is put under them and the privilege of using it for their benefit." *NET Bible Notes*, study note 59, Genesis 1:28

23 Bromiley, Geoffrey W., *Theological Dictionary of the New Testament* (Eerdmans 1985) entry for *entellomai* under A. *entole outside the NT*, p. 234

24 Meier, Sam, *Misunderstood Terms in the Bible 2020*, Lesson 1, Messianic Studies Institute, Term 4 2020

tive, this type of "righteousness is regarded as an eternal *duty* to the King of Glory."[25]

As we have said, in the world God created, sin always leads to captivity but obedience sets the captive free! We are not free to do whatever we wish. We are captives who have been set free to obey God's *entole*. The "new heaven and earth" that results refers to a universe "new in quality because [unhindered] righteousness has settled in and taken up permanent and exclusive residence."[26] The wicked have been forever cut off from God's presence.[27]

The entirety of Scripture – both Old and New Testaments – teaches that it matters to God what is in our heart when we obey His commands. We will be aided by a little side trip which will bring us to a right understanding of the true nature of salvation. Rightly understanding what it means to be "saved" will allow us see that a grateful heart of obedience flows naturally out of salvation. In fact, we are going to conclude that gratitude is actually part of the biblical definition of salvation!

Every book of the New Testament was authored by men who were well versed in Jewish life and thought.[28] That means their understanding of salvation came from their Jewish heritage and that definition was not changed by the Calvary cross. When the New Testament says that Jesus *saves* us from our sins neither Paul, nor any other writer, steps aside to define what it means to be "saved." A definition was not necessary because the entirety of the Old Covenant Scripture fully explains what the word means. So, let us go back to the most accurate New Testament dictionary there is

---

25 Rabbi Yisrael Ben Avraham, *The Standard Is Glory* (Xulon Press 2015) p. 147, italics added
26 MacArthur, John, *The MacArthur Study Bible* (Thomas Nelson 2006) study note to 2 Peter 3:13 under *righteousness dwells*, p. 1930, citations omitted
27 Psalm 37:9,10,20
28 As noted in the Preface, recent research suggests that absent evidence otherwise even Luke must be held to be Jewish. Henri Louis Goulet, Email to Deborah Roeger March 27, 2022, citing the work of Isaac Oliver on Luke

(i.e. the Old Testament) to gain an understanding of the fullness of this very important word.

The best place to start our discussion of salvation is back in the book of Exodus, the first time the word "saved" is used in the Bible. The foundational definition of biblical salvation comes from the exodus story as recorded in Exodus 2:16-17. We will look at these verses in two different translations.

> Now the priest of Midian had seven daughters. They came to draw water and filled the troughs to water their father's flock. Then some shepherds arrived and drove them away, but Moses came to their **rescue** [root word *yasha`*] and watered their flock. Exodus 2:16-17 HCSB, bold added

> Now the priest of Midian had seven daughters, and they came and drew water and filled the troughs to water their father's flock. The shepherds came and drove them away, but Moses stood up and **saved** [root word *yasha`*] them, and watered their flock. Exodus 2:16-17 ESV, bold added

The English Standard Version (ESV) translation of Exodus 2:17 makes it easy to see the idea of "saved/salvation" in this text. Although the Holman Christian Standard Bible (HCSB) is also an accurate translation of the Hebrew verb used in this text, the word "rescue" makes the connection with biblical salvation less obvious to us. A Word Study will be helpful.

### WORD STUDY

*The Hebrew word in Exodus 2:17 that is translated* **rescue** *in the HCSB and* **saved** *in the ESV is the verb vayyoshi'an. Although it is often translated in this verse as* *"help" or "rescue," it is best translated "and he saved them"* meaning he rescued and delivered them.²⁹

The verb *yasha`* {*yaw-shah'*} is the root word.³⁰ *Yasha`* is overwhelmingly translated as "save" in its biblical uses.³¹ It can mean to deliver, defend, help, liberate, rescue, give victory.³²

The concrete picture of *yasha`* is that of bringing one to safety. *Yasha`* pictures being led from a narrow strait (indicating distress and danger) to a broad pasture (a wide-open place of provision and safety).³³

In the Old Testament the Hebrew word *yasha`* "AL-WAYS – ALWAYS - ALWAYS refers to rescue from physical calamity, or distress, or illness, or deliverance in battle, and the like."³⁴

Exodus 2:16-17 gives us the first biblical example of someone being *saved*. The daughters of the priest of Midian had come to the well to water their flock, but Moses witnessed other shepherds

---

29   *NET Bible Notes*, study note 70, Exodus 2:17
30   Harris, Archer, and Waltke, editors, *Theological Wordbook of the Old Testament* (Moody Press 1999) word #929, p. 414
31   The *Theological Wordbook of the Old Testament* states that *yasha`* and its derivatives are used 353 times. Harris, Archer, and Waltke, editors, *Theological Wordbook of the Old Testament* (Moody Press 1999) word #929, p. 414; BibleWorks 9.0 identifies 205 uses of *yasha`*: 149 times translated as "save" and another 3 times translated as "salvation."
32   Baker and Carpenter, *The Complete WordStudy Dictionary of the Old Testament* (AMG Publishers 2003) word #3467, p. 484; Harris, Archer, and Waltke, editors, *Theological Wordbook of the Old Testament* (Moody Press 1999) word #929, p. 414
33   Baker and Carpenter, *The Complete WordStudy Dictionary of the Old Testament* (AMG Publishers 2003) word #3467, p. 484; Harris, Archer, and Waltke, editors, *Theological Wordbook of the Old Testament* (Moody Press 1999) word #929, p. 414
34   Meier, Sam, *Misunderstood Terms in the Bible* 2020, Lesson 1, Messianic Studies Institute, Term 4 2020, emphasis on word "ALWAYS" in original

forcefully pushing the women and their sheep aside in order to water their own flocks. Moses comes to the women's defense and in this sense he "saves" them. He stands up against those shepherds allowing the women rightful access to the well water. Moses' actions result in the gratitude of the women and their father who invited Moses into his home and gave one of the women to Moses in marriage (Exodus 2:21).

Even though we don't usually credit Moses with the first act of biblical salvation, his actions in context certainly help us understand what being saved meant to the Jews. In that first instance of someone being saved we learn the core meaning of salvation contains four interconnected elements:[35]

1. a situation or circumstance presenting a need for physical rescue
2. a literal rescue from danger by one called a "savior"
3. followed by the disabling or destruction of that which caused the danger
4. resulting in gratefulness and praise from the one "saved"

A standard dictionary definition of "save/salvation" from its Old Testament usage typically includes the first three of these elements (see for example *Theological Wordbook of the Old Testament*).[36] However, I'd like to suggest there is more than sufficient evidence to establish that the core definition of salvation always includes the fourth element of gratitude. Biblical gratitude can be defined as "a grateful attitude ... expressed in thanksgiving ... demonstrated by specifically suitable responsive actions of ser-

---

35 Elements identified in Exodus 2:16-17,20-22. All elements, except gratitude, are confirmed by the entry for *yasha`* in Harris, Archer, and Waltke, editors, *Theological Wordbook of the Old Testament* (Moody Press 1999) word #929, p. 414

36 Harris, Archer, and Waltke, editors, *Theological Wordbook of the Old Testament* (Moody Press 1999) word #929, p. 414

vice."[37] In other words, it is a heartfelt attitude that evidences our appreciation for salvation through our actions.

I'm going to provide three reasons why I consider it appropriate to include gratitude in the core definition of salvation. As an initial matter, gratitude is clearly a part of the narrative in this first instance of being saved. A rather straightforward rule of thumb in Bible interpretation is known as the "Law of First Mention." Simply stated, the first use of a word in Scripture is often very important as it establishes the primary or most significant meaning in the rest of Scripture. As a general rule, that first occurrence remains dominant and influences all later uses.[38]

> [T]he law of first mention ... simply states that the first time an important subject is mentioned in scripture is significant: God "introduces" it. He gives us important details or facts regarding the subject, which will, of course, help us understand the person or thing introduced, much like we do when "introducing" a guest lecturer, for example.[39]

The second support for regarding gratitude to be a standard part of the salvation definition comes from the work of scholar Jon Levenson. In his opinion, the inclusion of an element of responsive gratitude is *not* merely a *feel-good* tack on to the meaning of salvation. Levenson says gratitude arises naturally and serves an important function in the relationship between the "savior" and the one "saved."

---

37 Goulet, Henri Louis, *The Love of God*, Messianic Studies Institute Anytime Online Course Workbook, p. 71
38 Cooper, David L., *Rules of Interpretation, the Law of First Mention*, Biblical Research Monthly 1947, 1949, Biblical Research Studies Group (Publications from the Biblical Research Society). Retrieved from http://www.biblicalresearch.info/page56.html (last accessed February 4, 2022)
39 Sheets, Dutch, *A Serpent In The Garden*, GiveHim15, February 20, 2021. Retrieved from http://gh15database.com/2021/02/february-20-2021/

> [O]ne who properly experiences **gratitude** for favors received has in the process incurred a moral debt to his benefactor. His failure to discharge that debt would not be a defensible option: it would indicate a moral defect. If, moreover, the benefactor wishes the best for his beneficiary, he will discourage him from ... ungrateful behavior ....[40]

Naturally, we find this type of "moral debt" in the story of Moses. It is the precise response we see expressed without delay by the father of the "saved" Midianite women in the Exodus narrative.

> When [the women whom Moses rescued] came to Reuel their father, he said, "Why have you come back so soon today?" So they said, "[A man] delivered us from the hand of the shepherds, and what is more, he even drew the water for us and watered the flock." He said to his daughters, "Where is he then? Why is it that you have left the man behind? Invite him to have something to eat." Moses was willing to dwell with the man, and he gave his daughter Zipporah to Moses. Exodus 2:18-21

As soon as Reuel learns what Moses has done to benefit his daughters, he looks to express his gratefulness to him. We are told he first extends a dinner invitation, then invites Moses to remain with them and finally, he extends his daughter's hand in marriage. We can see in these actions that one who has benefited from saving acts can't help but express heartfelt gratitude to the "savior" for his salvation.

To the law of first mention and Levenson's learned conclusion I want to add supportive input from biblical scholar George Mendenhall. Mendenhall's area of expertise included ancient Near Eastern study. Based on his research, he delineated the differences

---

40 Levenson, Jon D., *The Love of God: Divine Gift, Human Gratitude, and Mutual Faithfulness in Judaism* (Princeton University Press 2016) p. 52, bold added

between ancient societies founded on law and those founded on covenant relationship. Being "founded on covenant" basically refers to a community that becomes bound together religiously and politically through a formal covenant ceremony. In that type of society, the covenant is viewed as a type of promissory oath which made the social group responsible to the covenant obligations.[41] Israel, of course, was a society founded on covenant relationship. The very basis of that type of society, according to Mendenhall, is "[g]ratitude: response to benefits already received, usually by grace."[42]

The three reasons I have cited above are examples of trustworthy supportive scholarship explaining how gratitude worked in the social setting of ancient Israel. They provide sound reason for my conclusion that gratitude is so naturally connected to being saved that it can reasonably be considered part of the biblical definition of salvation.

Let's turn our attention to how this Old Testament definition affects the New Testament understanding of salvation. After surveying all of the New Testament uses of "salvation," Dr. Sam Meier has concluded that in *every case* the New Testament use is consistent with the Old Testament meanings. The New Testament

---

41 Lundquist, John M., "Chapter 11. Temple, Covenant, and law in the Ancient Near East and in the Old Testament," in *Israel's Apostasy and Restoration: Essays in Honor of Roland K Harrison*, edited by Avraham Gileadi (Baker 1988) pp. 293-305 at original p. 275, including quote from Mendenhall's definition of the covenant process at Mt. Sinai as found in Mendenhall, George E., "Ancient Oriental and Biblical Law," Biblical Archaeologist 17, no. 2 (May 1954): 28. Reprint of Lundquist article retrieved from file:///C:/Users/Deb/Downloads/CH%2011%20 Temple%20covenant%20and%20law%20in%20the%20ancient%20 near%20east%20and%20OT.pdf (last accessed February 26, 2022)

42 Mendenhall, George, "The Conflict between Value Systems and Social Control," in *Unity and Diversity: Essays on the History, Literature, and Religion of the Ancient Near East,* edited by J. J. M. Roberts (Johns Hopkins University Press 1975) p. 211, adapted by Daniel I. Block as displayed in *For the Glory of God: Recovering A Biblical Theology of Worship* (Baker Academic 2014) pp. 82-84

uses are also consistently typical of how "salvation" was used in the first-century world.[43] To the authors of the New Testament, being saved meant "deliverance from physical calamity that is associated with present life."[44]

I believe Paul supplies us with one of the clearest understandings of how New Testament usage is consistent with the Old Testament. Those who believe in their heart and confess with their mouth that Jesus is Lord are described by Paul as being transferred (*methistemi* {meth-is'-tay-mee}) from the kingdom of darkness to the Kingdom of Light – a literal rescue by a Savior.[45] *Methistemi* means to remove or relocate from one place to another. This Greek verb was used for the common practice in the ancient Near East whereby a powerful ruler uprooted people groups and physically resettled them to a different location in his kingdom.[46] What a perfect image to explain how new Christ-followers are uprooted from the kingdom of darkness and resettled into the Kingdom of Light! Before the cross we were held captive by the ruler of this world – we could not free ourselves – we needed a Savior. This transfer of kingdoms is the aspect of salvation that we experience immediately. However, Paul also speaks very clearly about a future aspect of our salvation that likewise fits squarely with the Old Testament understanding of a literal rescue from physical harm.

---

43  Meier, Sam, *Misunderstood Terms in the Bible 2020*, Lesson 1, Messianic Studies Institute, Term 4 2020
44  Meier, Sam, *Misunderstood Terms in the Bible 2020*, Lesson 1, Messianic Studies Institute, Term 4 2020
45  "For [God] rescued us from the domain of darkness, and transferred us to the kingdom of His beloved Son." Colossians 1:13
46  Arnold, Clinton E., "Colossians" in *Zondervan Illustrated Bible Backgrounds Commentary*, Vol. 3, edited by Clinton E. Arnold (Zondervan 2002) Brought us into the kingdom [Colossians] 1:13, p. 378. Scholar Craig Keener likewise acknowledges this practice as a possible background image, but suggests Paul may have relied on other images. Keener, Craig S., *The IVP Bible Background Commentary: New Testament* (Intervarsity Press 1993) Colossians 1:12-13, p. 572

## The Power of Obedience

Every Christ-follower will be literally saved from God's wrath on the day of judgment.[47]

Just as Reuel outwardly expressed his gratitude to Moses for saving his daughters, the author of Hebrews makes clear that every Christ-follower should "show gratitude" in light of our salvation.

> Therefore, since we receive a kingdom which cannot be shaken, let us **show gratitude**,[48] by which we may offer to God an acceptable service with reverence and awe. Hebrews 12:28, bold added

In other words, the proper response of Christ-followers to our salvation is to express our appreciation to Him by living a life obeying His commands. "To live in such 'gratitude' [with] 'godly fear' is to live in the kind of obedience that flows from a heart on which God has written his laws …. Those who live this life truly 'serve' God by approaching him with praise and the obedience of good works …."[49]

Because this study is written as one of a series of Bible Studies titled *Lost in Translation*, a short history lesson is appropriate before we move on. In modern understanding, the words "salvation" and "save" are commonly "connected to a vaguely defined notion of religious experience or fundamentalist fervor, which [as we can now appreciate] is far from the biblical meaning of [those] term[s]."[50] In the New Testament salvation was **not** an abstract

---

47  See for example: Romans 5:9; 1 Thessalonians 1:10; 5:9
48  Scholar Gareth Lee Cockerill points out that while some translations render the Greek word used here as "grace" the original Greek contains an idiom that normally means "let us have gratitude." Cockerill suggests the immediate context combined with this normal meaning best determines the author's original meaning. Cockerill, Gareth Lee, *The Epistle to the Hebrews*, New International Commentary on the New Testament (Eerdmans 2012) Hebrews 12:28, footnote 47, pp. 671-672
49  Cockerill, Gareth Lee, *The Epistle to the Hebrews*, New International Commentary on the New Testament (Eerdmans 2012) Hebrews 12:28, p. 672
50  McCartney, Dan G., *James*, Baker Exegetical Commentary on the New Testament (Baker Academic 2009) James 1:21, p. 118

religious concept. It was very concrete and certain. As we have seen, in its first-century setting, salvation always included the reality of a physical rescue from Israel's enemies.[51] However, according to Dr. Sam Meier, in the second century A.D. the word salvation began to take on a strange *new* meaning.[52] Dr. Meier points out the first time we find this new interpretation (different from the one Jesus knew, different from the one His disciples knew) is in the writing of Justin Martyr.[53] Martyr interpreted Psalm 22 in a way that significantly modified the psalmist's original intent. In its cultural and historical context David, the author of Psalm 22, was understood to be crying out to God to be rescued from severe, life-threatening realities so he does not die physically.[54] Clearly that understanding would be wholly consistent with the historical biblical definition of salvation. However, ignoring that time-honored biblical context, Martyr decided that David was imploring God to rescue his immortal soul from the forces of darkness.[55] Dr. Meier points out that interpretation was not only novel, it was entirely manmade and resulted in an alarming change in meaning. Martyr's new explanation would have been totally unfamiliar to anyone knowledgeable of the Scriptures up until that time. In fact, *The Expositor's Bible Commentary* on the book of Psalms asserts that the more modern understanding of salvation has "[r]egrettably ....

---

51  Tucker, J. Brian, *Reading Romans After Supersessionism: The Continuation of Jewish Covenantal Identity* (Cascade Books 2018) p. 194. Tucker credits N. T. Wright for his impact on biblical interpretation with this understanding of salvation in the first century. Ibid., pp. 193-194

52  Meier, Sam, *Misunderstood Terms in the Bible 2020*, Lesson 1, Messianic Studies Institute, Term 4 2020

53  The writing in question is thought to have been authored between 150 – 160 A.D. Kirby, Peter, *Early Christian Writings*, entry for *St. Justin Martyr*. Retrieved from http://www.earlychristianwritings.com/justin.html?msclkid=cadad076ad4d11eca6d84ea6cd0cb1ad (last accessed March 26, 2022)

54  Meier, Sam, *Misunderstood Terms in the Bible 2020*, Lesson 1, Messianic Studies Institute, Term 4 2020

55  Meier, Sam, *Misunderstood Terms in the Bible 2020*, Lesson 1, Messianic Studies Institute, Term 4 2020

*The Power of Obedience* 239

robbed the NT of its rich OT background."[56] Sadly, when we don't put the biblical text in its proper historical and cultural context it ends up getting lost in translation.

Having established the clear connection between salvation and gratitude expressed as obedience, let's finish up our study of Matthew 28:19-20. In our Word Study on *entole*, we noted that the Greek word *entole* translates Hebrew *mitzvah* which is usually rendered in English as "command" or "commandment." The question naturally arises for Gentile followers of Christ, "what commands is Jesus referring to?" The ancient Jews knew 613 *mitzvot* (plural of *mitzvah*). Are Gentile disciples required to become Jewish and follow all of those *mitzvot*?[57] I believe a conclusively simple answer can be found in Scripture. In short, the answer is NO![58]

Here again we will turn to the writings of Paul, the Christ-appointed apostle to the Gentiles in the first century. In 1 Corinthians

---

56  Longman III and Garland, general editors, *The Expositor's Bible Commentary: Psalms*, Vol. 5, Revised Edition (Zondervan 2008) *Reflections: Yahweh Is My Redeemer* under *Conclusion*, p. 547
57  Hebrews makes clear that the 247 mitzvot (commandments) that pertain to the Old Covenant priesthood and animal sacrificial system are completely fulfilled in Christ and therefore not even Jewish Messiah followers are subject to these commands under the New Covenant. Cockerill, Gareth Lee, *The Epistle to the Hebrews*, New International Commentary on the New Testament (Eerdmans 2012) Hebrews 9:15, p. 402; Hebrews 10:1, p. 428
58  Old Testament passages describe Zion pilgrimage for teaching or worship in which Gentiles remain Gentiles and come with those who are ethnic Jews. For example, Zechariah 8:23 talks of a time when all nations will come to Jerusalem after hearing of the one true God. Isaiah 2:2-3 describes a future time when nationalism makes no difference, people will be drawn to Zion acknowledging the God of Israel as the true God of all nations. The New Testament describes the spread of the gospel to Gentiles absent any requirement that they change their ethnic identity. In both Romans 11:13 and 15:27 Paul refers to the Christ-followers in Rome as *Gentile* followers of Christ. In Romans 15:7-12 Paul envisions the continuing existence of Jewish and Gentile identity within the growing church without erasing the differences between them. Tucker, J. Brian, *Remain In Your Calling: Paul and the Continuation of Social Identities in 1 Corinthians* (Pickwick 2011) pp. 113-114

7:17-24, Paul plainly states his rule that those *in Christ* are not to seek to change their ethnic identification just because they begin to follow Christ. In other words, Paul says, "If you are ethnically Jewish when you become a Messiah follower then you remain Jewish; if you are Gentile at the time you are born again then you remain a Gentile."[59] Further supporting evidence is found in Dr. Ralph J. Korner's work on the first-century understanding of the word *ekklesia* (typically translated in our English Bibles with the word "church").[60] Scholars like Korner are suggesting that *ekklesia* was most likely a word chosen for the new "multi-ethnic assemblies" of Messiah-followers who were meeting together *because* the term was already well known. Dr. Korner has concluded that *ekklesia* was a well-suited word. It allowed for Gentile Messiah-followers to become full disciples of the Jewish Messiah "*without being required* to become Jewish proselytes and/or take up any one, or all, of the Jewish covenantal identity markers such as circumcision, dietary restrictions, and festival observances."[61]

That means on earth the Kingdom of God is purposely designed to include Jewish Messiah-followers and Gentile Messiah-followers. In God's design there is no disparity (i.e., no discrimination or inequality) between Jew and Gentile, nor between slave and free, male and female (Galatians 3:28).[62] All Christ-followers are in one

---

59  While some elements of both identities are continued in Messiah, other elements of each might be transformed. Goulet, Henri Louis, *Love of God*, Messianic Studies Institute online course, session 2.2

60  Dr. Ralph J. Korner serves as an Academic Dean and Associate Professor of Biblical Studies at Taylor Seminary (Canada). He is an active contributor to the Society of Biblical Literature, the Canadian Society of Biblical Studies, and the Evangelical Theological Society. Dr. Korner's dissertation addressed the origin and meaning on the term *ekklēsia* in the early Jesus Movement.

61  Korner, Ralph J., *Reading Revelation After Supersessionism: An Apocalyptic Journey of Socially Identifying John's Multi-Ethnic Ekklesiai with the Ekklesia of Israel* (Cascade Books 2020) p. 25, footnote 92, italics added

62  "[T]he two basic distinctions that separated people in [the early church] culture [was] race/religion and social status. In Christ these old distinctions have been obliterated, not in the sense that one is no longer Jew or

*The Power of Obedience*

body through the same Holy Spirit. *Everyone* who belongs to Christ is Abraham's seed.[63] Even though quite diverse in the natural, through new birth we are all one family unit who share a common salvation through Christ. Paul refers to this unity of diverse identity as the "one new man in Christ."[64] John's gospel explains that Christ-followers display God's glory through their unity.[65] The purpose is to show the divided world that *in Christ* they can walk in fellowship as one community despite their differences.[66] This is remarkable in that up to the time of the new creation initiated by Christ, the Jewish people did not even associate with Gentiles!

Having resolved that issue, let's move on to the question, "What are the commands Gentile Messiah-followers are to obey?" Jesus was asked, "Which is the greatest and most important *entole* (*mitzvah*) in the Hebrew Scriptures?"[67] He answered, "The first is to love God with all your heart and the second is to love your neighbor as yourself."[68]

Jesus understood perfectly well the absolute impossibility of what He was commanding. He knew the command to love those in need ranks in the second position because it is entirely depen-

---

Greek, etc., but in the sense of their having *significance*." Fee, Gordon D., *The First Epistle To The Corinthians*, New International Commentary on the New Testament (Eerdmans 1987) 1 Corinthians 12:13, p. 606, italics in original

63 "Seed" is used as a technical term for the family of Christ. Motyer, J. Alec, *The Prophecy of Isaiah: An Introduction & Commentary* (InterVarsity Press 1993) Isaiah 66:22, p. 543

64 Ephesians 2:15

65 John 17:22-24

66 Goulet, Henri Louis, *Love of God*, Messianic Studies Institute online course, session 2.2

67 Matthew 22:36

68 Matthew 22:37-38. Neighbor is a translation of the Greek word '*plesion* {play-see'-on} from a root word meaning "close by" or "near." It refers to "the person next to one," or more generally to a "fellow human being." Being strongly influenced by Old Testament understanding of neighbor, *plesion* presumes an encounter with another person who is in need. Bromiley, Geoffrey W., *Theological Dictionary of the New Testament* (Eerdmans 1985) entry for *plesion* under *C. plesion in the NT*, pp. 872-873

dent on our obedience to the command that is our first priority. Only when we love God with the entirety of our heart, soul, mind and strength can we truly encounter our neighbors with love. That wholly-devoted love for God provides the fuel for our obedience to *agapao* (love) those who are in need.[69] Whatever God commands and demands, He empowers and enables His *talmid* to accomplish through the power of the Holy Spirit. And that's the whole point! It is the life empowered by God's Spirit that displays God's Kingship in our hearts. Because "the entire law and all the demands of the prophets are based on these two commandments,"[70] Jesus said, "There is no greater *entole* than these two."[71]

In short, when we fulfill these two commands in practice, we have fulfilled the entire law. As one author noted, "These two commands sum up the heart and goal of the rest of God's commands in the Word."[72] Together they "stand to the rest of Scripture as source, sum, substance, and goal. This means that the rest of Scripture … provide[s] us with a commentary on these two responsibilities setting forth the means, manner, motive, method, and destination of our lives. Without the reality of these two commands in our lives

---

[69] 1 John 4:8,16. The love Jesus has in mind is a disposition of the heart to seek the welfare and meet the needs of others. It is not dependent on feeling or emotion, it is a matter of self-will. The motivation for *agape* love does not stem from the desirability or deservedness of the one we choose to love. Because this type of love is given unconditionally with no expectation of being reciprocated, you don't stop loving when the recipient doesn't love you in return. Christ-followers love because we make a choice to love. This type of love is possible because *agapao* is not human affection, it is a divine love produced by the Holy Spirit as fruit in the heart of an obedient disciple.

[70] Matthew 22:40 NLT

[71] Mark 12:31

[72] Keathley, J. Hampton III, *2. Hindrances to Loving One Another*, From the Series: 'One Another' Commands Of Scripture, Bible.org. Retrieved from https://bible.org/seriespage/2-hindrances-loving-one-another (last accessed November 22, 2021)

as both source and course, derivation and destination, obedience to the rest of Scripture will become merely legalistic demands."[73]

Obedience to God does not bring about salvation. We are saved by faith alone through God's amazing grace. However, obedience and transformation as an established blueprint of new life provide undeniable evidence of being born anew as part of God's new creation. As we are obedient disciples, we remain in fellowship with Him. "Jesus answered [His disciple], *'If anyone loves Me, he will keep My word. My Father will love him, and We will come to him and make Our home with him'* (John 14:23 HCSB)."

Allow me to make one more point before moving on. The commands of God are found in the Bible and much of our discussion has assumed that in general, we are referring to those commands. However, that is not the only way in which God can give us a command He expects us to obey. Because God still speaks today to those in covenant relationship with Him, He is certainly able to give us clear direction for Kingdom assignments which He expects us to obey as well. For example, He may provide instruction for you to leave the place you are presently living and move to another place. He may ask you to fast something for a season, like fasting shopping or turning off the T.V. He may impress on your heart His desire that you teach a class or serve another person in a certain way. He may give you a targeted prayer assignment that requires your travel to another city or state to complete. For the purposes of our study, I'll call these the "distinctive" commands of God as opposed to the more general commands of the Bible. I refer to them as "distinctive" because they are uniquely personal to you. The point is: it does not matter how you learn of the command, if it is something the Lord has asked you to do then He expects immediate desire-based obedience and that will always be for your best.

---

[73] Keathley, J. Hampton III, *1. Foundations and Motivations,* From the Series: 'One Another' Commands Of Scripture, Bible.org, bold deleted. Retrieved from https://bible.org/seriespage/1-foundations-and-motivations (last accessed November 23, 2021)

"The goal of instructing new disciples of Jesus is obedience to what He has commanded so that their lives increasingly become like their Master."[74]

> Therefore, be imitators of God as dearly loved children and live in love .... just as Christ loved the church and gave himself for her to sanctify her by cleansing her with the washing of the water by the word, so that he may present the church to himself as glorious—not having a stain or wrinkle, or any such blemish, but holy and blameless. Ephesians 5:1-2,25-27 NET

The way Christ-followers reflect God's character and present a witness to a lost and dying world against the very evil it celebrates is to "imitate God." As we have noted, imitation is another way of saying we are to obey God's commands. In Lesson 8 we pointed out that the model of evangelism we see in the Bible is that other people groups are *not* in large part reconciled to God by organized "outreach efforts." Instead, as God's redeemed people become walking billboards with obedient life styles, they display God's true character (in other words they glorify Him) and attract others to His growing Kingdom.

God left it up to us to use our life to paint an accurate picture of who He is. An artist whose talent is painting is skilled in the use of different brushes, materials and mediums. The artistic tool God has put in our hands is our obedience. He calls us to obey Him in our thoughts which will flow into our words and our actions. By our obedience in thought, word and deed we are RE•presenting His true nature to those around us – painting a picture of Him for the world to see.

In our last lesson, we used my imagined concept of a bone marrow transplant to think about how the desires of God's heart

---

[74] Wilkins, Michael J., "Matthew," in *Zondervan Illustrated Bible Backgrounds Commentary*, Vol. 1, edited by Clinton E. Arnold (Zondervan 2002) Teaching them to obey everything I have commanded you ([Matthew] 28:20) p. 190

become the desires of our hearts. Let's take that analogy one step further. How does God's Kingdom advance on earth? How is the new heaven and new earth ushered into existence? Our obedience provides God with His rightful Kingly rule on the earth. Every act of obedience evidences His sovereign rule. As *talmid* after *talmid* obeys their King, His rulership expands in scope. The Kingdom of God replaces evil in the same way in which the healthy bone marrow replaced the diseased marrow in our imagined bone marrow transplant. In due course, the power of evil is totally superseded by the power of God and what remains is the new creation which has chosen to obey and glorify God alone!

If we look around us in the Western world today it seems as if we are losing ground in this replacement battle. According to world-renowned author and social critic, Os Guinness, most of the problems in the church today are in fact rooted in cultural captivity which is especially true of the church in the West.[75] In his 2014 book entitled, *Renaissance: The Power of the Gospel However Dark The Times*, Guinness identifies some of the worst forms of Western worldliness as our worship of individualism and our insatiable consumerism.[76] He warns that a worldly church *fails to be* the church in that she: 1) betrays Christ, 2) does not live up to her calling to be dangerously different, 3) cannot provide a viable alternative to the world and 4) has no supernatural salvation to offer. In fact, that type of "church" is truly in desperate need of being saved herself.[77]

In a season when Israel failed to be the light to the nations she was called to be, God asked Ezekiel whether those dry (dead) bones could live again?[78] Then God answered His own question, in essence saying to Ezekiel, "Watch *me* turn these dry bones into a

---

75 Guinness, Os, *Renaissance: The Power of the Gospel However Dark The Times* (IVP Books 2014) pp. 34-35
76 Guinness, Os, *Renaissance: The Power of the Gospel However Dark The Times* (IVP Books 2014) p. 38
77 Guinness, Os, *Renaissance: The Power of the Gospel However Dark The Times* (IVP Books 2014) p. 119
78 Ezekiel 37:3

living army!"[79] By God's might those dry bones would be saturated with "lavish life .... [L]ife beyond measure, beyond hope, beyond suffering, beyond the shadow of death."[80] Os Guinness reasons this same question is relevant for the Western church today and he answers the question with similar encouragement.[81]

> The true answer is one we must both declare and live out: Yes, [these dry bones] can [live again] because God can [do it]—and he has in the past, and he is doing so elsewhere in the world, and he is able to do so again even here in the advanced modern world, because God is God, and his is the last word in human affairs.

God's answer to Ezekiel was to announce a new exodus and a new covenant, the very covenant under which we have our relationship with Him today. It is that metaphor of a "new exodus" I want to consider as we conclude our lesson.

Exodus is a common word in the Greek language that means "exit" or "departure."[82] Scholar G. K. Beale points out that the *new exodus* is a major theme in the Gospels, Paul's writings and Rev-

---

79  Ezekiel 37:4-6, my paraphrase
80  Levison, John R., *Filled With The Spirit* (Eerdmans Publishing 2009) p. 262
81  Guinness, Os, *Renaissance: The Power of the Gospel However Dark The Times* (IVP Books 2014) p. 144
82  *NIV Study Bible* (Zondervan Publishing 1995) Exodus Introduction, p. 83. The Bible reveals a recurring pattern of "called out ones." The pattern began with Abraham who was called out of his homeland to go to the land God would show him. That was followed centuries later by the seminal event which created and defined Israel as God's covenant people, the Exodus from Egypt. God called Moses out of Midian to lead that exodus. Through the leadership of Moses God called Abraham's descendants, the Hebrew people, out of Egypt to go to the Promised Land. Centuries later that mighty deliverance was followed by the Babylonian Exile. Even so, Isaiah prophesied their return to the land using new exodus terminology. Right on schedule, when 70 years of exile was complete, God called His covenant people back out of Babylon to return to the Promised Land.

*The Power of Obedience* 247

elation. In Beale's words it is a "metaphor for the new-creational kingdom [of God]."[83] The book of Revelation expresses its warning message to God's covenant people down through the ages using familiar Old Testament exodus imagery.[84] John heard a voice from heaven calling for God's people to come out of "Babylon."

> After these things I saw another angel coming down from heaven, having great authority, and the earth was illumined with his glory. And he cried out with a mighty voice, saying, "Fallen, fallen is Babylon the great! She has become a dwelling place of demons and a prison of every unclean spirit, and a prison of every unclean and hateful bird. For all the nations have drunk of the wine of the passion of her immorality, and the kings of the earth have committed *acts of* immorality with her, and the merchants of the earth have become rich by the wealth of her sensuality." **I heard another voice from heaven, saying, "Come out of her, my people, so that you will not participate in her sins and receive of her plagues**; for her sins have piled up as high as heaven, and God has remembered her iniquities. Pay her back even as she has paid, and give back *to her* double according to her deeds; in the cup which she has mixed, mix twice as much for her. To the degree that she glorified herself and lived sensuously, to the same degree give her torment and mourning; for she says in her heart, 'I SIT *AS* A QUEEN AND

---

83 Beale, G. K., *A New Testament Biblical Theology: The Unfolding Of The Old Testament In The New* (Baker Academic 2011) p. 172. Beale summarizes the theology of the New Testament as: "Jesus's life, trials, death for sinners, and especially resurrection by the Spirit have launched the fulfillment of the eschatological already—not yet new-creation reign, bestowed by grace through faith and resulting in worldwide commission to the faithful to advance this new-creational reign and resulting in judgment for the unbelieving, unto the triune God's glory." Ibid, p. 163, italics deleted

84 Revelation 1:4,11; 2:1,7; 2:8,11; 2:12,17; 2:18,23,29; 3:1,6; 3:7,13; 3:14,22; 22:16

I am not a widow, and will never see mourning.' For this reason in one day her plagues will come, pestilence and mourning and famine, and she will be burned up with fire; for the Lord God who judges her is strong...." Revelation 18:1-8, italics and all caps in original, bold added

In Lesson 11 we summarily said Babylon is the world system ruled by the antichrist spirit that sets up a false worship system and persecutes Christ-followers. In short, Babylon represents mankind in organized rebellion against God.[85] The command John heard to "come out of [Babylon]" is a call for a new exodus. However, this new exodus isn't prompting a change of physical location. The new exodus speaks of Christ-followers being physically located in the world but not being of the world. They do not value the things that the world values; they value only what God values!

To understand the type of exodus the New Testament envisions we need to think clearly about the mission and ministry of Jesus and the commission He gave His followers. The ministry of Jesus *never* took direct aim at overthrowing the Roman government (the Babylon of His day) even though "unseating the might of Rome .... for most ordinary Jews, was what the kingship of God was all about."[86] Jesus makes clear His blueprint for socio-political reform begins at the level of personal obedience. His Kingdom requires each Christ-follower to commit to a personal relationship with Him fully submitted to His Kingly rule. His Kingdom demands personal transformation with the expectation "a revolution of values" will be the inherent result.[87] As that type of radical transformation takes place person by person within the body of

---

85  Guzik, David, *Revelation Commentary,* Revelation 14 – Images of God's Victory and The Beast's Defeat. Retrieved from http://www.enduringword.com/bible-commentary/revelation-14/ (last accessed July 8, 2021)
86  France, R. T., *Divine Government: God's Kingship In The Gospel of Mark* (Regent College Publishing 1990) pp. 61,90
87  France, R. T., *Divine Government: God's Kingship In The Gospel of Mark* (Regent College Publishing 1990) p. 61

Christ, God's Kingdom advances – His kingship on earth becomes progressively more visible and as tangible as it is in heaven.[88]

In other words, the *new exodus* – the severance from the evil world system – does *not* come through physical uprising and revolt against the world. It calls for a holy separation unto God that takes place *internally* within each Christ-follower. That internal set-apartness manifests itself in a lifestyle of God-honoring behavior. It is the model of Joseph in his service first to Potiphar and then to Pharaoh although he is an Egyptian slave against his will. It is the example of Daniel serving Nebuchadnezzar in the midst of Babylonian exile. It is the way of Jesus amid the rule of the evil Roman Empire. And it is the pattern modeled and taught by His first-century *talmidim* in the face of intense suffering and persecution.

It is the story of untold numbers of *talmidim* since then who put their faith on the line to honor God in inconceivable circumstances. Missionary Martin Burnham is one modern-day illustration of the exodus mindset I'm describing. While he and his wife Gracia were serving with New Tribes Mission in the Philippines, they were taken hostage by a militant group and held in captivity in a jungle for more than a year. Martin was killed in the rescue operation, but Gracia would later tell the story of her husband's Christlike kindness to their captors. During the day as their captors kept on the move through the dense jungle, Martin offered to carry their heavy backpacks. Each night, in a sincere gesture of goodwill, Martin would look straight at his armed captors as they chained he and his wife to a tree and say, "Thank you very much" and then he would wish them good night. In each act of kindness, the Kingship of God that ruled in Martin's heart made God's Kingship on earth visible. Despite their unthinkable circumstances, Martin had resolved not to lose his joy, or his wit-

---

88  France, R. T., *Divine Government: God's Kingship In The Gospel of Mark* (Regent College Publishing 1990) pp. 62,72-73

ness![89] "'It's tempting to call their story a tragedy and to label the Burnhams "victims." But that doesn't sound right,' the Eagle editorialized Sunday. 'In a remarkable way, the Burnhams triumphed over their cynical captors and the cruel details of their captivity.'"[90] The Burnhams are part of the new exodus Christ set in motion. Our internal separation, highlights our unique "disciple of Christ" identity within a modern-day world system that scorns and dishonors the Christ we follow.

So, we wrap up our study by returning to the question asked by Os Guinness, "Is there yet hope for the Western church? Can these dry bones live again?" The resounding answer is, "Yes, God has done it before and He can do it again!" "We are to trust and obey God, and to follow His call in every inch of our lives, in every second of our time, and with every gift [He has given us]. And we are to leave the result as well as the assessment to God."[91] When we have done that, we will most certainly hear the words we long to hear as we are ushered into His eternal presence, "Well, done my good and faithful servant. Welcome to the place I have prepared as your eternal home!"

> Then I saw a new heaven and a new earth; for the first heaven and the first earth passed away, and there is no longer *any* sea. And I saw the holy city, new Jerusalem, coming down out of heaven from God, made ready

---

89  Various details of the Burnham's experience in captivity comes from my own recall of interviews with Gracia Burnham after her return to the U.S. Other details are found in a Baptist Press news report at the time of Martin's funeral. That article was retrieved from http://m.bpnews.net/13627/missionary-martin-burnhams-life-capped-by-joyous-funeral-in-kansas?msclkid=d45e1eeeadc311ec84c204403178d3d4 (last accessed March 28, 2022)

90  Olson, Ted, *Inside Martin Burnham's Funeral*, Christianity Today, June 1, 2002, italics added. Retrieved from https://www.christianitytoday.com/ct/2002/juneweb-only/6-17-12.0.html?msclkid=6785953bae8b11ec82a-21001c0a83f83 (last accessed March 28, 2022)

91  Guiness, Os, *Renaissance: The Power of the Gospel However Dark The Times* (IVP Books 2014) p. 111

as a bride adorned for her husband. And I heard a loud voice from the throne, saying, "Behold, the tabernacle of God is among men, and He will dwell among them, and they shall be His people, and God Himself will be among them, and He will wipe away every tear from their eyes; and there will no longer be *any* death; there will no longer be *any* mourning, or crying, or pain; the first things have passed away." And He who sits on the throne said, "Behold, I am making all things new." And He said, "Write, for these words are faithful and true." Then He said to me, "It is done. I am the Alpha and the Omega, the beginning and the end. I will give to the one who thirsts from the spring of the water of life without cost. He who overcomes will inherit these things, and I will be his God and he will be My son. But for the cowardly and unbelieving and abominable and murderers and immoral persons and sorcerers and idolaters and all liars, their part *will be* in the lake that burns with fire and brimstone, which is the second death." Revelation 21:1-8, italics in original

In a convicting commentary, Pastor and author Mark Batterson concludes, "Most of us are educated way beyond our level of obedience. We don't need to know more, we need to do more with what we know."[92] To the degree that those of us who call ourselves "Christians are not practicing what we preach, we cannot expect our society to enjoy the fruits of the way of life of Jesus, and our Christian faith is likely to be implausible and off-putting to the wider world."[93]

As we conclude this study, may this be the prayer on our lips, "Oh Father, give me an ear to hear and a heart to obey!"

---

92  Batterson, Mark, *All In: You Are One Decision Away From A Totally Different Life* (Zondervan 2013) DVD Session 3, All Out: Rim Huggers, italics added
93  Guinness, Os, *Renaissance: The Power of the Gospel However Dark The Times* (IVP Books 2014) p. 61

***Hear What The Spirit is Saying to the Church***: *Where are the ones who will devote themselves to draw close to Me? These are the ones I will use mightily to usher in the fullness of My new creation.*

## Appendix

# How to do basic Word Studies when you don't read Hebrew or Greek

To understand why Word Studies are important refer to "Preface: About Word Studies."

### Begin with prayer

The best counsel I have seen from anyone about how to do Word Studies on the internet comes from the Precept Austin website, "And so as you begin your word study, remember to begin with prayer beseeching our Father to grant that our Teacher, the Holy Spirit might guide us into all truth (Jn 16:13), for spiritual truth is spiritually revealed by the Spirit."[1]

There are multiple ways to do word searches using internet reference tools. As you become proficient at using these tools you will develop your favorites and find shortcuts to locating the information you are seeking. I am providing a basic starting point here for those just beginning.

As an initial matter, don't forget to check the English Dictionary for how your word of interest is defined in the English language. You may not be aware of all the nuances of a given English word. As a result, sometimes that research alone provides greater clarity to a word's usage.

Next, read your targeted Scripture in multiple Bible translations. Reading your passage in several translations may provide you with all the information you need.

---

1  *How to Perform a Greek Word Study*, Precept Austin. Retrieved from https://www.preceptaustin.org/greek_word_study#web (last accessed January 24, 2022). Note, as with the other materials on this website this is an overall helpful article regarding Word Studies.

As a general rule of thumb, I "over research" my word of interest to be as assured of accuracy as I can possibly be. When I am in doubt I check with someone more knowledgeable than I am.

### Strong's Numbers are the Starting Point for Your Research

When you've decided to proceed with an internet search the Strong's number associated with your word of interest is a must! A Strong's Number is the unique number that has been assigned to a word used in the Bible.[2] For example: the Hebrew word יָשַׁע *yasha`* {yaw-shah'} has been assigned the number: 03467. The Greek word δοῦλος *doulos* {doo'-los} has been assigned the number: 1401. Each number links the root meaning of the word back to the original meanings in the Hebrew and Greek manuscripts from which they were translated. *NOTE: When you use this number in internet searches you will generally need to add a "H" before the number for a Hebrew word or a "G" before the number for a Greek word.*

*Caveat:* Strong's concordance, keyed to numbers for roots in the original languages, is a valuable resource. Users need to be aware of some issues: 1) Strong's is old enough to almost be outdated. Because it is keyed to the language of the KJV it is advisable to check your results against more modern commentaries and other Bible translations. 2) Strong's provides glosses (words or phrases proposed as possible translations of a particular Greek or Hebrew word) rather than definitions.[3] That's because those Greek and Hebrew words have many potential meanings in different contexts. It

---

2   Strong's Numbers originate from a reference book known as *Strong's Exhaustive Concordance of the Bible.*
3   When a Greek student is taught that *"pistis"* means "faith" what he is learning is a "gloss." Contrast that with the following from the *Greek-English Lexicon of the New Testament Based on Semantic Domains*: "that which is completely believable—'what can be fully believed, that which is worthy of belief, believable evidence, proof'" [Louw, J. P., & Nida, E. A. (1996, c1989). *Greek-English lexicon of the New Testament: Based on semantic domains* (electronic ed. of the 2nd edition.) (Vol. 1, p. 370). New York: United Bible societies)].

The Power of Obedience 255

is imperative that you check carefully which word definition works best for the passage you are studying.

**HOW TO LOCATE A STRONG'S NUMBER ON THE INTERNET USING FREE RESOURCES:**

1. Go to https://biblehub.com.

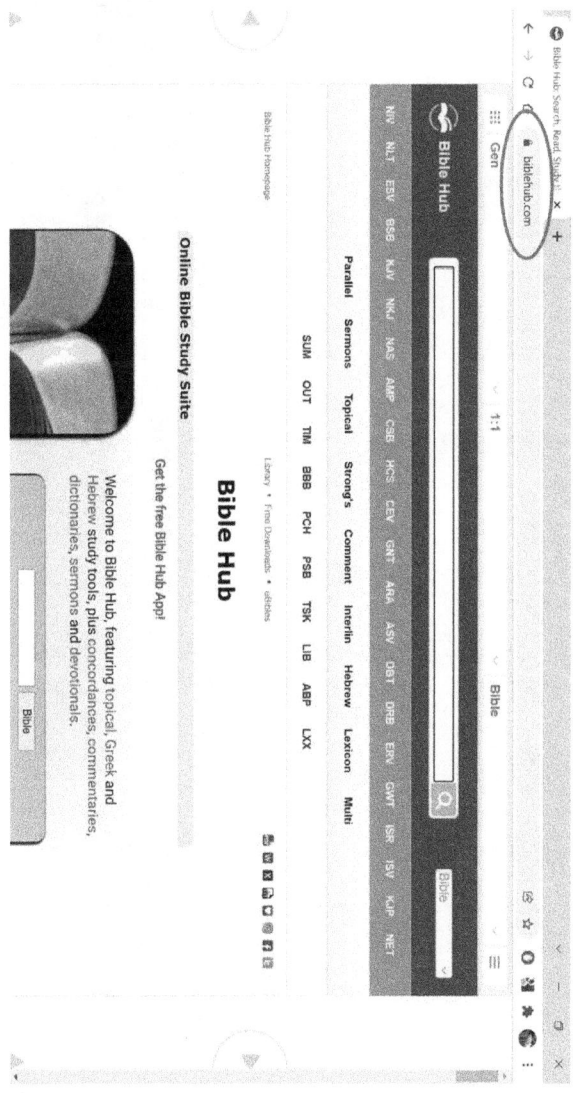

*256     How to do basic WORD STUDIES when you don't read Hebrew or Greek*

2. Across the tool bar find the header for "Interlin."

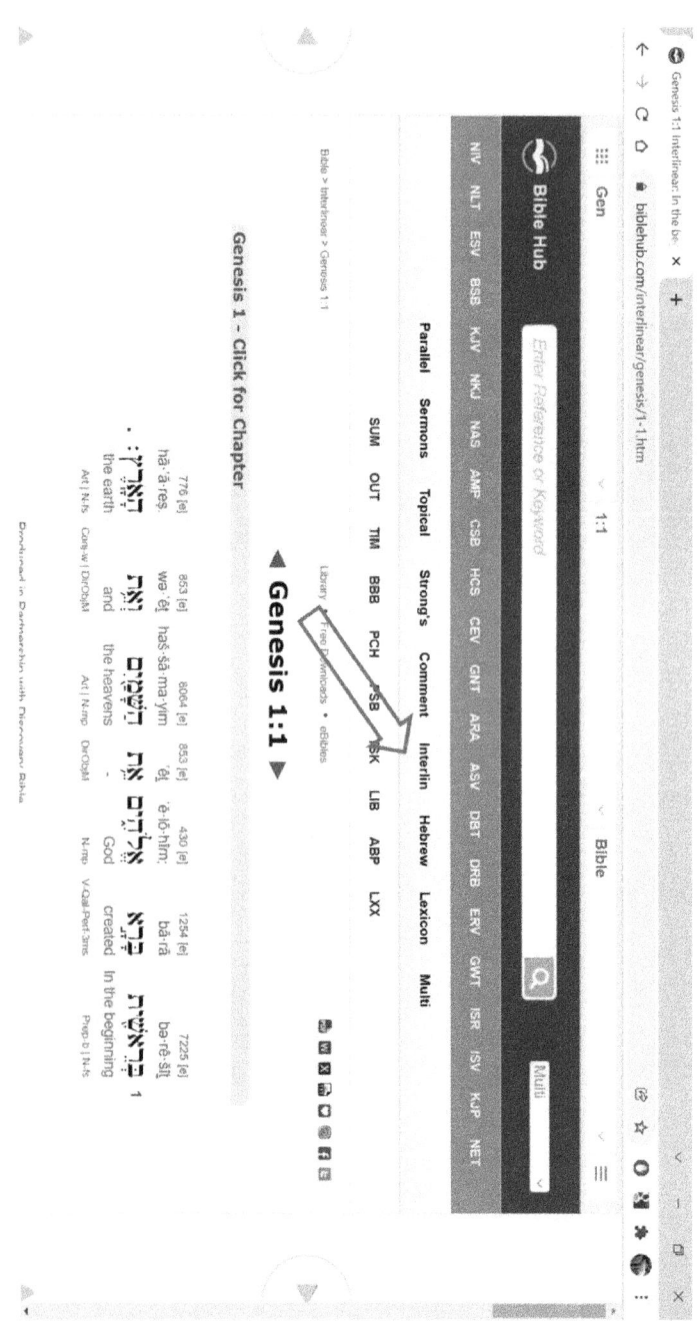

The Power of Obedience 257

3. When you click that header, it will take you to the Interlinear page for Genesis 1:1. Find the search box at the top of the page and enter the verse address containing your word of interest. The search engine will take you directly to the Interlinear entry (either Hebrew or Greek) for that verse.

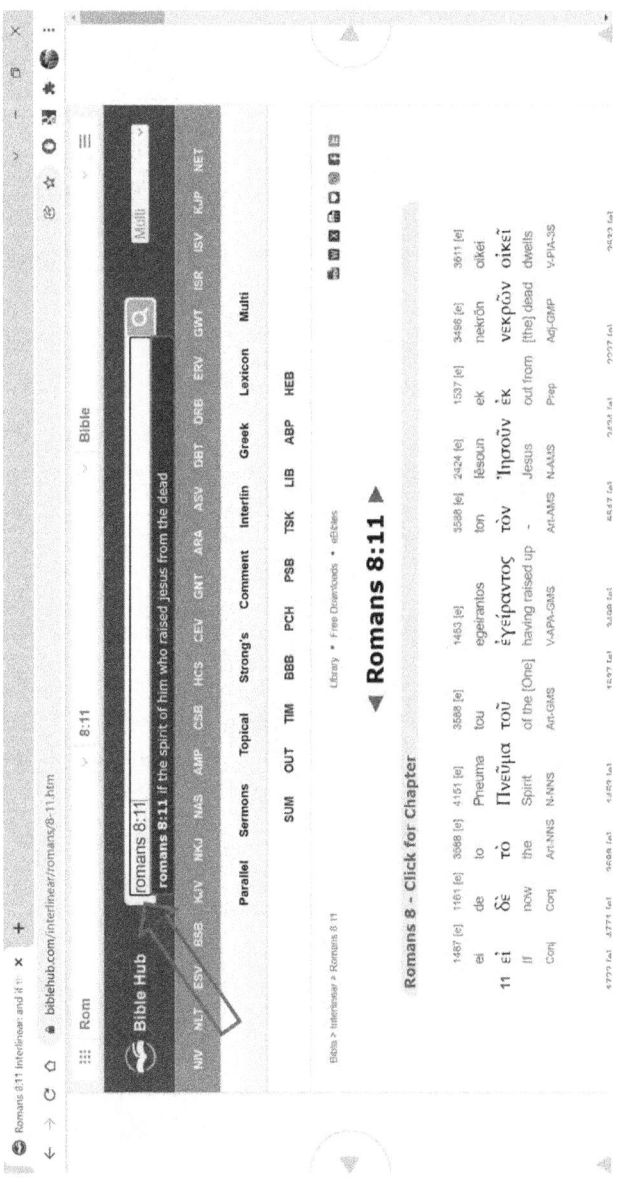

4. The numbers in blue across the top of each word is the Strong's number. You can click on that blue number and it will take you to a page with the Strong's Concordance information and other Bible Dictionary entries for that word. However, once you have the Strong's # you can research in a wide variety of other reference sources as well.

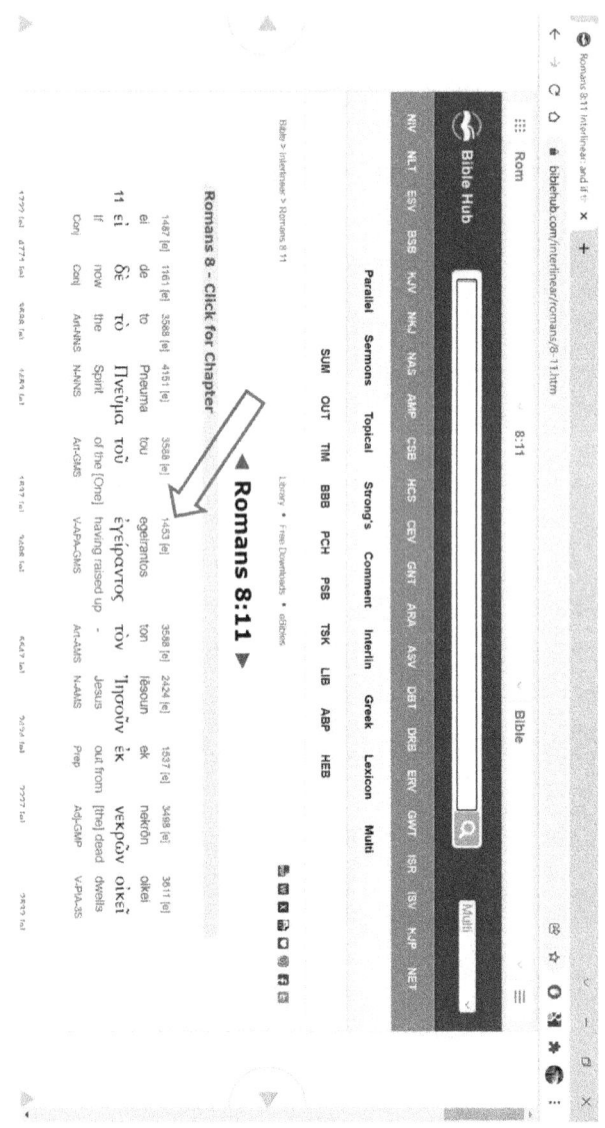

## COMMENTARIES CAN BE A GREAT SOURCE OF INFORMATION IN UNDERSTANDING HOW A WORD IS USED

Often the Commentary will define the word itself, but even if no definition is provided checking a variety of Commentaries for that particular verse/section of Scripture is a good way to gain additional understanding regarding the context surrounding your word of interest.

Bible Dictionaries and Bible Encyclopedias are another free resource worth searching to view any entries that might be available for the word you are studying.

Caveat: As you consider broadening your internet search a quote from Yale University Library helps us place the usefulness of internet resources in their proper context.[4]

> 1. Searching on the Internet. Care must be taken in searching for information on the Internet .... [F]reely available Internet resources have not necessarily been published by reputable academic publishers nor have they been selected by librarians with expertise in their subject area. Nearly anything can be posted on a website, and just because it is available online does not mean it is valid or authoritative. **However, this does not mean that you cannot find good resources on the Internet; the key to doing so is to carefully evaluate what you find on the web.** If you use web resources, be sure to ask these questions:
> 
> - Who is the author of the Web site? Are the author's credentials listed?
> - What institution or organization is behind the Web site?

---

4   Yale University Library, *Biblical Studies Guide: Websites*, Yale University Library Research Guides at Yale University, bold added. Retrieved from https://guides.library.yale.edu/c.php?g=295834&p=1972575 (site last updated Apr 30, 2021 1:08 PM) (last accessed January 24, 2022)

- When was the Web site created or last updated?
- Who is the intended audience for the Web site?
- Is the information provided objective or biased?
- How does information provided by the site compare to other works, including print works?

There are times when a website you are viewing provides you with the opportunity to view the beliefs and doctrines behind those who post articles on that particular site. Taking the time to read that information can provide valuable insight about the biases the author(s) may have about biblical points of view. Understanding the framework (lens) though which the author is operating may explain cases where their viewpoint is radically different than others you have read in your research efforts. It helps you evaluate the weight you may want to give to their characterization of your word of interest or its biblical context.

*A Caution Regarding Commentaries:* The advice provided by the Yale University Library quote above concerning internet searches is equally wise counsel when using Commentaries.

### A Few Remaining Observations

Words can have multiple meanings. As an example, the word "dig" has a wide range of meanings in the English language. It can refer to excavation (for archaeological or other purposes); an insult, taunt or sarcastic remark; a jab or nudge; to tunnel, to burrow or mine; or to plow a field. Dig can imply using large commercial equipment, a simple hand trowel or shovel; or it can refer to words that come out of your mouth. The same is true in Greek and Hebrew. However, generally speaking a word only carries one specific meaning at a time.

*Caveat:* Without getting too complicated, let me add one quick caveat to my last statement. The Apostle John is well known for using a word to mean two things at once (known as double entendre).[5]

The goal in a Word Study is to determine the author's originally intended meaning. It is a fundamental principle for Word Studies that the author's usage determines the word's meaning. In other words, the author's original intent, as determined by context, must be the guide you use to choose the most applicable meaning from the range of possible word meanings. The goal of your research is to find a working definition that fits precisely in the specific context. As my Publisher warns, "Most errors in interpretation come from focusing too narrowly on a single verse or even phrase. If you come up with an understanding of the meaning of a particular word that contradicts the teaching of that author in the rest of his writings, you might want to reconsider. Who is more likely to have made a mistake?"

A research technique I often use in Word Studies is to locate the first use of that word in the Bible. Let me first explain why I do that and then I'll provide an easy way to locate that first biblical usage for your word of interest.

---

[5] Keener, Craig S., *The Gospel Of John: A Commentary,* Volume Two (Hendrickson Publishers 2003) John 19:30b, p. 1148; Levison, Jack, *Filled with the Spirit* (Eerdmans 2009) p. 245. "One of the unique devices used by the author of the Fourth Gospel is that of double meaning. The author uses two meanings of a word, both of which are distinct enough that they could not convey one aspect of thought. He probably did not intend to present an either/or situation wherein a Christian must make a choice of meaning. More likely he was following a pattern of usage found in Qumran and the Old Testament wherein two meanings were intended to be conveyed through one expression." Wead, David W., *The Johannine Double Meaning,* Restoration Quarterly, 13 no 2 1970, pp. 106-120. Language: English; Publication Type: Article; (AN ATLA0001588405), citing 1. S. Cohen, "The Political Background of the Words of Amos," Hebrew Union College Annual 36 (1965) pp. 153-160

## Reason First Occurrence Can Be Important

The first time a key word or concept is mentioned in the Bible "gives us important details or facts regarding the subject, which will, of course, help us understand the person or thing introduced."[6] It is notable that "ancient Jewish commentators call special attention to [first mentions in Scripture], and lay great stress upon them as always having some significance. They generally help us in fixing the meaning of a word or point us to some lesson in connection with it."[7]

## An Easy Way to Locate First Usage

Using https://www.blueletterbible.org/lexicon/index.cfm enter the Strong's number for your word of interest, remember to use the "H" before the number for Hebrew words or the "G" before the number for Greek words. The search will take you to the Lexicon entry for that word. Scroll down past the definitions and reference section to the header: Concordance Results Shown Using the KJV. The first text box under this heading will show you how many times that particular word was used in WLC (Westminister Leningrad Codex) Hebrew. Following that entry will be a list of the verses where that word is used. You will be able to identify your word of interest by the superscript Strong's number next to the word. The first verse listed is the first instance of that word's biblical use.

---

6  Sheets, Dutch, *A Serpent In The Garden*, GiveHim15, February 20, 2021. Retrieved from http://gh15database.com/2021/02/february-20-2021/

7  Bullinger, E. W., *Number in Scripture: Its Supernatural Design and Spiritual Significance*, 4th Ed. (Eyre & Spottiswoode (Bible Warehouse) Ltd. 1921) Part II Its Spiritual Significance, One, First Occurrences of Words. Retrieved from https://www.levendwater.org/books/numbers/number_in_scripture_bullinger.pdf (last accessed January 25, 2022)

*The Power of Obedience*

**SOME ONLINE SOURCES OF COMMENTARIES (AND OTHER VALUABLE RESEARCH RESOURCES) ARE:**

**Biblehub.com** Retrieved from https://biblehub.com/ (last accessed January 24, 2022). From the Home Page, find the tool bar that lists resources. Select the header for "Comment" which will open a page containing Commentaries for Genesis 1:1. You can enter your verse in the search box on that page and it will take you to the available Commentaries for that verse.

**BibleStudyTools.com** Bible Versions and Translations Online (biblestudytools.com). Retrieved_from https://www.biblestudytools.com/bible-versions/ (last accessed January 24, 2022). From Home Page, locate study menu, drop down menu lists available resources such as: Commentaries, Concordances, Dictionaries, Encyclopedias, and others.

**BlueLetterBible.org** Bible Search and Study Tools - Blue Letter Bible. Retrieved from https://www.blueletterbible.org/study.cfm (last accessed January 24, 2022). This page lists Bible Commentaries, Bible References, Topical Indexes, among other resources. Blue Letter Bible also permits you to research a specific Hebrew or Greek word if you know the Strong's "G" or "H" number. By the way, this site provides you with the opportunity to hear how the word is pronounced. It's a great tool if you are planning to teach and need to say the Greek or Hebrew word.

**NetBible.org** Net Bible Translation with Notes. Retrieved from https://netbible.org/ (last accessed January 24, 2022). The NET Bible is a Bible translation containing almost 61,000 translators' notes from over 25 scholars. The translator's notes (identified with a number followed by the letters "tn" like this, [175]**tn**) document the decisions and choices they made for how/why they translated the original text. The notes make the original languages accessible to the reader who does not know Greek and Hebrew. Study notes (identified with a number followed by the letters "sn" like this, [2]**sn**) are often added to the notes section providing an additional layer of helpful information.

**PreceptAustin.org** Retrieved from https://www.preceptaustin.org/ (last accessed January 24, 2022). Home Page tool bar contains drop down menus for Commentaries, Verse By Verse (Commentaries), Study Tools with options for Greek or Hebrew Word Studies, among other resources. On the Home Page there is a search box that allows you to search for a particular Hebrew or Greek word using the common form transliteration (without markings) and/or search for a particular Bible verse. When you locate the verse you are studying, it will often have word study links to a particular Greek or Hebrew word used in that Scripture. You will also find a treasure trove of quotes from various Bible Dictionaries and Commentaries related to that verse.

**Note**: A transliteration is the form of a Greek or Hebrew word translated into letters in the English language making the word readable to one who does not read Hebrew or Greek. When you locate the Strong's number you will see your word of interest in its original language form and you will also see the common form transliteration for that word. It is important to point out that occasionally a given word has more than one acceptable transliteration. In those cases, you may need to research the alternate forms of transliteration. To be clear, let's use the examples I used above.

Hebrew word יָשַׁע *yasha`* {yaw-shah'} has been assigned the Strong's number: 03467. In this case "*yasha`*" is the transliteration; while {yaw-shah'} provides the reader with a key to pronunciation.

Greek word δοῦλος *doulos* {doo'-los} has been assigned the number: 1401. In this case "*doulos*" is the transliteration; while {doo'-los} provides the reader with a key to pronunciation.

**StudyLight.org** Retrieved from https://studylight.org/ (last accessed January 24, 2022). From Home page, the tool bar contains an option for "Bible Study Tools" that will take you to a list of available Bible Commentaries, Concordances, Dictionaries and Encyclopedias.

If you plan to do word studies often and have the ability to invest in a few published resources my recommendation for Greek words: Geoffrey W. Bromiley, *Theological Dictionary of the New Tes-*

*tament*, Abridged in One Volume (Eerdmans 1985)[8] and Hebrew words: Harris, Archer, and Waltke, editors, *Theological Wordbook of the Old Testament* (Moody Press 1999).[9] Additional valuable resources for your personal library include: Baker and Carpenter, *The Complete WordStudy Dictionary of the Old Testament* (AMG Publishers 2003) and Spiros Zodhiates, *The Complete Word Study Dictionary: New Testament* (AMG Publishers 1992) – both are keyed off of the Strong's Number. Suggestion: Search Amazon or eBay for used copies in very good / good condition to purchase these materials at a lower cost.

---

8   When you know the Strong's word number you can enter it in the search box on BlueLetter Bible website. You will have to inform the search as to whether you are looking for a Hebrew Strong's number or a Greek Strong's number. To locate a Greek # place a "G" in front of the number with no spaces. The TDNT Reference (if applicable) will be provided under the header "Dictionary Aids." For example, G42 will be listed as: TDNT Reference 1:114,14. In this case, you would go to page 14 of the Abridged Volume to find the TDNT entry for your word. Note: the first part of the TDNT Reference [1:114] is given for the unabridged volumes of *The Theological Dictionary of the New Testament*.

9   When you know the Strong's word number you can enter it in the search box on BlueLetter Bible website. You will have to inform the search as to whether you are looking for a Hebrew Strong's number or a Greek Strong's number. To locate a Hebrew # place a "H" in front of the number with no spaces. The "TWOT" (*Theological Wordbook of the Old Testament*) Reference (if applicable) is listed under the header "Dictionary Aids." For example, H3467 is listed as: TWOT Reference:929. In this case, you turn to word #929 on page 414 of *The Theological Wordbook of the Old Testament*.

# Index to the Word Studies

**Note:** Words are alphabetized according to their transliterations under the English alphabet.

## Greek

aisthesis 5
archegos 167
dynamis 209
energeia 208
energeo 208
entellomai 228
entole 228
epithumeo 177, 179
epithumia 177
oregomai 179
sarx 190
teleiotes 167
tereo 226
thelo 209

## Hebrew

`anag 200
Adonai 126
Adonay 126
'aven 141
buwsh 34
chafets 197
da`ath 5
derek 103
'esher 196
ḥāpēṣ 197

hazaq 85
ma'ac 152
maas 152
mitzvah 228
musar 149
nāsâ 46
qanna' 81
quwts 152
ra` 8
sane' 142
shama` 69
tob 6
tokachath 150
tov 6
towb 6
vayyoshi'an 230
yada` 93
yakach 149
yare' 60
yasha` 231

# Meet the Author: Deborah L. Roeger

Photo: Courtesy of Donna J. Barnett

I confessed Christ as my Lord and Savior in 1962 when I was 9 years old. I was baptized the same day and I can still visualize that experience clearly in my memory. When God knit me together He did so in a way that blessed me with a deep love for research. It is one of the reasons I excelled in academic study resulting in a Bachelor's degree in Business Administration, Master's in Human Resources Management and Juris Doctor – all with highest honors. All glory belongs to God that my research skills and giftedness as a quick learner brought me out on top in every academic environment and led to an extremely successful professional career.

In the months leading up to February, 1999 God was drawing me closer and closer to Him through worship and His Word. That season culminated in an earnest prayer to *know* Him more. On my knees I offered to *go wherever* He sent me or *do whatever* He asked me to do that I might truly *know* Him. God answered that prayer in a most unanticipated way. Seven months later He shockingly led me to resign from my job with a large wireless phone carrier. At that time, I was employed as a regional Senior Counsel, overseeing the company's legal resources for the Eastern region of the United States. Little did I know that at only 46 years old I had just *retired* from the professional work world. Before a full year elapsed God had unexpectedly reconnected my heart to something He had buried deep within me when I had visited a men's medium security prison as a young college student. He then divinely arranged an invitation from the Christian Warden of that same prison to serve there as a volunteer working with both inmates and staff.[1] Nine years later God called me to lay down the prison ministry work which had by that time expanded into other men's prisons, the women's prison and Ohio's juvenile correctional facilities. His astonishing instruction was that I begin teaching Bible studies in our local church. It was an extremely challenging transition for me to make. However, looking back I see that my love for learning, commitment to advance on my knees in prayer and my well-developed research skills gave me a jump start on lesson preparation.

I cut my teeth on facilitating DVD-driven Bible studies others had written, supplementing those lessons with historical and cultural background information. From there God began to give me assignments to teach various books of the Bible verse by verse. The next step was to instruct me to begin writing Bible studies I would then teach. Eventually teaching assignments grew to include an international teaching ministry. From the rearview mirror, I can see that the progression was a natural one. Each step along the way was undertaken cautiously and prayerfully – undergirded by my own prayers, times of prayer with my husband and the prayer covering of our faithful prayer partners.

At the Lord's direction, my husband and I co-founded Hope of the Nations International Ministry, Inc. a nonprofit ministry with a goal to disciple others. Our earnest desire is to see the body of Christ mature by growing up in the grace, knowledge and love of God through the study and application of His Word. Every Bible Study I've written is well researched and profits from the fact that I whole heartedly embrace the goal of being a life-long learner who seeks to apply the truth I teach others. I love drawing

---

1   In my first meeting with the Warden she asked me if I knew anything about mediation. I was in fact an experienced mediator and was presently mediating disputes for the Equal Employment Opportunity Commission. That began our working relationship which blossomed into a wide variety of ways in which God enabled me to serve both inmates and staff.

fellow Christ-followers into the biblical text for the purpose of life transformation.

My husband and I presently reside in Florida. We have celebrated 48 years of marriage and are blessed with two married children, Jeremy and Kimberly, daughter-in-law Jennifer, son-in-law Nathan and six amazing grandchildren: Jordan, Jackson, Hannah, Caleb, Jacob and Abigail.

www.ingramcontent.com/pod-product-compliance
Lightning Source LLC
Chambersburg PA
CBHW032035150426
43194CB00006B/288